"I picked up *The Brass Wall* and I started reading. And reading. And reading. And when I wasn't reading I found myself craving the next opportunity I could start reading again. David Kocieniewski hooks you on the first page. He knows narrative like a vintage mystery writer. Add to it superb reporting and you have one blockbuster of a book. *The Brass Wall* probes more deeply into the netherworld of cops and mobsters and the merciless New York streets than anything I have ever read."

—H. G. Bissinger, author of *Friday Night Lights* and *A Prayer for the City*

"Kocieniewski tells a gripping story that illuminates the historic fabric of the nation's largest and most prestigious local law enforcement agency. Well written and thoroughly researched, the book is part crime drama and part investigative exposé, and is sure to appeal to a wide range of readers, not just those who love a good detective yarn. . . . Some true-crime authors would ruin the story by taking shortcuts in their research or relying on well-worn clichés drawn from movies and hard-boiled detective novels. Kocieniewski clearly conducted hundreds of interviews and spent many hours peeling away the shells of his subjects." —*The Baltimore Sun*

"A vital, incendiary epic of crime, cops, and corruption in New York City. Kocieniewski brings insider knowledge and a flair for untangling complicated strife-ridden investigations to a shocking tale. Kocieniewski's wry, straightforward prose captures the moody desperation of a city reeling from crack-related violence and police scandals, as well as the tenacity of old-school organized crime in New York's less glamorous neighborhoods. He also paints a disturbing picture of IA compromising investigations and impeding straight-arrow cops in order to protect officers like the Wrynns, affiliated with the department's so-called "Brass Wall." Old style urban drama: hard to put down, and probably the best look into the NYPD since, well, James Lardner and Thomas Reppetto's *NYPD* (2000)." —*Kirkus Reviews*, starred review

"David Kocieniewski's *The Brass Wall* is a brilliant piece of nonfiction that reads like a novel. . . . *The Brass Wall* tells a human story, a mob story, and a cop story. It's a story as complex as its characters and one so saturated with rich cultural detail it seems destined for the cinema. But why wait? It's worth reading now." —*Trenton Times*

THE BRASS WALL

DAVID KOCIENIEWSKI

AN OWL BOOK

HENRY HOLT AND COMPANY

NEW YORK

THE BRASS WALL

THE BETRAYAL OF UNDERCOVER DETECTIVE #4126

Henry Holt and Company, LLC
Publishers since 1866
115 West 18th Street
New York, New York 10011

Henry Holt® is a registered trademark of Henry Holt and Company, LLC.

Library of Congress Cataloging-in-Publication Data
Kocieniewski, David.
The brass wall : the betrayal of undercover detective #4126 / David Kocieniewski.—1st ed.
  p. cm.
ISBN 0-8050-7695-6
  1. Armanti, Vincent.   2. Police—New York (State)—New York—Biography.   3. Undercover
operations—New York (State)—New York.   I. Title.
HV8080.U5A765   2003
363.209747'1—dc21   2003047764

Henry Holt books are available for special promotions and premiums.
For details contact: Director, Special Markets.

First Owl Books Edition 2004

Designed by Fritz Metsch

Printed in the United States of America

1   3   5   7   9   10   8   6   4   2

For Denise, Devin, and Katia

CONTENTS

THIS IS A true story.

It does not use composite characters, invented dialogue, or any other techniques of fictionalization. The only literary license taken by the author was to conceal the true identity of Undercover #4126, his relatives, and one other undercover who worked on the investigation. Because the detective work of #4126 has led to the conviction and imprisonment of dozens of organized crime figures and drug dealers, the publication of his true name might endanger him or his family, so he is identified by the pseudonym Vincent Armanti. The other undercover is identified by the pseudonym Terry O'Madden.

This book is based on hundreds of hours of interviews with more than one hundred people who participated in these events, along with thousands of pages of confidential police documents, fire department investigative files, FBI records, secret grand jury testimony, and trial transcripts. It also relies on transcripts and tapes of more than a hundred hours of secret recordings made by the NYPD and FBI in the streets of Throgs Neck, plus the surreptitiously tape-recorded conversations between Undercover #4126 and various officials within the FBI and Internal Affairs.

CAST OF CHARACTERS

THE FIRE
Thomas A. Williams, lieutenant in FDNY, commander of Rescue 4
Michael Milner, firefighter Rescue 4
Jack Ferranti, owner of Today's Styles, site of the suspicious fire
Shelly Anthony, resident of apartment above Today's Styles
Michelle Anthony, resident of apartment above Today's Styles

THE INVESTIGATORS
Vincent Armanti, undercover detective #4126
Edward Dowd, detective 104th Precinct
Cindy Peil, special agent for FBI
Richard Rudolph, special agent for FBI
George Stamboulidis, assistant U.S. attorney
Bobby Thomson, fire marshal
James Desocio, fire marshal
James Kelty, fire marshal
Anthony Lombardi, retired IRS agent

THE BAR
Michael "Myron" Dobbs, bartender

THE CAFÉ
Carlo Cuzzi, manager
Joey Scams, patron
Joe "Red" Bastone, patron

THE NEIGHBORHOOD

John K. Wrynn, NYPD detective

James Patrick Wrynn, his father, an inspector in Internal Affairs

Ann Wrynn, his sister

Jane Wrynn, his mother

Tommy "the Torch" Tocco, boyhood friend of John Wrynn

Vincent Basciano, Tocco's cousin, reputed soldier in Bonanno family

Mario Ferranti, Jack Ferranti's brother, boyhood friend of John Wrynn

Joey Ferranti, cousin of Jack and Mario Ferranti

Steve Turuk, John Wrynn's neighbor, boyhood friend

Tommy Gross, John Wrynn's neighbor, boyhood friend

Eric Mergenthal, John Wrynn's neighbor

Melissa Paradiso, John Wrynn's girlfriend

Linda Nelson, John Wrynn's girlfriend

Angelique Montemurro, John Wrynn's neighbor, later married and
   divorced Tommy Gross, then married Tommy Tocco

INTERNAL AFFAIRS

Robert Matthiessen, Internal Affairs sergeant

Sixto Santiago, Internal Affairs detective

John Shields, Internal Affairs lieutenant, supervisor of John Wrynn case

Michael Gagliardi, Internal Affairs lieutenant

Robert Beatty, chief of Internal Affairs 1988–1992

Walter Mack, commissioner of Internal Affairs May 1993–January 1995

Patrick Kelleher, chief of Internal Affairs January 1995–July 1996,
   then promoted to chief of detectives, and promoted to first deputy
   commissioner in April 1997

Jerry Walker, investigator assigned to Internal Affairs headquarters

William Gorta, Internal Affairs captain, driver for Chief Kelleher

Al James, deputy chief in Internal Affairs, longtime friend of
   James Wrynn

THE DEPARTMENT

Nancy McLaughlin, lieutenant in NYPD, married Inspector
   James Wrynn

Tommy Dades, narcotics detective, close friend of Vincent Armanti

William Plackenmeyer, captain in NYPD Detective Bureau

Michael McGovern, sergeant in NYPD, assistant to Patrick Kelleher

Raymond Kelly, police commissioner 1992–1994
William Bratton, police commissioner 1994–1996
Jack Maple, top adviser to William Bratton
John Timoney, first deputy commissioner under William Bratton
Howard Safir, police commissioner 1996–2000
Richard E. Mulvaney, assistant NYPD special prosecutor
Richard Kubick, special prosecutor

THE FERRANTI TRIAL

Jack B. Weinstein, federal judge
Lauren Resnick, assistant U.S. attorney
Sean O'Shea, assistant U.S. attorney
Vincent Marziano, cooperating witness
Thomas Klem, defense expert witness
Marion Seltzer, lawyer for Mario Ferranti
Jeffrey Hoffman, lawyer for Jack Ferranti
Lisa Ziccardi, former employee of Jack Ferranti
Gina Esposito, former employee of Jack Ferranti
Theresa Rodriguez, former employee of Jack Ferranti
Miriam Breyer, Jack Ferranti's wife

THE TOCCO TRIAL

William Zalenka, assistant Bronx district attorney
Ron Kuby, Tommy Tocco's lawyer
Marlene Besterman, lawyer assigned to NYPD Legal Bureau
Richard Lee Price, judge in Bronx State Supreme Court

THE BRASS WALL

"THEY'VE GOT ME doing *hand-to-hands*," said Myron Dobbs—cocaine dealer, drug addict, bartender to the mob—as if he were speaking any old words in the English language.

"I'm gonna get indicted, they've got me in the bathroom doing *hand-to-hands*," Dobbs said. Just like that—his voice so cool, so nonchalant, that had he been chatting up anyone other than Detective Vincent Armanti, New York City Undercover Detective #4126, there would have been no reason to expect gunfire.

But Armanti wasn't himself at the moment. He was posing as "Vinnie Blue Eyes," a Brooklyn street thug who had come to the Throgs Neck neighborhood of the Bronx three months earlier, looking to do business with associates of the Bonanno and Luchese crime families.

And the words Dobbs had just spoken, standing behind the bar at Sebastian's Pub on Tremont Avenue, were far more than just the workaday grumbling of some struggling coke dealer relegated to tiny deals with trifling profits. They were the exact words, the same hackneyed police jargon—"doing hand-to-hand cocaine sales"—that Armanti himself always used, the same words he had written on a confidential police report three weeks earlier. To hear them repeated here, from the lips of Myron Dobbs, was startling. As if Dobbs had told him: *You're going to be murdered, brutally, this very minute.*

During his three months undercover, Detective Armanti had been investigating the homicide of Lieutenant Thomas Williams, a decorated New York City firefighter who had died battling an arson blaze. During this strange tour of duty, Armanti had spent his nights sipping espresso with Sambuca, swapping war stories with Dobbs and the criminals who congregated in his bar, trafficking in a half dozen varieties of contraband. All the while, a concealed tape recorder was capturing it for posterity, the microphone wired just an inch from his heart.

Although Sebastian's billed itself as a sports bar, it was little more than a dive with a bookie in the back, named for Saint Sebastian, patron saint of alcoholics. Its decor was appropriately sullen: dingy wood paneling, a few strings of white Christmas lights, and—because it was the Bronx—a smoke-stained photo of the New York Yankees World Series team of 1961, arguably the greatest Yankees squad of them all. An odd rubber mat nailed to the floor beneath the stools ran along the length of the bar, ostensibly to keep spills and scuff marks from ruining the linoleum. But the clientele was such a collection of meat eaters and malcontents that Armanti had wondered whether it might be there to catch their drool.

With his pompadour hairdo, assorted scars, and that frightening glare, Vinnie Blue Eyes had made himself right at home on this hallowed ground. He seemed the perfect outcast: a guy so far beyond the point of caring that he'd do anything. So the Throgs Neck crew hadn't just accepted him; they'd begun to adopt him, offering him cocaine, whispering their secrets into his hidden microphone, and swapping stories about any of a hundred of their shadier ventures. Through it all, Armanti had begun to amass information about the main targets of his investigation, Jack and Mario Ferranti, two Luchese family associates who ran dozens of slum buildings, terrorized poor tenants with pit bulls and pipe bombs. They also happened to be the men suspected of ordering the fire where Lieutenant Williams had been killed. Armanti had already caught his first faint whispers about dead police informants, the crazy money that the Ferrantis had made shaking down store owners, and the victims they'd dismembered with power tools, minced like so much fresh basil.

Of course, Detective Armanti had no doubt about what would happen if anyone ever suspected he was a cop: The underworld code called for certain, vicious death. So before Dobbs had even finished his sentence, Armanti had shifted imperceptibly into self-preservation mode. While keeping track of Dobbs's hands, he scanned the bartender's black leather jacket, straining to see if it concealed a gun. Concentrating on the nerve endings in his own chest, he tried to gauge whether the cord from his tape recorder might be visible. Then Armanti pulled his hand out of his left pants pocket—where he always carried a string of red rosary beads and a small stone inscribed with the word *Courage*—and placed his fist on the bar, ready to fend off any attack. Trying to make it appear at least somewhat casual, he glanced outside to check if a car might be pulling up, loaded with hit men ready to get busy.

Nothing. And nowhere to run even if the Luchese family's enforcers did roll up. So Armanti took a deep breath, lit a Newport Light, and tried to play it cool. Myron's other bartender rinsed two pilsner glasses and shook them, sending a single drop of water hurtling through the air; it landed six feet down the bar just as Armanti noticed for the first time that Myron had a scrawny-looking throat.

"What do you mean *indicted*?" Armanti asked, picking up from Dobbs after a few seconds that seemed like hours and trying to prevent the ice ball in his stomach from causing a quaver in his voice.

Dobbs continued, but Armanti couldn't follow the words. He was too busy retracing his steps, trying to figure who might have leaked his report. He was a veteran undercover cop with a finely tuned ear for how things were said: Using "hand-to-hands" to describe low-level drug deals was a habit of his. It was a term used in police precincts, not on street corners. And as he stood at the bar that sweaty Bronx night, wondering if he'd ever see sunshine again, Detective Armanti was sickened by the knowledge that he had almost certainly been betrayed by a fellow cop.

During his ten years in narcotics, he'd purchased cocaine with a street value of $100 million—more than any undercover in the department's history. He'd posed as a hit man and arms dealer and had been put in charge of training new classes of narcotics detectives. All of those late nights and silk shirts, the death-defying raids and mindless street talk, all that marinara sauce—and for what? To be sold out by a fellow officer? To be done in by a mob wannabe, an Irishman named *Myron*?

"I think they've got an informant," Dobbs said, still not tipping his hand. "Someone here in the Neck."

Armanti exhaled cigarette smoke and silently made himself a promise: *If I get out of here alive, so help me God, I will find out who did this.*

And when I do, I will make him pay.

PART I

US AGAINST THEM

NO ACCIDENT

FEBRUARY 24, 1992

MORE THAN A year before Vinnie Armanti ever set foot in Sebastian's, at shortly after 7:00 A.M. on a cold winter morning, Lieutenant Thomas A. Williams was standing before a small group of firefighters inside the Rescue 4 firehouse. He had stopped talking just long enough to balance a quarter on his thumb. Rescue 4, one of the city's elite fire companies, based in Woodside, Queens, had just received a new chain saw to test. As shift commander, it was up to Lieutenant Williams to determine who would be the first to use it during an actual run.

Rescue companies have the most treacherous mission in the New York City fire department. Their special duty, beyond saving civilians unable to escape disasters, is to retrieve other firefighters trapped within blazes. They are the most highly trained, specially equipped members of the force, so the arrival of a new piece of gear is an important event. Each rescue company's rig is really little more than a huge, mobile toolbox packed with complicated apparatus: scuba gear for underwater work; acetylene torches to cut through metal locks, ducts, window bars, and pipes; block-and-tackle units to help move heavy machinery; and an assortment of ropes, clasps, and mountain-climbing gear to retrieve people trapped in inaccessible places or to snatch up a potential suicide too petrified to crawl back from a ledge or a bridge.

The shift had begun that day, at 6:00 A.M., with Lieutenant Williams showing the five men in his command the new saw they would be testing. It was an amazing product, specially engineered to help firefighters cut through walls and roofs more easily. One of two men would use it that day, and now Lieutenant Williams tossed the coin into the air to see which it

would be. Fireman Michael Milner won the toss; under another commander, that victory might have meant that Milner would carry the saw
into battle that night. But in Rescue 4, on nights when Lieutenant Williams
was in charge, things were a little different. The loser got the saw because
Milner chose to spend the night charging into fires alongside the lieutenant, as the "irons and can man" who carried his equipment.

It was a bit ironic that the men of Rescue 4 coveted every chance to be
near Lieutenant Williams when they were out in the field because, truth
be told, there were times inside the firehouse when many of them hid just
to escape his nonstop banter. He could talk sports, family, culture, current affairs, international relations—anything from the most personal,
private matter to the most far-flung theory. He beamed when he spoke, at
great length, about his two daughters and his wife, Patricia. In staggering
detail, he told the men how he spent his days off doing household work to
help Patricia, who held down a full-time job. But God help the poor soul
who mentioned a politician. Lieutenant Williams had always considered
them two-faced back stabbers, and in the two years since the city had
closed a nearby Queens firehouse as a budget-cutting move, his disdain
had turned to disgust.

Whatever the topic, Williams's fast-paced, playful voice was inescapable inside the station house, as indelible as the smell of soot, the hum of
fluorescent lights, or the chatter of the department radio.

"Like a broken record," the men would say to each other. "He was vac-
cinated with a Victrola needle."

Firemen work shifts that run twenty-four hours or more. They spend
more time cooped up with one another than they do with their families, and
at times, frankly, that familiarity frays the nerves. If Lieutenant Williams
had been a supervisor of lesser stature, it is more than likely that one of his
men would have bluntly addressed the issue of his jabbering. Yet no man
who worked in Rescue 4 could ever bring himself to embarrass Williams by
asking him to pipe down. Not even in jest. Some would feign sleep, hoping
he'd find another audience. Others would slip out of sight, tuck themselves away in the TV room or a bunk, hoping to sneak a few moments of
peace. But none of them could conceive of saying anything that might
bruise the lieutenant's feelings. They simply respected him too much.

Lieutenant Williams had earned that high regard because he knew
more than the best way to fight a fire; he seemed to grasp, instinctively,
how to bring out the finest in the men around him in the process. After

thirty-two years on the job, he had mastered as much of the science and art of firefighting as anyone in the department. But he never failed to ask every man for his input, and his constant inquiries forced his men to always keep thinking.

Lieutenant Williams also had one of the rarest attributes of any supervisor: the willingness to challenge his superiors on behalf of his men. His brother, Robert Williams, was a battalion chief who could have offered him an easy path to the status, security, and higher pay of the department hierarchy. But the lieutenant often said that the strength of the fire department and his love of the job both came from the men on the front lines. So he remained in his less exalted position and used his department connections to help his subordinates whenever they got into a jam. On numerous fire calls, when some battalion chief would ask Williams and the members of his crew to perform menial tasks, such as tearing down walls, he would curtly remind them that Rescue's job was rescues and the grunt work should be left to others. Then he'd gather his men and leave.

"We're outta here," he'd say, cultivating his reputation as a maverick but earning unwavering admiration from his troops.

Yet even if Williams hadn't been a motivator or a maverick, even if he'd been the most miserable, snarling lout who'd ever strapped on an FDNY helmet, there was one immutable reason why his men wanted to be near him. He made them feel safer. The most dangerous part of any call is entering a burning, smoke-filled building when you don't yet know where the fire is coming from. Lieutenant Williams was incomparable in those harrowing first stages because he had instinct, an uncanny ability to find the fire. That skill made his crew confident that whatever might happen, Williams would somehow find a way to get out safely. The closer you stayed to him, the more likely you'd wind up a survivor, too.

Milner had won the opportunity to partner up with Williams the night of February 24. But once that matter had been settled, fate decided to tease Milner by depriving Rescue 4 of any real fire to fight. On most days, the rescue squad averaged eight calls per shift, and it was not unheard of for them to make fifteen runs. But throughout the shift that day the squad had only a few minor jobs. The men enjoyed an uninterrupted dinner, which was a rarity. Afterward, they dispersed around the firehouse to watch television, catch a few minutes of sleep, or listen to Williams talk, talk, talk.

Finally, at about 10:45 P.M., a flurry of activity burst over the department radio. A dispatch operator fielded a call for a burning building in Maspeth, and Rescue 4 didn't wait for the alarm to sound. Williams ordered his men to suit up, and they scrambled into action. As he climbed aboard the truck, Lieutenant Thomas A. Williams shouted a reminder:

"Don't forget that saw."

LESS THAN THREE miles away, inside 66-45 Grand Avenue, apartment 2L, Michelle Anthony nuzzled tight against her husband, Shelly. Bundled in sensible flannel pajamas, they were too deeply ensconced in sleep to hear the first whine of the smoke detector outside their bedroom door.

Although it was not yet eleven P.M.—an hour when many young New Yorkers are just beginning their nights out—the Anthonys had neither the time, the energy, nor the inclination to stay out late. Michelle, a nursing student, was exhausted from a tough day at Long Island University. Shelly was a New York City transit police officer whose responsible nature was only further encouraged by his duties and his demanding work schedule. Married just eight months, they were already on something of an austerity budget, dutifully squirreling away money for a new home in the suburbs.

But the Anthonys were such upbeat newlyweds they never really felt deprived. Shelly had picked Michelle up from school that day, saving her the grueling subway commute. After a quiet dinner at home, they'd turned in at 9:30 P.M. and were fast asleep an hour later when the first spark ignited one floor below them and the flames began to spread their brilliant, terrifying light.

Their apartment was on the middle floor of a sturdy, three-story building on a noisy business strip. The traffic outside was so loud that the Anthonys didn't hear a sound as the fire chewed through the building's frame, sending clouds of smoke up stairwells and plumbing shafts.

It wasn't surprising that the wail of the smoke alarm had failed to stir them. Their home was a classic New York bargain apartment: dark, with few windows, and oddly configured—the kind of place where light and sound just disappeared. When she was in the bedroom, Michelle would often miss calls because the telephone was in the living room and its rings never reached her all the way down the lengthy corridor. It was annoying at first. Then frightening. What might happen if she was back there during an emergency and she couldn't hear the commotion until it was too late? A rickety fire escape led from their bedroom into the courtyard, but it looked unreliable, and the courtyard itself was enclosed. The only real exit was the front door, way down the hall in the living room.

Michelle put a night-light in the hall, just outside their room, and asked Shelly to install a smoke detector near their bedroom door. He teased her gently about being paranoid, but he did it anyway. By 10:30 P.M. on the night of February 24, however, the alarm wasn't enough to rouse them as the smoke spread toward their bed. Shelly had always been a heavy sleeper. Michelle was the one who usually woke more easily, but her body had an important reason to need more rest: Although the Anthonys did not know it, she was two months pregnant.

When the alarm finally roused Michelle, she looked toward the clock; when she couldn't see the numbers, she assumed it was still too early to wake. A wave of relief washed over her. Then, slowly, she realized that the alarm was coming from someplace infinitely more disturbing.

She took a deep breath and felt the smoke sting her lungs. Her heart began to sprint. Just as she had always feared, the building was burning and there was no way out. As she opened her eyes fully, she saw that the room was so thick with smoke she could barely make out the window.

"Shelly! Shelly, wake up!" she screamed, shaking her husband, uncertain whether he was asleep or unconscious. He stirred, but he didn't wake. Her thoughts began to scatter. She had to get out and she couldn't leave him, but how could a small woman like her carry a big guy like him?

"Shelly!" she shouted, her words cut short and her breathing labored from the combination of smoke and terror.

Finally he jumped up and bounded out of bed, instantly recognizing the smoke and making a seamless transition into a living, breathing version of the police department's emergency manual. Feeling the walls, he could tell by the heat that the flames had begun to climb up behind the plaster.

"We've got to get out of here," he said.

Michelle was too panicked to answer.

Smoke was pouring in from outside the bedroom door, but that was the only way out. Shelly told his wife to crouch down, and as the door swung open, they saw a wall of thick smoke from the ceiling to about waist level. Shelly looked back at her and started to crawl.

"Listen to my voice," he instructed, "and follow me."

Naturally calm, confident, and self-assured, he drew on those traits as he struggled to help Michelle find some strength within herself. On her hands and knees, half-paralyzed with fear, she heard his voice calling, trying to help her pull through. *What's going on?* Michelle kept asking herself as Shelly coaxed her into the hallway. *What could have caused this?* As they inched down the hall, that endless hall, she worried about everything she was leaving behind—her wedding gown, the hundreds of photos of her family. All her memories turning to ash.

Shelly kept calling her, reassuring her, repeating over and over that they were going to make it.

The smoke got thicker and the temperature hotter as the terrified couple moved toward the living room and the stairway. Halfway down the hall, Michelle was struck by a comforting thought: *At least if I'm going to die, Shelly will be here with me.*

"Keep moving," he called.

When they reached the living room, with the smoke sinking lower and the heat nearly searing their hands, Michelle saw a glimmer of light. It was Shelly opening the door to the hallway. Coughing and shouting, they scrambled down the stairs and sprinted out the door and onto the sidewalk. The cold, wet pavement chilled Michelle's bare feet, but it was the most beautiful sensation she had ever felt.

Shelly hugged her, held her until her crying and shaking started to slow. Moments later, as she tried to dry her eyes, she noticed a short, Mexican-looking man with a mustache standing next to Shelly. Her eyes began to well up again, this time with tears of joy. The man looked so concerned that she instantly assumed he was ready to run up and help.

"Is there anyone else up there?" he said, in a high-pitched, scratchy voice.

"I'm not sure, but I think so," Shelly replied.

Michelle was awed to think that some total stranger might actually risk his life by running into the hell she and Shelly had just fled. She was about to thank the man, whoever he was, when she heard the sirens growing louder. The fire trucks turned the corner, lights flashing. Suddenly, the man turned, without saying a word, and fled into the night.

WHEN RESCUE 4 pulled up to the scene at 11:05 P.M., black smoke was billowing out the windows of the building; the place was going up at a good clip. A few residents had escaped onto the roof and needed to be helped to safety. It was unclear whether anyone else remained inside, but even when a building appears vacant, rescue firemen try to search every possible room for survivors.

As they entered the building, Milner walked a few paces behind Lieutenant Williams carrying a metal can of water, for spraying back flames, and the iron—a tool resembling a whaler's harpoon that is used to poke through walls and grab burning pieces of debris. Partway up the first flight of stairs, Milner noted smoke rising between the gaps of the staircase, a sign that the fire was creeping up from the floor beneath them. He pointed it out to Williams, who nodded in acknowledgment, and they trudged on up. At the top of the stairs they found an open door. Entering some kind of office, they noticed what looked like a maze of metal desks, bookshelves, and filing cabinets visible through the smoke. About ten feet inside, Williams stopped in his tracks.

"Something's not right," he screamed, pulling his air mask off his face so Milner could hear his words.

He ordered the fireman with the new saw to head to the roof and forge a vent hole, then walked farther into the office, with Milner following. They were taking a beating from the waves of smoke and heat, and when they reached the front wall, Williams ordered Milner to break the large plate-glass window that ran from the ceiling to a ledge about four inches off the floor. Under most circumstances this would have helped clear the room: A fire's heat and pressure always rush toward the easiest escape route. But the window faced south, and the wind was coming from that direction, too. The stiff breeze blasted the smoke back at Williams and Milner, who attempted to continue their search, pushing on toward the center of the office. When they reached a set of bookcases jutting out into the aisle, a huge gust of smoke and superheated gases overwhelmed them, instantly reducing their visibility to an inch. Heat radiated through their boots, gloves, and face masks.

"Fuck!" Williams screamed. "Find that window! We've got to get out of here!"

In their eight years working together, Milner and Williams had survived countless heart-stopping exploits, yet Milner had never heard him use the word *fuck*, had never heard such urgency in his voice. Milner was determined not to fail the lieutenant now.

He reached for the wall with the iron, hoping to find something to guide him as he retraced his steps, but the sense of vertigo was unnerving. The smoke had literally whited out any visual point of reference. Then Milner remembered that the window was to his left, and he tried to use his hearing to do what his vision could no longer accomplish. He could make out the sounds of machinery, fire crews, and breaking glass off to his left, as well. Like a blind man with a cane, he began tapping the iron along the wall, trying to lead them out.

"Find that fucking window!" Williams screamed.

They had traveled only fifteen feet or so from the window, but as they inched their way slowly along, the distance seemed infinite, unattainable. Milner pushed as fast as he could, but he had to step carefully because he feared the fire might have chewed a hole through the floor. He couldn't see his arms, much less his feet. The smoke grew thicker and the heat continued to spike. He could feel the smoke and heat beating against his body, the taste of charred wood in his mouth and up his sinuses.

Suddenly, he heard the lieutenant shout, "Mayday! Mayday!"

It seemed unfathomable to Milner: Whenever he or the other firemen were beset with fears of disaster, it was always Lieutenant Williams who saved the day. Outside, the men who heard the *Mayday!* over the radio couldn't quite tell whose voice it was; but they knew it couldn't be Lieutenant Williams.

Instinctively, Milner pulled his mask back to repeat, "Mayday! Mayday!"

He tapped the wall quicker, tried to edge along faster.

"I'm over here!" he screamed to Williams. "Can you see me?"

Milner felt the crunch of glass beneath his boots and knew he was getting close. Then his iron hit the corner of the wall, and he followed it to the window's edge.

Slowly, he turned himself around, grabbed the window frame, and leaned out.

"We're here!" he shouted. "We're here!"

He could hear the firemen below calling back. But the wind had shifted again, and the smoke was so thick they couldn't see him. As he stood at the window ledge shouting, Milner sensed a black blur passing through the periphery of his vision, but he couldn't tell whether it was wood, a sheet of glass, or a darker cloud of smoke. Milner screamed into the void, the heat and the smoke wrapping around him tighter and tighter. He called out to Williams, but he couldn't see the lieutenant and he heard no response.

Milner grabbed the ledge and swung his body down under the smoke, hoping that the crew would see him and maneuver a ladder over. Instead, he just dangled there, hoping, praying, as the heat worked its way through his gloves and into his fingertips. After what seemed like a lifetime, his hands gave way. Although it was only fifteen feet to the street, the drop left plenty of time for Milner's mind to race. As he fell helplessly through the air, he heard no sounds, just felt the rushing air.

So this, he thought, *is how I'm going to die.*

Then a crash.

Milner landed flat on his back on the sidewalk. A few feet away, a crowd of firemen and paramedics were already stooped over Lieutenant Williams, who lay motionless, his face and head steeped in blood.

A thunderclap rumbled through Milner's body, followed by a flash and a wave of pain. As the noise receded, leaving just a ringing in his ears, it gradually dawned on him that, incredibly, he had not yet died. He saw the crews trying to revive Lieutenant Williams and, somehow, sprang to his feet. The numbness in his skull, the ringing, his throbbing back would have to wait. They were trying to get Williams to breathe again, but it wasn't working. Lieutenant Williams had taught Milner that air passages often get blocked by blood and mucus, so Milner ran to get a suction device to see if it might somehow help his friend draw another breath.

DETECTIVE EDWARD DOWD had almost reached the fire when he got a radio call telling him about another case: a cabdriver had been murdered. That's the way things went in 1992: The city had set a new record for murders the year before, more than six a day. There was simply more trouble than cops available to fight it. But Dowd, whose job required that he investigate everything from hostile phone arguments between spouses to homicides, was so close to the fire, which had already been pegged as a suspicious blaze, that he decided to stop in anyway.

The firemen there were so overcome that it took a few moments for Dowd to find someone willing to talk. A fire marshal was calling the blaze an accident; he kept saying it had been started by a space heater in the clothing store on the first floor. Dowd was relieved; if it was arson, he'd have another case on his hands, but an accident meant it was the fire department's problem. Glancing around, watching firemen still trying to douse the flames, he realized that the fireman who had fallen was in bad shape. Someone was administering mouth-to-mouth, but the men trying to keep him alive seemed raw, frantic, enraged. It occurred to Dowd that in his ten years as a cop, he'd been to hundreds of accidents and crime scenes, seen dozens of people receive CPR. Yet he couldn't remember a single one who had actually survived. *Not one.*

IN THE YEARS to come, Milner would replay those frenzied moments in his head incessantly, and each time he would find himself shaken by another wave of dread. At that moment, though, there at the scene, there were no feelings, no thoughts as he dashed through the cold. Just instinct playing itself out as he tried to revive the lieutenant. Milner had done his part inside; he'd found the fucking window, just like Williams had asked him to. But somehow, in the commotion, the man Milner had spent his professional life trying to emulate had plunged through the window so quickly that all Milner had seen was a blur he hadn't even recognized as human.

He had no idea how or why. Maybe his friend had become confused. Maybe he had seen the light from outside and had mistaken the window for a door. Or he might have slipped on a shard of broken glass, lost his balance, and gone out. In all the turmoil, Williams might have erroneously thought there was a window sash to lean on, then fallen through, heels over head. Or perhaps he hadn't seen the ledge four inches off the floor and had tripped. Whatever had happened, Williams had fallen headfirst to the pavement. Fifteen feet could be a treacherous drop, but it was one that plenty of firemen, house painters, window washers, tree trimmers, and even drunken college students had survived before with only minor injuries. Only Williams hadn't had time to prepare himself, and as he tumbled down through the air, his helmet flew off. His body did a somersault, and his fall was broken by his head striking the curb. His air tank also rode up his back during the descent, and when he hit the ground, it smashed into his head like a sledgehammer. His skull was broken in six places.

Blood had seeped down the back of his head as he lay there on the pavement. The dark red liquid formed a wide puddle on the sidewalk. The lieutenant's face was so splattered that one of his own firefighters didn't recognize him and asked if he should get Tommy to help.

"This *is* Tommy," he was told.

The firemen lifted Williams onto the stretcher, with Milner grabbing one side as they trundled the lieutenant to the ambulance. Years later, when someone showed Milner a picture of the frantic scene, it took a few moments for him to recognize himself. His face was so drawn, drained of any emotion. The face of death. At that moment, though, he felt nothing, thought nothing. Like a mechanical fireman on an overcharged battery, he was desperately trying to find a miracle.

The paramedic could sense the horror all around him. He stayed silent as Lieutenant Williams was set down inside the ambulance. Milner knelt beside it. Once the doors were shut and Milner was beyond the peering eyes of everyone outside, the paramedic looked up at him.

"Mike, he's not gonna make it," he said. "He's got air in his cranium. It's no use."

DETECTIVE DOWD WAS headed home on the Interborough Parkway later that morning, daydreaming about a few hours of uninterrupted sleep. Dowd, who had just completed a sixteen-hour shift, was eager to relieve his wife, who had been watching the couple's two young children and needed to go to work. He had handed the cabdriver's case off to another detective, who needed the overtime to help increase his final year's pay and fatten his pension. It had been 5:30 A.M. when Dowd swung back to the fire. At the scene, the fire marshals had said they wouldn't know for sure until the lab reports came back, weeks or months later, but it still appeared that a space heater with an electrical problem had accidentally started the blaze.

After finishing paperwork back at his desk in the 104th Precinct detective squad, Dowd had started for home around 9:30 A.M. He suffered from migraines, so the stress and sleep deprivation were already causing a sharp pain in his temples. He wanted to get some sleep before his headache turned into one of those crushers that rendered him unable to leave a dark room for two days. He was almost in Brooklyn when the announcer on the all-news radio station 1010 WINS reported that there was a development about the Maspeth fire that had killed Lieutenant Williams. It had been ruled an arson.

Dowd slammed a fist into the dashboard, cursed, and floored the accelerator, racing to the nearest exit so he could head back to the scene once again. Before he could even turn around, his pager rattled in his pocket. The numbers 911 lit up on the screen. He could already hear his captain screaming: *What the hell happened? You told me this was an accident!*

It was quickly evident that the Lieutenant Williams case would be beyond high-pressure. The official police department policy calls for detectives to treat every murder equally. But in reality, the media, the police department, and the public treat some murders more equally than others, using a complex and inexact formula involving the victim's class, race, gender, and ability to inspire a juicy tabloid headline. At the top of that hierarchy, just above the category RICH WHITE PERSON SLAIN IN POPU-LAR TOURIST DESTINATION!, are line-of-duty killings of police officers and firemen.

"Grab ahold of this one," Dowd's sergeant told him. "This could be the biggest case of your career."

Yet by the time Dowd screeched to a stop at the fire scene, it was clear that the chase had already begun without him. The building still smoldered, and in a few remote sections firefighters were hosing down piles of rubble. Investigators from the NYPD's Crime Scene Unit, which was supposed to recognize, gather, and preserve evidence, were taking photos. But they refused to enter the building, insisting the site was too dangerous. Meanwhile, on the first floor, where the fire had apparently begun, two fire marshals shoveled through the mounds of charred clothing, wood, and concrete in search of clues. It was never a good thing for a detective to lose control of a crime scene to another agency. Dowd hadn't ever worked with the fire marshals before this, but they had already blown the call on whether the fire was arson, so they weren't off to a promising start.

In the days to come, he would learn that the fire marshals had made an even more critical misstep. The morning Lieutenant Williams died, teams of detectives and police patrol officers had fanned out around the area to question shopkeepers, neighbors, commuters, and pedestrians in search of clues. So as to leave no potential witness undiscovered, they'd even interviewed a woman dressed as "Mini the Clown," whose job was to walk up and down the business strip and attract customers. But, incredibly, when the fire marshals had learned of a ridiculously obvious prime suspect, they'd set out to question him without telling Dowd or the NYPD.

Jack Ferranti, the owner of Today's Styles, the clothing store where the fire had begun, couldn't have appeared more suspicious if he'd had a bull's-eye tattooed on his forehead. Ferranti, who was affiliated with the Luchese organized-crime family, had twice been named to the *Village*

Voice's annual list of the city's ten worst slumlords. Bad things had a habit of happening to people and properties that had outlived their usefulness to Jack and his brother, Mario (who had a reputation as a street fighter and sex fiend). Jack's company had a history of using arson to rid itself of unprofitable buildings. Today's Styles, on the ground floor, had piddling sales, and such unappealing merchandise that people in the neighborhood suspected it was a front for some other, nefarious enterprise. One of Ferranti's former clerks told investigators that Jack had tried to talk her into buying the business. When she'd refused, he'd told her that his fire insurance would take care of the problem.

Ferranti's enemies also seemed to suffer unfortunate accidents. In 1988, a mortgage broker who took Ferranti to court for nonpayment opened his door and was gunned down in his doorway, shot in the neck three times, just hours before he would have foreclosed on the buildings. The next day, a man arrived at the mortgage broker's office saying he had to make a payment. He dropped off a card from F & J Management, Ferranti's company. No cash, check, or credit card number. Just a card. The mortgage broker sold Ferranti back the property for $400,000 less than it was worth. But it was a deal for the mortgage broker, too, because it spared him any further gunfire.

In 1985, a small-time criminal who agreed to rob a bank with Jack was shot three times because he backed out of the heist. Before Ferranti could be charged, his victim was jailed on unrelated robbery charges, and he died in custody.

By far, the most chilling example of Ferranti's methods involved Bruce Bailey, a Manhattan rent activist. Bailey, an icon of the New York counterculture, had been radicalized by the Columbia University protests of 1968 and educated by Allen Ginsberg, Jack Kerouac, and the Beat poets who socialized at the West End Tavern, a few blocks from the university. By 1989, at age fifty-four, Bailey was the head of the Columbia Tenants Union, a group that organized rent strikes in order to pressure the Ferrantis and other slumlords into making repairs on an assortment of buildings in Harlem. According to several reports, Bailey agreed to end the protests at the Ferranti buildings in Harlem in exchange for a $20,000 payment from Jack.

Then, emboldened by some inexplicable bravado, Bailey reneged on the deal and organized a rent strike anyway. But on June 14, 1989, shortly after he met with the managers of a building the Ferrantis owned on 164th Street,

Bailey disappeared. The next day, a truck backing up on a deserted South Bronx street accidentally ran over a black garbage bag dumped there. When it burst open, the driver was horrified to see a bloody torso, which was later identified as approximately one-third of Bailey's headless body. The remaining limbs, left in three other bags, were recovered in a vacant lot nearby.

Ferranti was clearly the person Dowd wanted to grill—fast, before Jack and his minions had a chance to synchronize their stories and threaten witnesses. But in their fury, the fire marshals had sped up to Harlem and barged into the home of one of Ferranti's employees. She stalled the fire marshals while Jack climbed out the window and ran off to concoct a cover story and confer with other witnesses.

Dowd wasn't able to speak to Ferranti until February 26, two days after the fire and two days before Lieutenant Williams's funeral. Nothing would have made Dowd happier than to have a suspect locked up before Williams was lowered into the ground. If he'd had the chance, he might have given Ferranti the kind of treatment usually reserved for cop killers: extracting the truth from him with intimidation, shouts, and threats of physical violence. But with the fire marshals, who were accompanying Dowd, in the room, everything had to be by the book. They conducted a proper interview, and Jack gave them an absurd alibi. He'd spent the weekend with a female friend in Jersey, he said, but he wouldn't say where, or who he was with, because the woman was not his wife. He wryly suggested that a disgruntled former employee might have torched the store. Or maybe the building owner had a motive, Ferranti suggested. He did everything but blame Mini the Clown.

AT LIEUTENANT WILLIAMS'S funeral on February 28, the firefighters seemed as infuriated as they were grief-stricken. Sensing their anger, Dowd felt relieved that they didn't know *he* was the one responsible for finding the killer. The Williams family had asked that only friends, relatives, and other firefighters attend the services. But by the time the funeral procession rolled through a two-mile stretch of Kings Park, Long Island, ten thousand people had jammed the streets, bringing the town to a halt. Firemen poured in from around New York, and as far away as California. In their dress blues and white gloves, they stood ten deep along much of the route. Despite the family's request that the service not be exploited, news reporters from every city paper and camera crews from a half dozen television stations descended as a red fire engine draped in black-and-purple bunting carried the coffin from the funeral home to St. John's Roman Catholic Church. The church was filled far beyond capacity. Outside, Michelle Anthony had come to pay her respects. Beside her stood her husband, Shelly, wearing a borrowed jacket and trembling in the cold because his police uniform and warm clothing had been lost in the fire.

The firemen saluted as the casket slowly passed by, their gloved hands flashing white against the overcast sky. The drum corps played a death march, and when the coffin was lowered from the rig and carried up the church steps, bagpipers launched into "Amazing Grace." Although tears ran down the faces of many mourners, Patricia Williams and her two daughters were so determined to be strong that they hugged but did not cry.

There were noteworthy absentees, however. Out of respect for Lieutenant Williams's wishes, his wife and the other firefighters had barred all elected officials from attending. The choice seats customarily reserved for the mayor and other dignitaries were filled instead by the lieutenant's coworkers from the department. It was an incredibly defiant political statement. The media tried to make it a racial thing: the unpopular African-American mayor, David Dinkins, and his Hispanic fire commissioner snubbed by the predominantly white fire department. But anyone who had known Lieutenant Williams knew that when it came to politicians he was an equal-opportunity curmudgeon.

By standing up to the world and closing ranks in Williams's honor, some of the firefighters momentarily found a place to focus their rage. But nothing could overshadow just how deeply the lieutenant's death had unsettled the department. Watching the firemen grieve, feeling their disbelief, Dowd saw that the tragedy had undermined their sense of security. If it could happen to Lieutenant Williams, it could happen to any of them. No one had to tell Dowd the rest of the equation—that as long as Williams's killer remained free, nobody would have any peace of mind.

THE INTENSE ANGUISH was soon directed at Dowd, and he often felt he was bearing it all alone. Williams's friends and relatives never stopped calling to check on the status of the case. At first, they offered assistance. Then, as the weeks and months passed with no tangible signs of progress, some firemen began to question whether the police department, which the FDNY had always considered a rival, was giving the case its best effort. One of Williams's daughters worked in a dentist's office that participated in the NYPD's union plan, so a few times a month some cop with a fresh filling or new root canal would call Dowd, asking, "What's going on with the fireman case?" or "You gonna get these fucking guys?"

Spring turned to summer, but Dowd just couldn't get any traction. The fire marshal assigned to the case was often missing in action. And the more time that passed, the more Dowd ached to give the Williams family some peace of mind by locking up the killers. Burn patterns in the store showed unmistakable evidence that some sort of fuel had been used to set the building ablaze. Lab tests established that the door lock had not been picked and confirmed that the heater had not caused the fire. To bring a solid case to court, however, Dowd needed something solid, and to get that he needed to get close to the Ferrantis, whose home turf in Throgs Neck was so incredibly ingrown it seemed impenetrable.

Although the pressure mounted as time went by, the police department was so overwhelmed with murders that resources became scarcer. The first team of fire marshals assigned to the case grew harder to find. Dowd's colleagues in the 104th Precinct grumbled that they were being forced to work harder while he was off on special assignment. Several accused Dowd of loafing; others stopped talking to him altogether. The NYPD bureaucracy made it difficult to get cars, equipment, or cash to pay informants. Dowd used his own money to cover some expenses. He worked nonstop—weekends, nights, days off, holidays—searching for leads among Ferranti's neighbors, enemies, former cell mates, business partners, and victims.

All he found was one dead end after another.

Finally, on the last day of June, as Dowd staked out the home of one of Jack's former girlfriends, he got his first real break, and he grabbed it ferociously. Someone told Dowd about a street corner where Jack Ferranti's cousin Joey sold heroin. It didn't take Dowd long to locate Joey Ferranti selling ten-dollar bags, and he flung the dealer into the car. Joey was reluctant to incur his cousin's wrath by talking, but his glassy eyes and the needle marks on his arms told Dowd that the junkie had other, more pressing worries. It would be awfully hard to maintain a habit in Rikers Island, or some upstate prison, where Joey would be sent for violating his parole.

As they drove over the Whitestone Bridge, Dowd took two heroin packets off the stack he'd seized from Joey, waved them in front of the open window, and ordered his passenger to talk. Joey looked at Dowd quizzically. Then he told Dowd how Jack had ordered an arson once up in Harlem and—*Whaddaya know!*—two bags flew out of the car and fluttered down toward the East River. Joey was astonished, but Dowd planned to keep pitching the dope; if he stopped the guy might quit talking and he wanted information on other arsons, preferably the one in Queens. When Joey managed to offer up a few more details—*Presto!*—two more bags scattered in the wind. Dowd was breaking any of a dozen department regulations, but he felt as desperate as the addict he was dealing with. By the time they reached the precinct, Joey's stash was gone, but Dowd had his first glimpse of Jack Ferranti's operations and how the arson had been arranged.

Word on the street was that one of Jack's cronies, Tommy "the Torch" Tocco, had been paid to burn the store, Joey said. When Dowd conducted a photo line-up with the Anthonys they identified Tocco as the man with the raspy voice who'd been lurking on the night of the fire. Joey even steered Dowd to a neighborhood addict, Steve Turuk, who was friendly with the Ferrantis and might work as a snitch.

Dowd found Turuk and talked him into wearing a wire. Then Dowd pressured Turuk into finding a second informant—Eric Mergenthal, another junkie who was close to Tocco. He rode both informants hard throughout the summer, threatening them, giving them money to support their drug habits, and even driving them to score heroin before wiring them up. Dowd shuddered to think what his bosses might say if they knew how many NYPD rules he was violating. But what else could he do? He had no other leads. The flack from the fire department, all the reminders and telephone calls, never seemed to stop. (In the fall, when the Anthonys gave birth to a son, Cory, they gave the child the middle name Thomas, in honor of Lieutenant Williams.)

By early November, Dowd's hardball tactics appeared to be paying off. Turuk had learned quite a bit about Jack Ferranti's business. He provided Dowd with the name of a city police officer from their neighborhood in the Bronx who still did drugs with some of Ferranti's crew and had worked for Jack in the past. Turuk also gave Dowd some tantalizing information linking Ferranti and his brother, Mario, to the gruesome murder of the rent activist Bruce Bailey. A few weeks before Bailey was dismembered, Turuk said, the Ferrantis had hired him and Tocco to stalk

Bailey and "beat him badly." Later, Turuk had even lent the Ferrantis a Sawzall—a construction tool resembling a large, electric meat-carving knife. The Ferrantis returned it spattered with a reddish-brown substance that Turuk had assumed was mud.

Eric Mergenthal worked on Tocco and gradually arranged to purchase an illegal gun from him. Mergenthal and Tocco had known and trusted each other since boyhood. Even though Tocco suspected that the police had informants in the neighborhood, he agreed to do business with Mergenthal.

At one point, Mergenthal got cold feet. But Dowd wasn't about to let him leave, not with Tocco ready to commit a felony. Dowd threatened to send Mergenthal to jail, cutting him off from both his freedom and his easy access to heroin. When that didn't work, Dowd roused Mergenthal one day and hauled him into his unmarked police surveillance van. With one hand clutching Mergenthal's blond, curly hair, Dowd used the other to show him photos of Bailey's desecrated corpse.

"You want to end up like this?" Dowd screamed. "You want Ferranti to find out you were working for us?"

Mergenthal came back in. On November 19, he introduced Tocco to "his cousin from Long Island," who was really an undercover from the firearms task force. Two days later, Tocco took $750 from the undercover and said he'd deliver a nine-millimeter Beretta. The wait was nearly unbearable. If Tocco could be arrested on a gun felony, he'd face such serious prison time that Dowd was certain he could squeeze him into cooperating and describing how Ferranti had hired him to set the fire. All Tocco had to do was produce that illegal gun.

At first Tocco stalled, saying his new supplier was taking a bit longer than expected. Then, on November 23, Tocco went cold. He told Mergenthal the deal was off and warned him not bring his "cousin" around anymore.

There was something unnerving about the abruptness of Tocco's about-face. Had he simply been unable to resist the temptation to rip off a hopeless, defenseless addict like Mergenthal? Had he been tipped off? Dowd wasn't sure, but he knew that something had gone very wrong, and his investigation was once again nowhere.

Dowd was frantic. He went to the FBI's organized-crime task force, hoping that Ferranti's mob ties might convince the feds to bring additional resources to the investigation. He had also begun reaching out to an old friend from Brooklyn, Detective Vincent Armanti, to ask if he'd help with the case. Armanti had a reputation as a bit of a loose cannon, but he and Dowd had been friends in Brooklyn narcotics, and his productivity had made him one of the department's star undercovers.

On February 24, 1993, the one-year anniversary of Williams's death, four hundred firemen held a memorial service as the city named a street near the Rescue 4 station house Lieutenant Thomas A. Williams Place. The ceremony received widespread media coverage, all of which noted that the firemen were heartsick that the killers remained free.

Then on March 19 came the most chilling development. Eric Mergenthal was found dead in his bedroom, clutching a syringe. The cause of death was said to be an accidental overdose. But Dowd had gotten to know Mergenthal well during their five months together in the field, and was more aware than he should have been of Eric's savvy and experience as a drug user. Dowd felt a sickening certainty that Mergenthal's death had been no accident.

2

ONE LAST CASE

MARCH 1993

DETECTIVE VINCENT ARMANTI was so enthralled by the ragtag mobsters ambling across his TV screen that he never heard his front door creak open upstairs. For hours, Armanti had been lost in his Staten Island basement, clutching the VCR remote as if it were the key to heaven. He could go on like this for days during the early stages of an investigation. The beginning—figuring out a way into his target's world—was always the toughest part of the game he'd learned to play so well. He just wasn't exactly sure why he was getting ready to play it again. Back in December, against his saner instincts, Armanti had allowed Ed Dowd to coax him into dusting off his undercover act. Now here he was in March, with spring practically beginning, studying his surveillance tapes—eight hours of surly, hairy-backed thugs trudging in and out of Sebastian's bar in Throgs Neck. His job was trying to conjure up some way to make these charmers into his pals—without being bludgeoned, shot in the face, or having his head cut off like Bruce Bailey.

Once he was inside, on "the set," as the pros called it, Armanti was a masterful improviser—full of fast talk, a scam artist's instinct, and bent-nose sex appeal. Compact and powerful, he had the look of a Sicilian middleweight fighter, which instantly translated into street credibility. Born Brooklyn Italian, he was inherently hip to the rhythms of the underworld's unspoken idioms. Depending on the moment, he knew when to flatter or threaten, when to challenge or brag or cajole. During one investigation in Bensonhurst, he spent six months buying cocaine and fending off advances from the matriarch of an unusual drug operation, a stylish fifty-year-old dame who directed the narcotics sales of a dozen of her own children and grandchildren.

Another case had nearly ended disastrously when he was sitting in a mobbed-up coffee shop and an off-duty detective recognized him. "Hey, I know you," she announced. "You're Vinnie Armanti." He gave her the brush-off, but she chased him, shouting his real name a second time. Meanwhile, a roomful of heavily armed wiseguys had stopped what they were doing to observe. Armanti turned toward the detective, stared her down, then dropped his pants and asked her to refresh his memory. The detective ran off, and the mobsters howled.

That freewheeling style earned Armanti a reputation as the resident eccentric of the narcotics unit, and gave his supervisors palpitations. Other undercovers resented the way he defied authority and got away with it, especially because Armanti seemed incapable of passing up a chance to needle his fellow detectives. But in the end, narcotics commanders are judged by statistics: arrest figures, the aggregate weight of their drug seizures, and the number of positive headlines they ring up for the commissioner and the mayor. Assessed by these criteria, Armanti was definitely a star, nabbing hundreds of kilos of cocaine, smashing dozens of drug operations, and catching a group of Russian mobsters planning to rob a Brinks truck with an armor-piercing missile, a murderer with two bodies in a freezer, and a drug dealer who had faked his own death to escape prosecution. Did it really matter if some of his attitude might be interpreted as a middle-finger salute, daring the bosses to try to rein him in? Armanti's supervisors shook their heads and worried that one day he might go too far. Everyone got it, though: There was no real choice but to let Vinnie be Vinnie.

But now, before he could get his new routine up and running, he had to find an opening, and the search was making him irritated, because he was a perfectionist. Five years as an undercover had taught him to interpret the subtle distinctions in customs and dialects among New York's colorful Mafia clans. He rarely missed a nuance. Like an urban anthropologist, he could spot the difference between the Cosa Nostra showboats of Bay Ridge or Rego Park, the Little Italy old-timers, and the working-class gangsters of Bensonhurst. Armanti's experienced eyes and ears picked up everything.

These guys in Throgs Neck were a new variation on the old bloodstained pinstripes and crucifixes. They dressed differently, usually in construction boots and T-shirts or cotton baseball jerseys. They had jettisoned the back slaps, hugs, and ostentatious greetings, like "How's it goin', Sallie Boy!" Instead, they'd exchange a nod, a slight wave, at most a "Hey." They didn't even kiss, for Christ's sake. They were more like the leg breakers Armanti had rumbled with in Sunset Park—street toughs with no mob connections. All this familiarity made the case seem more engrossing and, somehow, more threatening.

Alone in the dark, oblivious to the hushed sound of someone creeping down the stairs, Armanti whirred the tape back and forth, trying to stitch together a new self, a persona worthy of the occasion. Most of the key players at Sebastian's were in their early thirties—a good start, because Armanti was thirty-three. They had a certain scruffiness—also a plus. Armanti came from New York's struggling classes; he'd survived enough hockey fights and street brawls that his scars helped him blend in with any group of men who earned a living with their hands and hardiness.

He also had his most disarming feature: those eyes. On anyone else's face, they would have undoubtedly been notable for their color, a shade of clear blue that glinted like some exotic gem. But on Armanti they were weapons. His stare was so unrelenting that even glancing away he was still sizing you up. The sheer intensity of his gaze at first made suspects choose their words carefully, but it eventually seduced them into opening up. Whatever crimes they might be considering—rape, murder, narcotics, dismemberment—was there any point in being shy in front of a guy whose eyes had so obviously seen worse? Sometimes, off duty, Armanti would absentmindedly slip into the stare, and his friends would have to remind him to knock it off with "the SKL"—his serial-killer look.

Armanti lit a cigarette—a Newport Light, the streetwise brand of choice—and made a mental note that they'd be a suitable prop for his work in the neighborhood he'd soon know as da Neck.

Then he felt a hand on his shoulder and nearly jumped off the couch. It was his girlfriend, Judith, back from her job at a travel agency in midtown. She gave his cheek a quick kiss—too quick, he thought—as he scrambled to shut off the tape and distract her with a warm welcome and some small talk. No luck. Judy, no pushover, had already recognized the grainy police-surveillance footage.

"What the hell are you doing?" she asked, though they both knew already. Armanti was breaking his solemn vow to give up the thrill of undercover work and stay at a desk job. Now the fight was on again, and neither of them could really bear to consider how it might end this time.

SEX, MONEY, AND relatives may spark arguments between average couples, but in police households most battles revolve around the Job. The rumblings may start with quibbling about a cop's brutish and unpredictable schedule, the lousy pay, or the stifling calendar of promotion ceremonies, funerals, communion breakfasts, and retirement bashes. Some wives or husbands or beaus worry about the way the work deadens the soul, all those chilling little workaday stories played out in four-letter words, bloody endings, and macabre punch lines. At heart, though, anyone who loves a cop lives in mortal fear of that knock on the door, the moment they'll find two men in uniform on their stoop with long faces and bad news to deliver. They grow to despise anyone, anything responsible for placing them in such ungodly proximity to death.

Armanti was surprised, even touched, when Judy first admitted how scared all the undercover intrigue made her. Given all the things they fought about (and they tangled frequently and audibly), he'd never suspected that her worries about his safety would grow into an unbridgeable chasm between them. After all, she was the free spirit, the woman he admired precisely because she was nothing like the obedient Italian girls from Our Lady of Perpetual Help, the Marias and Catherines and Angies he'd been raised to accept as his moussed-up destiny.

Armanti had been set to marry a butcher's daughter when Judy came along with her English lit, her Save the Whales slogans, and a style all her own. He was twenty-five, an ex-marine bound for the NYPD. Really, people had badgered him, after eight years dating the same girl, wasn't it time to propose? His relatives and neighbors and their relatives and neighbors formed a chorus: Marry the nice girl, leave her home with the kids while you carouse with the Goumada a few nights a week. On Sunday, everyone's off to church, then the mother-in-law's for macaroni. It's the way things worked.

Then one night, as a cousin bragged about his Manhattan connection for cut-rate engagement rings, *beauty-ful* stuff, Armanti saw Judith. It was a Thursday, at Jasmine's Nightclub on Third Avenue in Bay Ridge, and in 1986, that meant enough gold chains, silk shirts, and perfume to dazzle Marco Polo. And there she was on the dance floor, wearing a T-shirt, dungarees, and a backpack. A blond Puerto Rican girl with a smile that blared *Who says I can't?*, flaunting the fact that she was dressed to hike Mount McKinley. Once they'd exchanged glances, he walked up and introduced himself with some subtle line like "What's goin' on?" In no time, they were like a TV ad for togetherness. After six scandalous months of being spotted around the neighborhood with the girl people called the "Hot Tomato" and the "Alley Cat," Armanti took a deep breath and broke it off with the butcher's daughter.

Alone, Armanti and Judy dreamed up their own world. She was the devoted student who introduced her rough-hewn lover to the finer things. He was the tough guy who'd almost been tossed out of FDR High School for fighting and who'd finally had some sensitivity dragged out of his testosterone heart. She loved his exuberance, his passion. And while Judy was surprised to learn that he carried a copy of Khalil Gibran's *The Prophet,* which he called his bible, she found his lack of college-boy pretentiousness refreshing. Nor was she embarrassed when she took him to galleries or parties with her clients in the Hamptons. She'd read to him, Shakespeare and Keats, and she introduced him to Monet and Caravaggio.

"You've got this whole other side," she said early one morning, when they'd walked to the playground at five A.M., rapt in one of those intoxicating conversations during love's first bloom. "You just needed someone to bring it out of you."

Judy was the first person who cared enough to really encourage Armanti to rely on his brains rather than his fists or his terrifying eyes. The butcher's daughter had initially hated the fact that her intended was a roughneck: A year before Armanti left for the service, her father had set him up with a job at a friend's supermarket in Hell's Kitchen. But the effort to soften up Armanti's edges backfired when he was given a baseball bat and instructed to pummel any wino, junkie, transvestite, prostitute, or gang member who decided to shoplift. Judy, from a different world, detested violence, wouldn't tolerate it, and threatened to leave him if she ever saw him throw a punch.

To encourage him to open up, she refused to accept any expensive gifts from Armanti, asking him to write her letters instead. The words just seemed to rush out of him. He told her about street fights, growing up in a home ravaged by alcoholism and drug abuse, his fears of the future, and the countless kicks, slaps, and slights of growing up poor. He even confided about how his extended family added to his problems. When Vinnie was ten, his cousin and uncle would pick him up at two A.M., smudge dirt on his face, and pour water on his crotch. Then they took him to the loading docks to ask for donations so the poor kid could get a kidney transplant. Armanti's cut averaged ten to twenty dollars a night. He had never trusted anyone enough to really share these things before, but telling Judy didn't make him feel weaker. It made him stronger.

The one topic he found it difficult to talk about was his work. When they'd met, he'd told Judy about his part-time work on the docks in New Jersey. But he'd waited a few weeks to mention the day job as a cop. He figured that anyone who spent weekends at rallies for Native Americans might have a few issues about dating a soldier of the armed oppressor. When he finally fessed up, she seemed more amused than anything. But Armanti still sensed that he'd best spare the gritty details about his undercover work.

Besides, for the first time in his adult life, Armanti wasn't really focused on what his career was putting him through. Armanti had never held even the slightest romantic notion about being a cop—he'd taken the police exam in 1981 because it had seemed like a path to something approximating respectability, good benefits, and a pension. His application had been rejected when the NYPD's screeners learned that his cousin had been indicted for racketeering. Those legal problems had nothing to do with Armanti, but he had no connections in the department, so it was enough to keep him off the force.

He joined the marines instead, and found boot camp a relief from city life, although his Brooklyn accent and big-city style made him an easy target for the drill instructors. (They called him "Flatbush," because it was the only part of Brooklyn any of his platoon mates could name.) For months, the Good Ol' Boys tried to break Armanti, assigning him every demeaning job they could think of, inflicting innumerable push-ups on him, and practically begging him to throw a punch. Armanti survived the test so well that after thirteen weeks of boot camp he graduated at the top of his platoon and was promoted to Private First Class. He was shipped out to 29 Palms, California—a marine base in the Mojave Desert. Here the promotion earned him more than just bragging rights; it also helped him finagle the occasional furlough and spend weekends in Palm Springs. Just the kind of place where a kid from Brooklyn could sit by the pool, take off his shirt, and impress vacationing West Coast women with his ginzo gigolo routine.

A year into his military tour, the NYPD unexpectedly informed Armanti that there was an opening and offered him a job. Homesick for the action of the city and eager to see how his newfound self-discipline might play on the streets of New York, Armanti finagled his way out of the marines and headed back East to the police academy. He spent his first three years patrolling the Eighty-fourth Precinct in Brooklyn Heights and two more in the precinct's anticrime unit. He was drafted into the narcotics division almost by accident. One day in 1987, Armanti was waiting for his best friend Tommy outside the Brooklyn South narcotics office when a supervisor mistook him for a street creature and ordered him to get away from the police officers' parking lot. Armanti walked away, and when the lieutenant went inside, grumbling about a "neighborhood punk" loitering outside the office, Tommy, an undercover, glanced out and realized he was talking about Armanti.

"He's not a neighborhood punk," Tommy had shouted, breaking into laughter. "He's a cop."

Within a month, the lieutenant had successfully lobbied the police brass, and Armanti was conscripted into the NYPD's war on drugs—as an undercover detective.

Finally, Armanti had found a place where his gritty past and dramatic range were truly assets. Most undercovers played it safe during street buys, either coddling the subject of their investigations or simply walking up to a crack dealer and nervously muttering, "Gimme two." But Armanti made every set a Broadway production, even the penny-ante buy and busts. He'd usually start by hovering around a corner, all keyed up while nursing a beer and smoking a cigarette in his inimitable way. Between each drag he'd stare at the smoke curling off the tip, check out the filter, examine the paper so intently you'd think it was covered in secret code. Then he'd exhale luxuriously, sensuously, unforgettably. (A friend of his once remarked, "You don't just smoke a cigarette, you fuck it.") If some unsuspecting dealer watched a little too closely, Armanti sprang into action.

"What the fuck you staring at?" Armanti would scream. "You want to fuck *me*? How about I split your head open! Right now, you and me!"

In any other context it would have been laughable for a mauler like Armanti, whose attraction was strictly grit, to suggest that someone considered him fey. But in the macho world of drug dealers and wiseguys, his challenge was such heresy it never failed. Armanti just kept pushing, forcing his flustered target to defend his manhood. He figured he was smart enough to call it quits just before things exploded, tough enough to handle himself if they did. Usually he would find some way to let the suspect save face just before the first punch or bullet flew. Then—*voilà!*—Armanti's first theory of street etiquette: Confrontation + Confrontation = Friendship. After he passed the buddy stage, Armanti would pull back and wait for days, or sometimes months. He'd just hang out and listen to the clock tick, smoking, drinking, watching. When the talk inevitably turned to crime, no one suspected that Armanti was tape-recording every word. They all figured the guy was too crazy to be a cop.

Most amazingly, Armanti's rap worked in virtually every neighborhood in the city, no small feat in the racially balkanized New York underworld. Armanti's spin on a mafioso wannabe was so dead on that real mobsters often thought they'd met before. A wiseguy Armanti sent to prison in 1997 still tells relatives that there's no way the guy could have been a cop—even though he watched Armanti testify, saw it with his own eyes, for days on end. In black and Latino neighborhoods, Armanti's edgy goombah swagger also managed to touch chords, familiar as it was from their B-movie impressions of the mob. At one time in the Dominican neighborhood of Washington Heights, his chilling stare had street dealers whispering about the mobster nicknamed *El Diablo*.

IN LESS THAN seven years, Armanti progressed from rookie beat cop to a legend of the narcotics division. Yet his most effective deception came later—at home, where he offered Judy only vague, thoroughly sanitized tidbits about his sweaty crucible of a vocation. Covering his tracks wasn't difficult, given the circumstances of their life together. She traveled for weeks at a time to resorts in Monte Carlo, Tahiti, and Thailand. When she was in town, he pretended he was a clock puncher, sharpening pencils in some cubicle. Any cop who nabs a purse snatcher can end up with his name in print or a picture in the neighborhood newspaper, but undercovers always cut out before the cameras arrive and, by necessity, leave the press conferences to the chiefs and politicos. So even though Armanti's stature grew within the department, and even though he handled cases sensational enough to inspire screaming front-page headlines in the *New York Post* and the *Daily News,* his name never got bandied about.

It was a workable arrangement until Judy's brother joined the force as a patrol officer in Coney Island during the crazy, smoke-filled era of the crack wars. From his street post in the Sixtieth Precinct, her brother heard whispers about Armanti's exploits. When Judy complained one day about Armanti's intrusive work schedule, her brother blew his fuse and his fellow cop's cover. "Why are you busting his balls?" he said, hoping his own awe would prove contagious. "Don't you know how much pressure he's under at work? He's one of the top undercovers in the country."

Later, Armanti tried to soothe Judy's wounded, out-of-control temper by explaining how much he enjoyed working as an undercover and how he'd lied to protect her from her own fears and sleepless nights. He told her how the job made use of everything he had suffered so hard to learn: his calm in the midst of chaos, his knack for reading strangers cold, and his improbable charm. She flared back, suggesting vocational guidance and an occupation with a lower mortality rate. But Armanti knew there was nothing that could match the sheer buzz of undercover work.

It wasn't that he was a zealot about drugs. Armanti had been surrounded by narcotics during his entire upbringing. Cocaine was such a popular recreational drug in Brooklyn during the mid-1970s that it wasn't unusual for young Vinnie to be at a friend's house watching television while a grown-up sat in the next room cutting up piles of it and stashing them in Polly-o ricotta containers in the freezer. While Armanti was still in grammar school, the owner of the corner fruit stand would occasionally send Vinnie to the local marijuana dealer to score joints, and tip him $3 each delivery.

And Judy already understood that the glory of being an undercover had nothing to do with the pay. To work in narcotics is to be mocked by money. Armanti had told her about risking his life chasing kids rich enough to buy and sell them both. He handled obscene amounts of cash, usually alone, in godforsaken alleys where no one would ever notice if he slipped a bundle of hundreds under his belt. Yet an honest cop like Armanti—the first undercover entrusted with a million dollars in flash money during a single deal—made only about as much as a decent cabdriver.

No, the reason he loved working as an undercover was because it was the one place where he felt accepted, and exceptional, by being himself. All his life he had been punished for being a street fighter, or smart-ass, the parts of his personality he liked best. Now he was not only paid to play all those roles, he was admired and rewarded because they seemed to come to him so naturally.

"Please," he told Judy, "don't try to change me."

She fumed for a while, then abandoned the argument. But Armanti knew that with her, the first woman who ever told him *Fuck you* during a fight, silence didn't necessarily mean the negotiation was closed. Sure enough, during a cozy moment a few weeks later, the whole thing came back with a vengeance. At dinner, Armanti was fantasizing about the day they'd settle down and she would leave her fast-lane job to raise a family. Their fights usually evolved into protracted battles of psychological chess, but this time Judy moved like a grand master mercilessly crushing a novice.

"You quit your job, I'll quit mine," she said. Check and mate.

The chill still hadn't exactly thawed three months later, when Judy learned about the shooting. Armanti had been driving to work along Ninth Avenue in Sunset Park, when he happened to buzz past a street-corner drug rip-off that turned into a shoot-out. He jumped out of his car, rushed toward the gunman, and found himself with a nine-millimeter automatic against his temple. Somehow, he hadn't wound up with his brains spewed across the pavement. That night, without telling her why, he took Judy to dinner at her favorite restaurant and bought her flowers to celebrate the fact that he had survived. When they returned home from what she had thought was merely a romantic dinner, his answering machine was crammed with messages from concerned cops who wanted to make sure he was still in one piece.

"Vinnie, we heard you almost bought it today," blurted out the voice in the answering machine before Armanti could shut it off.

Judy had had enough. So, after weeks of furious arguments and escalating threats to leave him, Armanti relented and told her his days as an undercover were over. When the narcotics division training unit was looking for a new instructor a few months later, Armanti was ordered by his superiors to apply. During his interview, Armanti made sure to tell the captain he'd miss undercover work because he liked drinking on the job. It was no use. The captain had already been warned about Armanti's warped sense of humor and reluctance to leave the streets. By the time Armanti drove from One Police Plaza back to his office in Brooklyn, the transfer had already been approved.

Armanti's concession began a blissful new era between him and Judy. They talked seriously about wedding plans, kids, even when they might start trying to get pregnant. They traveled to Greece and France, and as a birthday present, Judy took Armanti to Giverny to see the gardens that had inspired the Monet paintings he so loved. In Paris, when some Frenchman flirted with Judy a bit too persistently, Armanti reacted without a second's hesitation, belting him with a left hook. Judy fumed for a few days, but after all Armanti had sacrificed, how could she refuse to forgive him?

On the day they moved in together, into his tidy house on the Jersey side of Staten Island, Armanti unpacked a sheaf of journals he had written as a teenager. Rereading the alienated, existential ramblings of his former self, he just shook his head. "What am I asking for?" read one entry, written when Armanti was fourteen. "A kiss that I don't reach for or maybe a thought that I didn't think of? What? How long does my existence last? How long?" Armanti felt blessed that he could finally bid that poor kid good-bye.

All in all, life together with Judy might have settled into a steady, upbeat momentum if Armanti hadn't decided to drop in on the Brooklyn South Narcotics Unit Christmas party in December 1992. For what seemed like forever he had been dodging Detective Ed Dowd, a classmate from the police academy (and quite possibly the only homicide detective in the history of the NYPD to carry books on Matisse and van Gogh alongside his murder files). Dowd was trying to lure Armanti into his case involving the highly publicized and painfully unsolved death of fireman Lieutenant Thomas Williams.

With his lanky build, unshorn hair, and laid-back demeanor, Dowd had always struck Armanti as an absentminded-professor type. In the late 1980s, Armanti and the others who worked in narcotics had dubbed Dowd "Shaggy," after the beatnik character in the Scooby-Doo cartoons. But like all skilled detectives, Dowd had a gift for using whatever he had— strengths, weaknesses, warts, whatever—to get his way. Some investigators bullied or badgered their suspects. Dowd lulled them into a false sense of security, then used his quiet, relentless common sense to outsmart them.

For him, the party was the perfect opportunity to put Armanti in the vise. Sidling up to his old friend at the buffet table, Dowd started recounting war stories about the cases they'd worked together, as they dug into the veal cutlets and chicken francese while Frank Sinatra crooned "White Christmas" in the background. As Vinnie wondered what the hell had happened to Bing Crosby, he bobbed and weaved away from the other detective. But Dowd steered Armanti to the bar and waited for the liquor to help him with his task. Finally, Dowd pulled his pal into the bathroom and tried to close the deal.

"You gonna help me with this fireman case?"

Armanti had ad-libbed something he knew wasn't even half convincing, some nonsense about cops hating firemen—even though Dowd was well aware of the fact that Armanti considered firefighters the only people in the world more heroic than undercovers.

"Come on, Vin, you're trying to tell me you're happy doing what you're doing? In the office?"

"Yeah," Armanti said. "It's not bad."

Dowd cocked an eyebrow, and reached into his jacket pocket. Lo and behold, he just happened to have a newspaper article about the case, complete with a photo of Lieutenant Williams, all spiffed up in his dress uniform. Armanti looked at the picture and shook his head.

"Jesus, that's a shame."

Dowd waited a moment, then pulled out the heavy artillery: the case folder, with photos of the suspects.

"His family can't sleep," Dowd said. "They keep calling to ask about the case, and they can't sleep knowing that whoever did this is still out there."

Armanti wouldn't admit it that night, but by the time he walked out to Dowd's car and agreed to take the case folder home for a closer look, he was already hooked. Within a day, he was in training, sculpting his body to attain that hard, pallid, jail-yard look. He used a low-fat, high-protein diet, and lots of push-ups and pull-ups, trying to accentuate the muscles most likely to be built up in a prison cell. He'd even begun practicing a few of the tics he'd observed watching prisoners in the marines military brig—sitting with his heels together, speaking only when spoken to. He coached himself to remember to always stick close to walls. (In prison, only guards walked down the middle of hallways.) Two days later he called Dowd, and during the two weeks it took for the chiefs to approve Armanti's assignment to the case, he called again nearly every day.

By the time headquarters gave the go-ahead, Armanti had already spent days in the Bronx alone, taking surveillance videos outside of Sebastian's bar without so much as mentioning it to Dowd.

ON THE AFTERNOON in March when Judy caught him hunched over his gangster tapes, Armanti knew it would take a miracle to hold their relationship together.

"You promised me, no more."

"I know. It's just one last case. The guy's family is all torn apart."

"I don't want to hear about his family," she said. "What about me? I'm supposed to spend my entire life worrying about whether you're coming home?"

"What about you? You're in planes, flying around the world all the time. Every time there's a plane crash I have to wonder if I'll ever see you again."

"I don't go around getting guns stuck in my face, thinking it's cute."

"It's not cute," Armanti said. "It's what I do."

The truth was, Armanti had felt diminished sitting behind a desk. On the streets, he was the Man. Some people thought he was cocky, others were certain he was crazy, but no one doubted that he could get the job done. Working as an "inside guy," Armanti felt ashamed of the fact that many cops assumed he must have had a connection to land such a cushy job. Shortly after Armanti began working as an undercover he hung a plaque in his locker, a quote from Teddy Roosevelt:

It is not the critic who counts, nor the man who points out where the strong man stumbled, or where a doer of deeds could have done them better. The credit belongs to the man in the arena whose face is marred by dust and sweat and blood, who strives valiantly, who errs, and who comes up short again and again, who knows the great enthusiasms, the great devotions, and spends himself in a worthy cause. The man who at best knows the triumph of high achievement and who at worst, if he fails, fails while daring greatly, so that his place will never be with those cold timid souls who never knew victory or defeat.

In his locker, the plaque had inspired Armanti; but sitting framed on a desk, under the numbing hum of fluorescent office lights, it seemed like a curse.

Things with Judy had undeniably been smoother since he'd agreed to leave the streets. But at home, Armanti had only one thing: the way he loved her. Even if he could have put those feelings into words, though, how could he tell her? And how could he ever answer her inevitable comeback: *So what you're saying is, loving me isn't enough?*

There was also something about this case, the cruel way the Ferrantis ruled over their turf. Mobsters in Brooklyn and Queens are usually embraced by the communities they control because the wiseguys are savvy enough to donate to churches, put on fireworks displays for neighborhood kids, and handle all the little problems that people can't take to the police. The Ferrantis ran their neighborhoods like the slumlords they were. They didn't just control the people in their ghetto empire; they seemed to take a sadistic glee in dominating the powerless. And during his research into the case, Armanti had also seen a newspaper photo of Lieutenant Williams and his kids. He thought of those bright-eyed girls knowing that their father's killers were still out there laughing. The Ferrantis hadn't even had the courtesy to wait until he was buried before they'd begun filing their fraudulent insurance claim.

Armanti looked at Judy, his fearsome eyes reduced to pleading.

"You fell in love with me. This is what I do. It's what makes me who I am."

"I fell in love with you," she said. "Not the police department."

When Armanti crawled into bed that night, he and Judy didn't say a word before they made love. If he had known anyone else he could confide in, he might have told them that this night was the most intense romantic experience of his life, kissing away the tears as they ran down her face.

Over coffee the next morning, they avoided the question for a while, although they both felt it between them, like a radioactive iceberg on the breakfast table. It was Judy, of course, who finally had to ask.

"So what are you gonna do?"

Armanti waited a moment to reply.

"I've got to do it," he said.

She stormed off, and Armanti turned to watch her, wondering if he'd ever see her again. He took another sip of coffee, heard her start the car and pull out of the driveway. Then Vincent Armanti, New York City Undercover Detective #4126, walked to the basement and opened up a dresser drawer. He wanted to see if any of his clothes had the right look for Throgs Neck.

3

BOTH ENDS

JUNE 1, 1993

ALWAYS MAKE THEM come to you. This is the first rule Armanti drummed into the heads of his undercover trainees: that the essence of narcotics investigation is patience. No one is more keenly attuned to telltale nerves than a drug dealer. Nothing is more obvious, or endangered, than an undercover who seems overeager. So the most vital lesson Armanti strove to teach young detectives was the high art of sitting back, dangling like a human lure, and drawing suspects gradually toward yourself.

Yet as he leaned on the bar in Sebastian's on this warm night, fumbling to read the message on his pager, Armanti also knew it was much easier advice to give than it was to heed. He was not predisposed to considering patience a virtue, yet he'd been on the set nearly three months and still hadn't managed to get close to Tommy "the Torch" Tocco. As he headed to the pay phone to call the number on his beeper, careful to hide his impatience and maintain his best Vinnie Blue Eyes strut, Armanti wondered: *How much longer? What would it take to finally get these guys to engage?*

The first step in creating his new character—finding a name—had been simple. Armanti had decided to resurrect one of his trusty old undercover aliases, Vincent Penisi, taken from a gravestone in the wiseguy section of Greenwood Cemetery in Brooklyn. On a whim, he'd added the middle initial J., to honor his late grandfather, Joseph. Forming Vinnie's back story and calibrating his personality traits was a far more complex endeavor. Armanti's initial instinct was to mimic the look of the neighborhood and wear dungarees, baseball shirts, and work boots. But as he had studied the tapes, he noticed that the characters at Sebastian's were so socially stunted that they barely acknowledged their peers; he realized that if Vinnie was really going to connect with these guys, he'd have to stand out from the crowd. Watching the videos over and over again, Armanti sensed a vulnerability at Sebastian's: The guys there seemed a bit unsettled by the occasional visitor who appeared better dressed or better paid. So Armanti decided to nudge Vinnie a rung up the social ladder, to make him someone that members of the Throgs Neck crew might feel a need to impress.

Armanti added a few ostentatious flourishes to make Vinnie the kind of guy who, in the words of any street creature from Bensonhurst, "thinks who he is." With a gold chain here, a designer label there, and some big talk about grand schemes and lucrative scams, Armanti could make Vinnie a comer, someone they just had to watch.

To contrast with the flash and finery, Vinnie would adopt the standard undercover character's explanation for showing up in the Bronx. He was running from the law, keeping clear of his home turf in Brooklyn until the investigation into some unspecified, but tantalizing, crime cooled down.

During every undercover operation, Armanti kept two things in his pocket. One was a small rock with the word *Courage* chiseled into it, a memento that had been with him so long he couldn't even recall where he'd gotten it. The other was a string of red rosary beads that had been left to him by the one person who'd actually managed to make him feel protected during his boyhood, his grandma Rose. During his parents' fights, and all the assorted turmoil of his adolescence, Armanti had often taken refuge in her apartment. There she'd calm him with a hot meal, telling him: "Don't worry, Dolly, everything's going to be all right." She died when Armanti was eighteen, shortly before he joined the service. But he had such frequent dreams about her promising to watch over him that he began carrying her rosary as a good-luck charm.

THROGS NECK IS a world unto itself, the kind of place where even the law-abiding keep to themselves, and they expect the same from everyone else, thank you very much. Tucked into a forgotten corner of the Bronx, New York's forgotten borough, the neighborhood lies far from the glare of New York's bright lights and the gaze of the city's powerful. Geographically, Throgs Neck is quite literally an enclave, a peninsula separating the East River and Long Island Sound. Residents here are predominantly Italian and Irish, the civil servants and tradesmen who form the working-class backbone of New York's infrastructure. People are not so much wary of outsiders as resistant to them. So while much of the Bronx was transformed into bustling pastiches of Latino and West Indian culture during the 1970s and '80s, Throgs Neck's predominantly European-American residents used a combination of cliquishness, stubbornness, and no small amount of redlining to beat back the waves of the immigrant tide.

By the time Armanti first set foot on Throgs Neck's streets in March of 1993, it had the outdated look and languid pace of the New York he'd seen on old reruns of *I Love Lucy*. Its main drag was a run-down collection of chintzy neon storefronts, bagel shops, delis, pizzerias, gin mills, banks, and shoe-repair places. In contrast to most New York neighborhoods, both in the Bronx and beyond, the overwhelming majority of the faces hurrying along its avenues were white.

As in so many New York neighborhoods, Throgs Neck's underworld characters were also fixtures on its street corners and business strips, landmarks every bit as essential and recognizable as the stop signs or lampposts. One such figure was Louis Inglese, whose profoundly obese frame won him the nickname Louie the Whale, and who could often be seen sunning his estimable self on a lawn chair in front of a funeral home on East Tremont. Tocco's cousin Vinny Basciano, a soldier in the Bonanno family, lived closer to the water, and anyone who had the bad manners or misfortune to allow his dog to relieve itself on the Basciano lawn quickly learned that this particular patch of turf needed no additional irrigation. More than one dog owner in the neighborhood can recall the lady of the Basciano household responding to the sight of a squatting beagle or a lifted hind leg by leaning out the window and warning:

"I'm gonna have Vinny break your fucking legs!"

When the Bascianos expanded their home on the end of Revere Avenue in the early 1990s, they weren't shy about depriving every other house on the block of its precious glimpse of the water. But it was when the family installed huge plate-glass windows facing the river—only to find the view obstructed by a stand of about thirty trees on a vacant city lot—that the truly miraculous transpired. One day, neighborhood residents awoke to find the timber reduced to a collection of stumps, like some clear-cut forest chewed up by a runaway chain saw.

"Vinny wanted to see the water," they were told with a smile.

There was grumbling and a great deal of fear, but it wasn't like you could call the forest service—or anyone else, really. The same city officials who couldn't stop the drug dealers or the blatant influence of organized crime weren't exactly going to vault into action for a Save the Trees campaign. In a community as inward as Throgs Neck, where people knew their places and kept to themselves, there was little reason for wiseguys to hide their power or influence.

In Throgs Neck, their base of operations and home turf, Jack and Mario Ferranti had pioneered new levels of brazenness in the way they flouted existing laws. Not only did the brothers earn steady incomes and brutal reputations from their slums in Harlem; they also liked to boast about their powerful connections in law enforcement and city government. Around the time that Armanti was preparing to go undercover, Dowd and the other detectives met with a retired federal agent named Anthony Lombardi, who had once investigated charges that the Ferrantis had law enforcement officials on their payroll. Lombardi said that he had received information from a lawyer describing how the Ferrantis paid off the Bronx district attorney to fix cases. What's more, the lawyer told Lombardi that the Ferrantis gave payoffs to Rudolph W. Giuliani, then the U.S. attorney for the Southern District of New York, which encompassed Manhattan and the Bronx. Lombardi said he later met with Jack Ferranti, who was trying to make a deal with prosecutors to beat an illegal weapons case, and Jack told him that both the Bronx DA and Giuliani were on the take.

Nothing had ever come of the accusations. Lombardi, who worked for Giuliani on the President's Commission on Organized Crime at the time he heard the information, said he passed the allegations to the Justice Department. Ultimately, they were determined to be unfounded. Nonetheless, in the spring of 1993, when Giuliani was running for mayor on his record as an aggressive crime buster, it was chilling to even consider that the Ferrantis might have that kind of influence.

As the Williams case progressed, Dowd and the other investigators tried to examine the evidence Lombardi had gathered, to determine whether the charges were true or just campaign-season character assassination. But, when they asked for the investigative file, things got murky. Lombardi had obtained six tapes of Jack Ferranti's secretly recorded telephone conversations about the payoffs and had turned them over to the FBI. When Armanti and the FBI agents involved in the Lieutenant Williams case requested the tapes, however, the agent running the evidence room returned empty-handed and panicked.

"They're gone!" he claimed. "Somebody took them and they weren't signed out."

Cindy Peil, the FBI agent working with Armanti, was puzzled, to say the least. "Who the hell would steal those tapes," she asked, humiliated that her own agency couldn't be trusted with sensitive evidence. "And why the hell would they want to?"

Armanti was having his troubles out on the streets, too. The Ferrantis' reputed political connections and the bunker mentality of the neighborhood made things complicated enough. But his main target, Tommy Tocco, was beyond slippery. Short, squinty-eyed, with a high-pitched voice that was simultaneously gravelly and whiny, Tocco was hardly a figure to instill fear in any survivor of New York's streets. Yet he had parlayed his dim wit and malleability into a surprisingly privileged position. Simultaneously he had ingratiated himself with two competing mob families, running numbers for his cousin Vinny Basciano and, later, crossing party lines to marry the daughter of a Luchese soldier. These dual alliances provided Tocco with his most intimidating feature—his proximity to toughness. Throughout the late 1980s and early '90s, he used it to build a formidable reputation.

Watching how the Torch kissed up to his wiseguy superiors—then talked down to his equals with a teacher's pet's self-importance—Armanti figured that goading Tocco into a confrontation would be pointless. Tommy was just too light weight to fight his own battles. Armanti also realized early on that he couldn't connect with Tocco on any intellectual level: It was readily apparent that no one would ever accuse the Torch of being cerebral. Somehow, Tocco had managed to graduate from Lehman High School, but his limited dexterity with simple arithmetic made his work as a numbers runner an accountant's nightmare. On more than one occasion he'd returned from his rounds collecting money from Basciano's numbers spots with too much or too little cash. Anyone else might be fired for such a serious infraction, or maybe even accused of stealing and then beaten or killed. But Tocco's bosses understood the limitations of his low-watt intellect, laughing off the errors as "fuckin' Tommy." Tocco was once fired from a numbers job, too, but the cause was bad manners. Picking up the daily take from a numbers spot in Harlem one day in 1990, Tocco felt the urge to relieve himself in the hallway on his way out of the premises. Unfortunately for the Torch, one of the hoods inside made such a fuss about the stench that Basciano was forced to replace Tocco, just to shut his clients up.

That minor indiscretion aside, Tocco was still in good standing with Basciano in 1993, and he also worked as a kind of boy Friday for Jack

Ferranti. Tocco liked to boast that he worked as a carpenter in Ferranti's buildings; but his craftsmanship was so shoddy and the buildings so ramshackle that a more accurate job title would have been "guy with a hammer." He also dabbled in gun sales, cocaine dealing, and using his Doberman to harass Ferranti's tenants. Any little thing to earn a few dollars or help out the boss.

Despite his lack of sophistication, Tocco had been wily enough to slip away from Dowd the previous fall. That incident, coupled with the way Ferranti and Tocco bragged about their moles in the NYPD, had raised a troubling possibility: namely, that someone inside the force might have warned Tocco not to sell a gun to the now-interred heroin addict Eric Mergenthal. But Armanti had been so obsessed with crafting his persona and plotting strategy that the remote possibility of a leak from within the NYPD seemed like just one of an infinite number of obstacles between him and Tocco.

WHEN ARMANTI SKETCHED out his battle plan, he had known, intuitively, that Vinnie's entrance into Throgs Neck would have to include some sort of fight. So when he walked into Sebastian's for the first time, in April 1993, he wore dress slacks and expensive Italian loafers. Then Vinnie fired the first shot, ordering a Dewar's and soda. In most taverns, this sort of mundane detail would go unnoticed. But Armanti had a hunch that this request might serve to ignite the class resentments of the beer drinkers crowded around Sebastian's bar. Sure enough, before the ice in Armanti's Scotch had completely melted, the biggest lunkhead in the bar, some burly Irishman in a flannel shirt and construction jacket, came a-blustering. A time-honored ritual in cell blocks, sports bars, and most other all-male societies is a bit of etiquette known as Test the New Guy, so when the Irishman swaggered over, careful to nudge the bar stool into Armanti's legs, it was clear that the welcome wagon had arrived and the initiation was about to begin.

"Jerkoff," he said under his voice, kicking the stool a second time.

"What the fuck did you say?" Armanti shot back, not yet looking at him.

"You heard what the fuck I said," the Irishman growled. "Jerkoff."

"I hope you're talking to your girlfriend over there," Armanti said, pointing to the Irishman's companion, who was quite obviously male. "Because you better not be talking to me."

A round of "Whooas" circulated like a stale draft through the bar. Then silence fell, as the guzzlers and beer drinkers looked on glassy-eyed, waiting for Armanti to start to bleed.

"You've got a big mouth."

"Why don't you do something about it?" Armanti said, glancing at his would-be assailant for the first time.

"You wanna go?" the Irishman said, thrusting out his chest to emphasize the fact that he was far taller and beefier than Armanti.

"You wanna walk, let's walk," Armanti said.

Armanti took a sip of his drink, removed his leather sports jacket, and folded it, ever so neatly. He ran his hands over it repeatedly, reverentially, attempting to chase away the evidence of every last potential wrinkle. Then, delicately, he laid it over the back of the chair and smiled.

"Let me tell you something, my friend—you've got some problems," Armanti said, his voice suddenly calm, his eyes burning with the full SKL. "Because we're going to go outside and the first thing I'm gonna do is beat your ass. Then I'm gonna come back in here and drink with your money."

One of the onlookers scoffed. The Irishman looked puzzled.

"But if you beat me, ain't no big deal," Armanti added with a sneer. "Because everyone here expects you to beat me. I have nothing to lose. You have everything to lose. Let's go."

With that, Armanti strode toward the door, walked outside, and waited. As the Irishman slowly approached, Armanti searched for a bottle, a rock—anything to help him compensate for his disadvantage in height, weight, and strength.

But when the Irishman reached the door, he took a half step, then stopped. He looked at Armanti, waved him over.

"You've got one big set of balls," he said, throwing an arm around Armanti's shoulder and breaking into a grin. He turned Armanti toward the beer drinkers, who were still hoping for some carnage.

"His money's no good here tonight," the Irishman laughed. "This guy's got some set of balls."

Having passed the entrance exam, Armanti was introduced around the bar like a long-lost relative. He met all the beer drinkers, even the old man taking sports book in the bar's back room. The bartender, Myron Dobbs, was a friend of Tocco's, so Armanti took a chance and tried to forge a special connection. He had noticed a small café under construction across the street, a place with an Italian name, and wagered that the predominantly

Irish crowd in Sebastian's kept it at a distance. When Dobbs shook hands and asked what line of work he was in, Armanti appealed to him as a fellow small businessman and said he would be working at the café.

"Oh yeah," Dobbs said. "Welcome to the neighborhood."

Two weeks later, with Café d'Oro nearing completion and its real owners inside, Armanti's gamble paid off. He introduced himself to the owners, Carlo Cuzzi and Joe (Red) Bastone, welcomed them to the block, and offered to help them out if any neighborhood kids gave them trouble.

"I'm from across the street," he said, pointing to Sebastian's.

With his dual bases of operation established, Armanti looked for ways to make himself part of the neighborhood's routine. He'd drop in once or twice a week for a drink at Sebastian's and an espresso at Café d'Oro. Every now and then he'd show them some merchandise he had for sale, cheap. Everyone assumed the clothing or perfume or boxes of shrimp he was selling must have been stolen from the loading docks at the nearby Hunts Point trucking terminal, and they appreciated the bargains from their well-dressed new drinking buddy. In reality, most of the goods came from the unclaimed-evidence section of the police property clerk's warehouse in Queens, and when the police department was too cheap to provide money for more merchandise, Armanti used his military experience to his advantage. The headquarters for the investigation into Lieutenant Williams death was in the fire marshal's office at the Fort Totten army base in Queens, so Armanti bought duty-free cigarettes from the PX, where they cost four dollars a carton less than most retail outlets, then resold them in Throgs Neck as bootlegs.

The cut-rate smokes quickly made Vinnie a welcome sight in both the bar and the café.

"Hey, hey," Joe Red announced one day as Vinnie strode into the café. "Here comes Vinnie Cigarettes."

For all his hard work, however, Armanti still hadn't even come close to Tocco. The Torch had been banned from Sebastian's because of some slight or other, and the café was too new to be a hangout. So Armanti would watch him walk by—usually accompanied by Mario Ferranti—and wait eagerly for his moment. Mario seemed too busy to be concerned about his banishment from the bar. It was clear, though, that Tocco couldn't handle being excluded from any group. He would walk past Sebastian's with his head down, then stop for a drink at a Chinese restaurant across the street. Witnessing this, Armanti finally realized how Tocco could be had. Every undercover operation is a kind of perilous seduction, and Armanti sensed that the best way to win the attentions of a hanger-on like Tommy Tocco was to play hard to get.

He began by staking himself out in front of the café, staring down Mario and ignoring Tocco as they passed. In tough neighborhoods, as in wolf packs, direct eye contact is considered a full frontal challenge, daring someone to either fight or flee. The stares never seemed to register with Ferranti. But Tocco looked insulted that Vinnie acted as if he weren't there. Armanti figured that any man that desperate to be noticed couldn't resist for long.

VINNIE'S VERSION OF *Let's Make a Deal* had become a running joke among the detectives and fire marshals eager to snare Tocco. As one of his ostensible sources of income, Vinnie sold small kitchen appliances, auto supplies, perfume. He even found a pair of suede baby overalls, such a hideous brown color and tacky lederhosen style, that Dowd and the other investigators bet he'd never be able to sell them. Armanti took it as a personal challenge, telling the crowd in Sebastian's that the overalls were from the new babies' department at Bloomingdale's and had a retail price of $180. He sold them for $25.

But selling swag is a long way from buying cocaine, and during his first few months in Throgs Neck, Armanti grew frustrated that no one had broached the subject of drugs. By late May he noticed that Dobbs occasionally came out from behind the bar to meet with customers in the bathroom, presumably to do a few hand-to-hand transactions. Armanti was tempted to discuss cocaine with him, but thought it was best to lay back, just waiting, waiting.

He was so frustrated by the pace of his progress that when his pager went off that evening of June 1, his first impulse was to suspect it might be Judy calling. He hadn't seen her since the morning she'd stormed off, and he spent his nights on a cot at Fort Totten. A few weeks after their fight, Armanti had left her a note on the kitchen table, promising that she'd soon be the sole focus of his life. But when he returned home a few days later, he found the note crumpled on the kitchen floor and all of Judith's belongings moved out. The slow pace of the investigation, all that downtime, had given him the chance to daydream about changing her mind, somehow patching things up. So when he saw the number on the pager, his heart sank. It was someone from the department. Worse than that, it was someone from the Internal Affairs Bureau.

Given the allegations that Tocco and the Ferrantis had hooks in the police department, Internal Affairs had been brought into the investigation to see if there were grounds for a corruption case. There were rumors about a cop who hung out at Sebastian's passing confidential information to some of the wiseguys who hung out there. To Armanti, who had been raised in a neighborhood where cops and capos often lived on the same block, it seemed like an overreaction. In many sections of New York, only a saint in a cloister could avoid coming into contact with wiseguys. Even now, Armanti's part-time job on the docks in Jersey involved a union legendary for its mob connections. Big deal. Unless the cop was actively involved with Tocco and the Ferrantis' schemes—and there was no indication he was—who really cared where he went for a drink? So Armanti didn't jump to conclusions, even when he heard that the cop, a detective, was the son of someone high up the police department's chain of command.

In the beginning, Armanti naively welcomed the involvement of Internal Affairs detectives. Even though city officials and police brass loved to make public proclamations that their top priority was the war on drugs, the narcotics division could be incredibly miserly when it came to providing its troops manpower, equipment, and buy money. Internal Affairs, which had taken lot of heat in recent months for blowing high-profile investigations, had received a huge influx of cash and new equipment, so Armanti figured that the department's largesse might come in handy. Working alongside the Internal Affairs investigators, who were notorious for their ineptitude, also allowed Armanti and Dowd to keep an eye on them. Left to its own devices, IAB was liable to do something amateurish, like pull up to the set in a patrol car and get Armanti killed.

But now that Internal Affairs was pestering him, Armanti began to get a little anxious that they might be more of a distraction than a help. When Armanti called the number on his pager, the Internal Affairs sergeant told him that the suspect police officer's motorcycle had been spotted outside the bar and to watch for him inside. Of course, Internal Affairs had never shown Armanti a photo of the guy, so he had absolutely no idea who it was he was supposed to be looking for.

Just like clockwork, a few minutes after the phone call, Myron Dobbs, the bartender, introduced Vinnie to his friend John. There was no telling whether he was an officer, no talk about police work or even crime, for that matter. Just harmless banter about baseball and neighborhood girls. When Armanti left the set and made his way back to the base, Internal Affairs was all over him. Did you see the cop? Was that him?

"I met someone named John," Armanti said, "but I don't know if he was a cop."

He still didn't see what the fuss was about. They had never discussed anything the least bit illicit. There were so many New York bars where gangsters socialized that you'd need a police force full of teetotalers to avoid crossing paths with them. But the Internal Affairs detectives were insistent, desperate to know whether the John in the bar had been their John.

"Show me his picture," Armanti demanded. To his annoyance IAB was unprepared yet again. Armanti had noticed one distinguishing feature about the guy, so he grabbed a piece of paper and drew two letters side by side, two upside-down V's.

"All I know is, his eyebrows looked like this," Armanti said, handing the Internal Affairs detectives the paper.

One of the narcotics detectives, Benjamin Gozun, lit into Armanti.

"You didn't see John Wrynn in there," said Gozun, who had worked with Wrynn in the Organized Crime Investigation Division. "That wasn't him."

Armanti was caught off guard by Gozun's vehemence. "What the fuck's his problem?" he demanded.

"He's never even seen John Wrynn, he doesn't know what he's talking about," Gozun bellowed.

"I'm just telling you what I saw," Armanti said.

"You don't know him!"

Armanti shouted at the IAB supervisors, "You better get this fucking guy out of here!"

The next day, Lieutenant John Shields from Internal Affairs called Armanti into his office and handed him a stack of ten police officers' ID photos. Armanti flipped through the pictures and quickly picked out the man whose eyebrows were arched in the same cartoonish fashion he'd drawn the previous day.

"That's him," said Shields, nonchalant. "John Wrynn."

"Fine," Armanti shot back, upset that the episode had disrupted the hunt for Williams's killers. "Can I go back to work now?"

4

"A GOOD GUY"

JUNE 1, 1993

THAT NIGHT, AFTER he left Sebastian's, Detective John Wrynn climbed on his blue-and-white Suzuki motorcycle and kick-started the engine. The bar was only six blocks from his parents' home on Hosmer Avenue, through a neighborhood where he'd lived most of his twenty-eight years, streets familiar enough to travel half-looped with his eyes shut tight. But as he cruised through the warm night air, dressed in a leather jacket, earring, cowboy boots, and chunky silver belt buckle, many of his neighbors might not have immediately recognized John as the cop's kid who had been brought up straight-laced and churchgoing. His attire—classic outcast biker regalia—was a look he had carefully honed since he'd joined the New York City Police Department seven years earlier. But it was no disguise. It was a statement of his own essential difference, his way of asserting that John K. Wrynn had become his own, very complicated man.

The rebelliousness of Detective Wrynn's style was unsettling to many neighbors who, for a quarter of a century, had considered the Wrynn clan an upstanding part of their upstanding community. His mother, Jane, was a meticulous homemaker and a staunch pillar at St. Francis de Chantal Roman Catholic parish. His father, James Patrick Wrynn, was dutiful to a fault, a police inspector entrusted with the awesome responsibility of disciplining errant cops.

The two Wrynn children, John and his younger sister, Ann, seemed by all outward appearances to be the kind of sensible kids whose parents could sleep soundly. John wasn't a good enough student to follow his father's footsteps at Fordham Prep (a Jesuit institution and the borough's preeminent private school) but he had still gotten a solid education at Monsignor

Scanlan High School, a Catholic academy closer to home. He had also held down a part-time job at Baker's shoe store in a mall a short drive away in White Plains. Ann Wrynn, a year younger than her brother, attended all-girl Preston Academy. Like her mother, she was often described as having a kind heart and a sweet disposition, and was generally considered one of those nice Catholic girls who could be counted on to pitch in whenever a friend needed help.

The Wrynns had always been known as a quiet family whose small bungalow was modest but immaculately scrubbed and scrupulously kept. While they were not particularly outgoing, they weren't by any means reclusive. The Inspector's imposing physical stature (he stood six foot two and weighed 220 pounds), coupled with his somewhat off-putting reserve, made some think him a loner and assume that his social life revolved around his badge. But he could occasionally be seen sharing a drink with pals at Sebastian's or, on Saturdays, smacking a handball outside Intermediate School 192 near the service drive to the Throgs Neck Expressway. He was also chummy with the D'Erricos, an Old World Italian family whose son was a buddy of John's and who, for years, had dated Ann. In the summer, it wasn't unusual to see the Inspector's mountainous body wallowing in the D'Erricos' pool.

John and Ann, unlike many siblings so close in age, were also exceptionally tight. Both children were considered fairly attractive, too, although their dark hair and matching dark eyes made many neighbors marvel that two Irish kids could look so Italian. This kind of ethnic observation came as second nature to many residents of Throgs Neck. Although the neighborhood was named for John Throckmorton—an English merchant who'd settled thirty-five families there among the Siwanoy Indians in 1642—it was transformed from its WASPy beginnings by Czech, German, Italian, and Irish immigrants. Many Swedes and Finns came too, settling in an area derisively called Square Head Hill. The opening of the Throgs Neck Bridge in 1961 and the completion of the Cross Bronx Expressway in 1965 made the area accessible to a whole new generation of commuters.

Yet in 1968, when James Wrynn moved his young family to Throgs Neck from a cramped walk-up in the University Heights section of the Bronx, Hosmer Avenue still had the feel of a place far removed from the city. Although immigration and overflow from the Throgs Neck Housing Project had begun to infringe on the seclusion of the neighborhood's western edge, the Wrynns' corner of Throgs Neck proved stubbornly resistant to change. Its tree-lined streets were as sleepy and insular as a New England mill town or a Chesapeake Bay backwater, allowing John Wrynn and his friends the kind of simple, innocent childhood that most city kids have to take a bus trip to experience. During the 1970s and '80s—while much of New York wrangled with fiscal crises, racial problems, rampant crime, and the glitz and moral uncertainty of the Studio 54 era—it was possible to grow up in Throgs Neck and believe that the universe revolved, rather slowly, around Tremont Avenue.

By far the most compelling thing about the Wrynns' end of Throgs Neck was its proximity to the East River. Unlike much of New York City, daily routine here is often tied to the rhythms of the river. Each spring, the neighborhood begins to bustle as boaters and fishermen crowd the marinas and waterfront. Schoolchildren learn to keep an eye on the tides, which can cough up abandoned barges, rafts, or sunken boats raised from the river's bottom.

The Wrynns' home was just a few hundred yards from the water. John, Ann, and their friends spent summers swimming in the calm (though slightly polluted) current. Skipping stones, they waited for one of their parents or an older kid to take them for a spin in a boat. John Wrynn developed into a strong swimmer and, as an adult, a scuba diver who hoped to be assigned to the NYPD's harbor unit.

The streets near Detective Wrynn's childhood home were also set off from the rest of the urban world, both physically and culturally, by the odd collection of structures that gave their section of Throgs Neck its unofficial nickname, German Stadium. The stadium itself was part of a larger complex, several hundred acres known as German Gardens, which for generations stood as the hub of the area's social life. It had picnic grounds and ball fields, a beach house and bathing area, tennis courts and a fashionable restaurant called the Riviera, located in an old Greek Revival mansion. For decades it drew thousands of people for weekend tennis tournaments and soccer games featuring touring teams from abroad. Here, the Wrynns were known to occasionally pass the day watching tennis or just enjoying the outdoors with neighbors. In 1989, however, the stadium was demolished, replaced by a few blocks of nondescript town houses, leaving the section of Schurz Avenue near the Wrynns' home just another anonymous dead end by a river that gradually seemed to grow less enticing.

———

THE RIVER'S EDGE was the unofficial headquarters for the gang of kids who became John Wrynn's friends. They'd spend summers diving off the dock, or swimming out to abandoned barges. In winter, they'd congregate by the water, ribbing each other as they gazed across the bay and warmed themselves around bonfires built in metal trash barrels.

They'd also spend hours down the block, exploring the swamps at Ferry Point Park, an old landfill that the city had turned into baseball diamonds and playing fields. The group—about a dozen young boys and a half dozen girls—was notably disinterested in sports. Aside from the occasional game of touch football or softball, they played their own game, Manhunt, the neighborhood's version of Capture the Flag. Players were divided into two teams—the hunters and the hunted—and spread out amid the hills and sea grass to try to defend, or capture, a pre-appointed home base. John had an average build but was a plodding runner; if he wasn't the last one selected when choosing sides, he wasn't far from it.

In parts of Ferry Point Park commonly called "the dumps," the kids built forts out of scrap wood and furnished them with bits of carpet and old car seats they'd pull from abandoned autos. (One year, when a punishing nor'easter hit, many parents were amazed that these makeshift clubhouses managed to survive the lashing wind and rain.) As John Wrynn and the other boys grew into their early teens, they would ride minicycles and dirt bikes around the park's hills. "There was so much fun for those kids, with the water, the fields, the boats, so much to do," said Charlotte "Millie" Mergenthal, whose boys Artie and Eric grew up with John and Ann Wrynn. "It was, really, the kind of childhood you'd read about in some storybook."

But all stories change, and try as they might, Mrs. Mergenthal and the other parents couldn't prevent the outside world from seeping in or the children from growing up. Soon, teenage girls were being chased by older guys—guys with cars, who offered them a taste of life far beyond the piers. When the neighborhood boys got old enough to drive cars of their own, they gradually started venturing farther and farther into unfamiliar, and often less pastoral, venues.

New music filtered into their lives, starting with what was then called hard rock: bands like Led Zeppelin, the Doors, the Who, and the Rolling

Stones. In the 1970s, while teenagers in Brooklyn embraced the flashy disco style of *Saturday Night Fever* and trendy Manhattanites gravitated toward the British punks, Throgs Neck was strictly heavy-metal territory. Head-banger bands like AC/DC, Black Sabbath, and Van Halen were the music of choice. For Wrynn and the neighborhood's other head bangers in training, that meant a dress code of jeans, bandannas, work boots, and black T-shirts with the insignias of the most hard-driving stars.

Like many teenagers, John Wrynn's friends also began to experiment with drugs and alcohol. In New York it wasn't hard to find someone to buy a teenager a six-pack and, by the time John Wrynn entered high school, it was no big deal to see marijuana passed around at parties or hear talk of cocaine or PCP. Although the neighborhood was sheltered by Ferry Point Park and the river, it was also less than a mile from the Throgs Neck Houses, a city project where a wide range of narcotics was easy to acquire. Within a few years, this unchecked access would destroy the lives of many of the young men growing up in Throgs Neck during the mid-1980s. It would profoundly affect even John Wrynn, who was considered too cautious and obedient to really push the limits, and often socialized with conservative Catholic-school kids from Queens.

Steve Turuk, the unofficial leader of the old neighborhood's pack, had little use for the meek or mild. He wasn't the oldest, strongest, or best looking, but he was the most daring and found ways to make the other boys crave his approval. According to several friends, Turuk took turns treating each guy like his bosom buddy for a brief spell, lavishing him with attention, then unceremoniously replacing him with a new best friend. John was the chosen one for a few months, then Eric Mergenthal.

Later, an Italian kid named Tommy Tocco was in favor. At Lehman High School, Tocco was teased because his dog, Pirate, would often follow him to school and was usually waiting outside when the recess bell rang. Tocco's look was a little bit slick for Throgs Neck's heavy-metal sensibility, but he had a sense of humor and charmed many of the girls. As the group moved into adolescence, Tocco also began to flaunt something else that enhanced his place in the pecking order: his association with gangsters. Tocco occasionally bragged that his cousin was Vinny Basciano, the Bonanno-family gangster who lived in an opulent home a few doors from John Wrynn's grandparents. The connections gave Tocco access to important status items unavailable to John Wrynn and the others.

He had an impressive car and cool clothes and was always able to flash around more cash than his peers.

Tocco was particularly friendly with Mario Ferranti, who drove the ultimate muscle car: a '69 Camaro, with a Chevy small-block 350 LTI and the name THE BRONX SCREAMER emblazoned on the driver's door in glittery flash paint. On weekends, Tocco, Ferranti, and a few others would take their vehicles to the midnight drag races at Hunts Point Market, a scene straight from a Bruce Springsteen song, where the winning driver could pocket $200 a race.

Wrynn's first automotive experience was considerably less glamorous. His first car, a blue Dodge Dart, was so nerdy and practical that the neighborhood kids joked that it looked like a police department "narc car." No one would refuse a ride to Jones Beach, the mall, or a club with John just because his car looked like it belonged to their grandparents. But no one ever got a date by wowing a girl with his Dodge Dart, either.

Eric Mergenthal and his brother, Artie, came from a scrupulously law-abiding family, but they, too, were drawn to the gritty bravura of drag racing. Eric's first car was a red '69 GTO, and the day he brought it home, Ann Wrynn helped give it its first official cleaning. Eric had always been a practical joker, but by the time he got his license, his wild side had also begun to emerge. On weekends he seemed as if he were on a mission to outparty everyone in sight. Even on school days, he'd occasionally skip classes at Lehman High School, asking his friends to spend the day drinking with him and Turuk. John and the Catholic-school kids were stunned. One of the girls, a student at Preston, wanted to know how Turuk and Mergenthal could get away with their flagrant truancy.

"You just don't go," Turuk explained. "What can your parents do about it?"

Such blatant insubordination would have been unthinkable in the Wrynn home. Inspector Wrynn was stern and unassailable. Mrs. Wrynn was the classic old-school wife; she did all the cleaning, made sure dinner was on the table, and trained her daughter to one day assume those duties in her own family. John would later tell friends that it was that clear division of responsibility and power that made his parents' marriage so solid. For all her conservative family values, however, Jane Wrynn was a strong woman who taught her daughter to stand up for herself. In 1976, during the bra-burning era, Ann raised a few eyebrows in the neighborhood when her fourth-grade yearbook—celebrating the bicentennial—included a short feminist essay she wrote on the under-appreciated role of women in the Revolutionary War.

Mrs. Wrynn also demanded that her son treat women with respect, a factor many friends credit with fostering the close relationship between John and Ann. To many teenage boys, the thought of hanging out with a little sister would be mortifying, the ultimate act of uncool. But John never seemed to mind.

As adults, John and Ann would remain close enough friends that they would frequently double-date. In high school, however, John's love life was stagnant; he lacked the self-confidence to pursue even the girls who flirted with him. He was also uncomfortable with the other kids' public displays of affection. One day during his high school years, Wrynn and a few friends were on a boat when two kids aboard began to make out. Wrynn glanced over, shook his head, then shouted a classic New York put-down.

"Why don't you two go get a room?" he said.

His lack of ease with the art of seduction was so notable that in 1982 John was given a new nickname, taken from the title of a low-budget film about a hapless high school student's search for love: the "Last American Virgin."

Wrynn did many of the things other teenagers did. He'd drive to the beach and nightclubs, go to parties and rock concerts. In the winter, he'd stand near the river downing beers with his buddies. But as he progressed through high school, his friends began to notice John developing a tendency to brag and exaggerate, as if to prove he was as cool as everyone else was. He also became fixated on heavy metal, the heavier the better. Ozzy Osbourne, the former lead singer of Black Sabbath (who gained notoriety for biting the head off a live dove during a meeting with record company executives), was a particular favorite, although John later became infatuated with bands like Poison and Queensrÿche. John Wrynn might not have been as self-destructive as some of the head bangers, and he may have appeared a bit distant socially, but he could go on about metal with the hardest of the hard-core.

After high school ended and kids from the neighborhood were forced to contend with the first phase of adulthood, it quickly became clear that John had been wise to keep his distance from those friends who excelled at chemically induced forms of rebellion. It would be hard to imagine a circle of friends who were paying a higher price for their indulgence than John Wrynn's pals. Wrynn was in his early teens when Billy Cornish, his next-door neighbor, came home from the hospital paralyzed. Cornish won't talk about the incident that left him permanently confined to a wheelchair. But his neighbors, including Inspector Wrynn, hold it as an article of faith that the accident happened when he was intoxicated, dove into a pool, and suffered a crippling spinal injury.

John Wrynn was one of the few neighborhood kids who went to college. Ann Wrynn and a few other girls went to secretarial school. Tocco and Ferranti seemed destined to enter the family business. Meanwhile, the party animals appeared lost. Some, like Tommy Gross and Mike "Myron" Dobbs, didn't seem to have any long-term plan for themselves. Others, like Steve Turuk, Eric Mergenthal, and Steve Scarpetta, went to a technical school they saw advertised on television. They were pleased with the choice because it provided a quick payoff in the form of a good paycheck, even though the others teased them for setting their sights too low, saying they'd never amount to anything.

JOHN'S BRIEF EXPERIMENT with college was his first step toward leaving Throgs Neck. He enrolled in a business program at a community college—a far cry from the academic achievements of his father. Despite John's levelheaded choice, it was an uneasy time for him—and the Inspector. To pay his way through school, John occasionally met up with Tocco to do construction work renovating apartments at the Ferrantis' buildings in Manhattan. The Inspector wasn't overjoyed. The Ferrantis were reputed to be wiseguys, slumlords, and God knows what else. No police officer's son should be seen taking pay from such people. When the Inspector came home from work and saw John spattered with paint or covered with dust from drywall, he'd make it known that he didn't approve of whatever the hell it was John was doing with his life.

John stood his ground. He didn't do drugs and, besides, he told a classmate, he was paying for college himself: How could the Inspector complain if he was out there sweating to make a buck? "My father says I have to work my way through school myself," he explained to friends. "Just like he did."

When Wrynn left college, he worked for a few months in a low-level supervisory position at a shipping company, hating every minute. He bellyached that he didn't like managing others and felt cooped up in an office. In 1985, he and a neighbor, Gabriella Stolz, went to Manhattan one Saturday morning to take the NYPD entrance exam. Many of John's friends and relatives were stunned. He had always appeared conflicted about his father's line of work; Inspector Wrynn's grim seriousness had never made life on the police force appear very appealing. John never acknowledged it, but many of his friends suspected that his family had pressured him into joining up. Maybe he hoped to finally win his father's approval, they thought, or, at the very least, get a glimpse of what made the old man tick.

While the Inspector could hardly be pleased that the girl down the block outshone John on the exam, John went off to the police academy in 1986, and the Wrynns became another link in the long, blue line of father-and-son teams in the NYPD.

After an uneventful stint at the academy, John was assigned to a six-month training program patrolling midtown; he made just three arrests for minor administrative violations during his apprenticeship. In 1987, Wrynn received his first real assignment, the Fifty-second Precinct. The Five-Two—which encompasses the neighborhoods of Woodlawn, Kingsbridge, and Fordham, as well as the New York Botanical Garden and the Bronx Zoo—was considered one of the most desirable assignments in the Bronx. Relatively safe, it was a place where an ambitious officer could be active, rack up arrests, and qualify for promotions without placing his life in too much danger. It also covered the area around Fordham University, which had a wide selection of good restaurants for officers to choose from during meal breaks. Those factors made the Five-Two what was known as a "hook house," one of the coveted spots where a connection, or hook, somewhere in the chain of command was required for admission.

Even though he was placed among other rookie officers with connections in the department, Wrynn was given such wide latitude that other cops began to grumble. A few months into his assignment, Wrynn began appearing in uniform wearing an earring and with a ponytail tucked under his cap, both violations of the NYPD's strict paramilitary dress code. Most other cops would have received written warnings, known as command disciplines, or CDs, for such infractions or been ordered to cut the ponytail and lose the earring immediately. But Wrynn somehow managed to ignore the regulations with impunity. Low-level NYPD supervisors, sergeants and lieutenants, were always reluctant to write up relatives of any higher-ranking officials, especially the son of an Internal Affairs veteran who could easily destroy someone's career. So Officer Wrynn was allowed to make a few more outspoken fashion statements than his peers, and no one was foolish enough to make an issue of it. In a family business like the New York Police Department, John Wrynn was an untouchable.

At the time John Wrynn entered the force, police commanders were wrestling with issues far more important than the dress code. Crack cocaine had hit the streets in 1985, and by 1986 it had thrust many of the city's poor neighborhoods into a state of chaos. So potent and so profitable was the drug that it spawned waves of street violence bloody enough to shake New York's unshakable self-confidence. Even in the Five-Two, events were veering out of control. Murder, rape, mugging, and assault became far more menacing problems. The same month John was assigned to the Fifty-second, an off-duty police officer who lived in the neighborhood was killed by a mugger who had watched him cash a paycheck. The next year, a police officer reporting for work at the Fifty-second was stabbed in the face as he tried to interrupt a car theft.

Few people in Throgs Neck realized that the neighborhood was becoming a different place. One day in late October 1988, Gabriella Stolz got worried when her boyfriend, Steve Scarpetta, was ten minutes late to pick her up. Thirty minutes later, she fell apart when two police detectives arrived to inform her that Scarpetta had been shot and killed at a drug-infested corner of the Bronx. He had apparently bought heroin from a dealer down the block just a few minutes before he died. In her grief, Gabby told her confidants that Steve had been struggling with a habit for more than a year. Then Gabriella's brother, Chris, stunned his family by confiding that he, too, had a drug problem and desperately wanted help to avoid ending up like Scarpetta.

It didn't stop. Within a year, Eric Mergenthal and Steve Turuk were both arrested on drug charges, as was Turuk's older brother. People began to openly question whether the erratic behavior of Myron Dobbs and several other young men who had grown up with Wrynn might signal drug use. Several years later, when Eric Mergenthal died, John Wrynn seemed overwhelmed by what drugs had done to his friends. Mergenthal's parents tried to hide their embarrassment by claiming that Eric had died of asthma. But it was widely known that Eric had an addiction, so John and others assumed it had been an overdose.

Wrynn's coworkers at the Fifty-second Precinct did their fair share of partying, too, but most of that involved alcohol. The Fifty-second was known as a party house, and once the afternoon tour went off duty at 11:00 P.M., officers would meet in the New York Botanical Garden for beers. If it was a slow night on the streets, on-duty officers would often join them. Even supervisors and detectives would occasionally stop by during meal breaks for a little libation. Wrynn fell in with a clique of young, good-looking officers who met at French Charlie's, a bar on Bainbridge Avenue, and Pauline's on Broadway and 236th Street. Occasionally, he'd bring friends from the NYPD back to Throgs Neck, and they'd socialize at Sebastian's or Casey's, a sports bar across the street.

In the years after Wrynn joined the department, his social circle began to extend beyond Throgs Neck, and people in the old neighborhood started to notice a flashy side emerging. It had begun with little details: the earring, then the ponytail. Pretty soon there were louder accoutrements, like cowboy boots and the big silver belt buckle. Before you knew it, the kid who used to drive the dowdy narcmobile was cruising the streets on a motorcycle. The makeover occurred over the course of months, maybe even a year or two, but the transformation was stunning.

Life as a cop also made Wrynn act differently. Shortly after he became an officer, some neighborhood friends bumped into him and some fellow cops at Jones Beach, on Long Island. One of the officers bragged about harassing a homeless man by smacking him on the legs with a nightstick. Another joked about rousting crack users; because all parties to the conversation were white, he used the word *nigger* freely, and to great comic effect. Gene Gross, who had grown up with Wrynn but was inherently distrustful of cops, finally asked them to lay off.

"You guys are fucked up," Gross told them, according to one witness. "Someone's gonna shoot you guys out there. And I don't blame them."

Others still saw John Wrynn's sweeter side. Melissa Paradiso, a neighborhood girl who dated John during his early days in the department, was captivated by his good humor and old-fashioned kindness. They both loved football, and she was a fan of the New York Giants, the same team John and his father followed. When her grandmother died, John was so attentive that Melissa told several friends she didn't think she could have made it through the grief without him. (John had been shaken by the death of his grandfather "Big Jimmy" Wrynn, an Irish immigrant, who'd passed away on March 17, 1989—St. Patrick's Day. As a tribute, John told his friends, he vowed to forgo celebrating the holiday ever again.)

The rift between Wrynn's professional life and his neighborhood roots reached the level of caricature the day Tommy Gross, one of his boyhood friends, married Angelique Montemurro, the daughter of a local wiseguy who once ran with Henry Hill and the crew behind the legendary Lufthansa heist. It was quite the event in the Throgs Neck social circle, and Wrynn showed up without a date, looking very Italian: dark suit, boots, and gold chains. Partway through the reception, Wrynn caused a frightening scene in the men's room when one of Angelique's friends lit a cigarette with a lighter shaped like a pistol. Mistaking the novelty item for a real gun, Wrynn leapt into action, reaching toward his boot and drawing his own firearm—a full-sized and fully operational .38 revolver. To the alarm of the other guests, he wrestled his opponent to the bathroom floor, cursing and screaming, "Drop it! I'm a cop!" After throwing the man against the bathroom wall, Wrynn frisked him while a handful of guests looked on, aghast.

While Wrynn's eagerness might have made for awkward social moments, it wasn't out of place on the job. As crack ravaged neighborhood after neighborhood, it became clear that narcotics units were both the most dangerous assignments in the NYPD and the best way to get ahead. John volunteered to work in Bronx narcotics and was accepted after less than two years on the force—an incredibly short time span for such a promotion. In 1989, good fortune found him again, when he was promoted to detective at the tender age of twenty-six, making him one of the youngest members of the department to be awarded the detective's gold shield. Given his father's lofty rank, Wrynn's rapid-fire advancement inspired plenty of insinuations that he was surfing a wave called nepotism. But John worked harder than ever, frequently volunteering for overtime, special details, warrant duty—anything to stay up front and highly visible. The Bronx Narcotics Unit specialized in low-level buys and busts, but no one ever accused John of cowardice. Even as a member of the backup team, he wasn't shy about busting down a door or leading the charge into hostile territory.

Wrynn had another valuable, intangible asset: charisma. The detectives, assistant DAs, and defense lawyers who saw him on the stand thought he made an impressive witness. Confident and well spoken, he projected a warmth and professional detachment that seemed to connect with jurors. And more than one judge noted Wrynn's persuasive presentations. Wrynn had such a winning way in the courthouse that he even managed to date an assistant Bronx DA.

By the time Wrynn finished his first year in Bronx narcotics, he was credited with two dozen arrests, most for small amounts of cocaine. His colleagues noticed that John seemed energized by the excitement and proud to be building a successful résumé. As Wrynn moved up, he also grew more self-assured with women. The neighborhood girls slowly began to find him more outgoing, and he was popular with women at work, too. In fact, it wasn't unheard of for Wrynn to have two girlfriends at the same time. Part of his allure was the tough-guy nature of his work, but his kindness was also appealing. When one of his women fell ill, John usually responded with the kind of doting that would have made his mother proud, becoming a virtual home-care attendant and babying his patient back to health. As a lover, he had a reputation for being attentive and tender, sometimes to a fault. It was as if the Last American Virgin was trying to become the Marathon Man.

But Melissa also experienced the downside of John's machismo, his investment in his status as a ladies' man. One day in 1993, suspecting that John was seeing someone else, she sneaked into his bedroom and caught him—literally—in bed with another woman. Melissa belted him in the nose, leaving a visible bump, which he had a difficult time explaining.

AT TIMES IT looked as though police work and his budding social life would wrest John away from the neighborhood completely. In 1992, Wrynn moved to Manhattan for two months to live with Linda Nelson, the Bronx ADA he'd started dating while working narcotics. Her parents had bought her a one-bedroom co-op on East Fiftieth Street and Third Avenue, on the same block as the legendary restaurant Lutèce, and right across the street from Paul Newman. The boy from the Bronx was suddenly surrounded by international embassies, exclusive shops, and all the rarefied trappings of cosmopolitan New York. Those who worked with Wrynn noticed his pleasure at announcing, "I'm living on the East Side." Some colleagues figured Linda was such a great catch for a cop—smart, cute, accomplished, and from a well-off family—that he'd be a fool not to marry her.

Others doubted the union could last—and just waited for their cultures to begin clashing. "What's a nice girl like you doing with him?" Tocco asked one day during a chance encounter. Wrynn laughed off Tocco's joke and told her Tommy was a bookie, but said little else. At work, Wrynn's colleagues noticed that his new home in Manhattan seemed to bring out the Bronx in John. He raved about the great restaurants but had nothing else positive to say about Manhattan living. The traffic made him crazy. He was spared one of the biggest urban headaches, the scarcity of parking, because he had a NYPD placard, which allowed him to leave his car nearly anywhere without being ticketed. But John still felt alienated. With his flamboyant, urban cowboy look, he could have passed for a Eurotrash tourist who had gotten lost on his way home from Times Square. Yet Wrynn confided to friends that the class differences made him uneasy.

"Everyone's so hoity-toity," he told a coworker.

Less than three months after he'd moved in with Linda, they broke up and John moved back with his parents. Then in 1992, he moved to Pound Ridge, a rural upstate hideaway about half an hour north of the city, near the Connecticut border. It appealed to the outdoorsy side John had developed in the years since joining the police force. As a kid he'd loved scuba diving, but recently he'd also begun bow hunting and hiking, and he sometimes went on solo overnight camping trips along the Appalachian Trail. Even though he suddenly fancied himself as some kind of nature boy, Wrynn never completely lost touch with his friends in the old neighborhood. Since he'd become a police officer, his father had started nagging him to stop associating with Tocco and the Ferrantis. John insisted that he spoke to them only if they happened to bump into each other. "I used to have paragraph-long conversations—now they're a sentence long," he explained.

The Inspector had little reason to doubt his son, but sometime in 1992, other members of the police department began to hear differently. The original source was Steve Turuk, who by the summer of 1992 had become Detective Dowd's informant in the Lieutenant Williams case. He told detectives about a house party in Chris Stolz's basement, where Wrynn was offered cocaine. Wrynn didn't snort it, Turuk said, but he soon lit up a joint of marijuana.

"Aren't you afraid of getting a drug test?" Turuk asked him.

Wrynn laughed and told him that he didn't worry. Although the NYPD policy called for random drug screenings of a predetermined number of officers each week (not to mention automatic dismissal of any officer who tested positive), Wrynn said he always got tipped off beforehand. He said he knew of an herbal tea that he could drink a few hours before a test to mask any trace of marijuana in his urine.

"How do you know the test is coming? Your father?" Turuk asked.

"Are you kidding me?!" Wrynn said, mortified at the very suggestion. "My father'd kill me if he knew I was doing drugs."

Turuk also told detectives about another occasion, sometime in 1990, when Wrynn had reportedly helped Turuk's brother avoid being arrested in a drug sweep. Turuk's brother had been standing outside a crack house when John Wrynn happened to walk by, spot him, and call him over.

"We're gonna bust this place in a few minutes," Wrynn reportedly whispered to his old friend. "Get the hell out of here."

Neither incident involved a particularly serious investigation. The party was harmless. The drug bust involved a dime-a-dozen roundup of addicts and low-level dealers. In fact, one could argue that Wrynn was preventing the NYPD from wasting its precious time and scarce resources on a small-time knucklehead whose crimes were victimless and whose arrest would be just a distraction from the real, dangerous criminals.

Obviously, that wasn't the way the department said things were supposed to work. But in the real world, decisions were usually more complicated than the catechism of the police patrol guide. Wrynn's father had been forced to make countless judgment calls during his career, deciding which officers to squeeze, which to let slide, and what best served the interests of the department. In fact, the biggest knock against the Inspector was his intolerance, his unwillingness to overlook low-level infractions by street cops.

Despite John's more flexible view of department rules and regulations, his career remained on a trajectory straight upward. In 1991 he was promoted to the High Intensity Drug Trafficking Area team (HIDTA), a federally funded effort to choke off major shipments of cocaine at crucial distribution points. It was a drastic upgrade in the level of case Wrynn was allowed to handle. The Bronx Narcotics Unit had focused on street-corner sellers, half of whom were junkies themselves. HIDTA targeted traffickers far up the distribution chain, mainly wholesalers who bought kilos directly from the cartels in Colombia. Wrynn, exhilarated by the high stakes, spoke endlessly to his friends about the intrigues.

HIDTA was such an elite unit that Wrynn's job there also offered him entrée into some of the department's more exclusive social functions, events like the 1992 Christmas party thrown by employees of the Organized Crime Investigation Division at the Beaten Path restaurant in Manhattan. There Wrynn mingled with some of the best narcotics investigators in the city. Near the end of the evening, he struck up a conversation with a detective who had been working on a gun case in Throgs Neck and asked for a little background on the neighborhood. Wrynn listened intently to his description of the case, and when the detective mentioned that the target of his investigation was someone named Tommy Tocco, Wrynn couldn't stop himself.

"He's a good guy," Wrynn said. "You should leave him alone."

Wrynn's incorrect, and inappropriate, character reference for Tocco was not reported to Internal Affairs. By early 1993, however, new information had been discovered during the investigation into Lieutenant Williams's death, making Wrynn a secondary target of the arson-homicide case. And when he popped into Sebastian's on the night of June 1, 1993, John Wrynn walked onto a set monitored by a task force of FBI agents, fire marshals, and detectives from NYPD's Organized Crime Control Bureau and the Internal Affairs Bureau—the unit where his father was considered a shining star.

5

"THESE GUYS ARE MINE"

JUNE 9–16, 1993

"*THEY'VE GOT ME doing hand-to-hands...*"

Over and over again during Myron Dobbs's grim, split-second pronouncement, Armanti heard the horrifying echo of his own words being repeated. As he stood at the bar inside Sebastian's, suddenly uncertain whether he would live or die, Armanti envisioned himself three weeks earlier, pecking at the keys of his clunky IBM Selectric, writing the very words that Myron had just tossed off. He had been describing the kind of cocaine trading he'd witnessed at Sebastian's in order to give his superiors a complete rundown of the place. He could see each letter of the phrase as it had appeared on the daily-occurrence form known to police officers as a DD5. One copy of his report had gone into the locked file drawer in his desk. Another was handed to his supervisor in narcotics. The third went to Internal Affairs. Paperwork was such a chore that Armanti performed it mechanically, without bothering to engage his brain at all. Yet the images of those words were now suddenly so clear they were almost tangible. Armanti knew it would have been virtually impossible for a direct quote to travel from his work sheets to Myron Dobbs's lips without the complicity of someone inside the department. But just in case there was any doubt, Dobbs's next sentence put the matter to rest.

"How do you know you'll be indicted?" Armanti asked, stalling, as he cased the barroom for possible gunmen.

"My father heard," Dobbs said. "A detective friend told him."

Armanti had felt the chill of a loaded gun pressed against his temple before. Early in his undercover career, he had gone into a Brooklyn apartment to buy cocaine and had found himself in the middle of a mob feud. A .45 automatic had been shoved into his face and he was ordered to strip, kneel, and bow his head—so a dealer could clip him, execution-style. But his current situation was far more complex. Never had Armanti had to navigate on a set where his identity had been compromised. He realized that *maybe* it hadn't gone that far. Maybe the "detective friend" talking to Dobbs's father hadn't found out that Myron and his buddies were being observed by an undercover. Maybe they hadn't identified him specifically, *yet.* But Armanti had to brace himself for the worst-case possibility—that the detective had revealed Vinnie Blue Eyes's real identity.

Armanti instantly suspected the detective he'd met at Sebastian's eight days earlier: Wrynn. Who else would it be? But the real question was: Who on earth was leaking information to Wrynn? Could Dowd or one of the fire marshals have mistakenly let a copy of his report slip out of his hands? Would Internal Affairs really go so far as to burn him on the set? With his life on the line?

Armanti tried to breathe evenly, appear calm, wrestle his brain away from the task of trying to track down the leak, at least long enough to focus on Dobbs and find some way to make it out of the bar in one piece. Armanti studied Dobbs, looking for signs that Myron had figured out who he was. Judging by Dobbs's demeanor, Armanti had to assume there was at least some doubt in his mind, so he tried to put Dobbs on the defensive and, hopefully, hide behind a shroud of possibilities.

"Who the fuck told the cops? Someone in here? Someone who works at the bar?"

"I don't know. I've been—"

"Who did you tell?" Armanti said. "Someone in here is a fucking rat?"

"I don't know."

"Maybe they set you up," Armanti said. "Is there someone pissed about what you sold them? Did you sell to some motherfucking under-cover? To anyone at all you didn't know?"

"I don't think so," Dobbs said.

"If it's that fucking Joe Red, I'll fuck him right in his ass," Armanti said, referring to one of the hoods in the café across the street.

Armanti turned up the intensity with every threat, but it was impos-sible to gauge whether his smoke screen was generating any true camou-flage. When Dobbs dashed off to the bathroom, Armanti realized that he had to stay cool. Was Dobbs really unsure who the leak was or was he just stringing him along? There was no way to figure it out for sure. Armanti had to just let it ride. But Dobbs grew more tense as their conversation continued, and when he took an inordinate amount of time to return from the bathroom, Armanti braced himself for gunfire. All the while, he wracked his brain, trying to figure out *how?*

Then Dobbs walked back to the bar, apparently unarmed, hanging his head and announcing, "I just puked." In Armanti's state of hyperalertness, even that offered no real consolation: He couldn't be sure if Dobbs was nervous about his legal problems or sickened because he was about to take part in the murder of an NYPD undercover detective.

It wasn't until the conversation quieted down that Armanti began to recognize real panic in Dobbs. Even though the bar was chilly, Dobbs glistened with sweat. His eyes looked dilated, desperate. Maybe he'd done a bump of coke in the john.

"What the hell should I do?" he pleaded. "I don't want to go to jail. What do I do?"

Dobbs was either truly freaked or really smooth. Armanti twitched when his pager went off, rattling silently; then he coughed in an attempt to compensate for the fact that it had made him jump. There was no way he could answer it now, so he took a deep breath, tried one last time to figure it all out, then leaped at the chance to play Dobbs's mentor. "Look, you gotta watch out for yourself," Armanti told him. " Don't sell to anyone you don't know. Don't sell at all until we find out who the rat is."

Somehow, Armanti managed to appear calm, despite the fact that his pager kept jerking madly in his pocket. He figured that the backup team knew he'd been burnt and was trying to get him out of there. Studying Dobbs's face and body language, he tried to assess whether it was safe to turn his back and head out. But there was just no way to be sure. Armanti knew he had to get outside somehow; he had always trained young undercovers that if shooting was imminent, they'd be more likely to survive if it happened in the street. The Narcotics Division's radio transmitters were so delicate that the sound of a gunshot could cause the microphone to short out. If shots were fired indoors, an undercover might be left wounded for several minutes, his life draining out of him, before the backup team or anyone else knew he'd been hit.

Armanti took one last sip of his drink and decided to chance it.

"Look, I've got to go take care of some business across the street," he told Dobbs. "You just watch yourself. Lay low, don't talk to anyone about anything. And I'll let you know what I hear."

Armanti put his hand on Dobbs's shoulder and headed toward the door, still scanning the room. Each step seemed interminable, as if he were running into a gale and was unable to advance forward. Then, finally, he felt the night air hit his face as he passed through the doorway in a kind of extended slow motion. He reached the sidewalk. All his senses seemed sharper. He felt as if he was in shock, yet every car that droned by, every movement on the street was perfectly clear.

The pager went off again, but Armanti was still too shaken to answer. He knew what they wanted. And he didn't want to speak with them until he'd figured out how to fend off the inevitable call to shut down the investigation. His heart still racing, Armanti charged toward Café d'Oro to assess how badly the case had been damaged. As he approached the door, Joe Red was standing outside. Armanti scanned him and saw no obvious sign of a weapon. Joe Red kissed him hello, just like always, and Armanti paid close attention to see if Red might be checking him for a gun. Nothing discernible; Armanti thought it was worth a venture inside.

Patrons of the café had always been more suspicious of him than their counterparts across the street at Sebastian's, so Armanti tried to remain hyperaware. (A few weeks earlier, in fact, the Internal Affairs detectives had parked their white surveillance van in such an obvious location outside the café that Joe Red had banged on the side of it and asked if he could pick up any coffee and doughnuts for the officers inside.) When Armanti saw Carlo Cuzzi behind the bar and a few of the regulars seated at tables—nothing out of the ordinary—he decided to stay. First he went to the bathroom, threw cold water on his face, and checked to see whether he had managed to retain even the faintest semblance of composure. Then he walked back out into the café and said a few hellos. Armanti was still so rattled that he offered to give Cuzzi a few cartons of cigarettes as an excuse to duck out to his car and get his gun.

He returned, sat at his usual table by the window, and ordered a glass of wine for his nerves. A few minutes later, as he was wracking his brain to figure out who had burnt him and how to keep the case from falling apart, Tommy Tocco walked to the front of the café and started talking to Joe Red. Armanti was jolted by equal measures of excitement and fear. For months he had been trying to lure Tocco into proposing a drug deal, but the Torch hadn't budged. Now, today—less than an hour after one of Tocco's friends had made it clear that Armanti's cover might be blown—

Tocco wanders up to the café, a few yards from Armanti. Maybe it was just a coincidence. But Armanti felt a whole lot better when he reached under the table to check his .380 automatic, which was taped to the inside of his thigh.

He briefly considered leaving, going home, counting his blessings, getting laid, and planning a new approach to apprehending the killer of Lieutenant Williams that was not tantamount to suicide. But the chance to finally meet Tocco was too much to resist. He finished his wine and approached Joe Red, consciously avoiding eye contact with the object of his true interest. As if on cue, Tocco reached out to Vinnie at last.

"You're Vinnie, right?" Tocco asked.

Armanti glanced away and sighed. Tocco had taken the trouble to learn his name.

"Who wants to know?"

"I've just seen you around," Tocco said, slightly sheepish. "I'm Tommy."

Armanti shook his hand, grudgingly.

Armanti wasn't sure whether it would be days, weeks, or months until Tocco sold him cocaine, but he knew now that it was just a matter of time.

"Yeah, how ya doing, Tommy," he said, then turned and walked back into the café.

Armanti waited for Tocco to leave before making his own exit from the café, his pager hectoring him yet again. As he walked to his car, then drove to the headquarters, Armanti tried to calculate just how much the danger had escalated and what precautions he'd have to take if he was reckless enough to press on. Could he get away with wearing a bulletproof vest on the set? How many guns could he discreetly strap to himself? Was it possible to bring the backup team closer? *Was he out of his mind?*

Later that night, Armanti would awake drenched in sweat, then rush to his car to search for places to conceal guns, knives, any protection. But that afternoon, when he reached the detectives' meeting room, Armanti knew he had to provide the enthusiasm to keep the game going, and he had to play it so smooth and easygoing that they might actually believe he was thinking clearly. Detectives are always reluctant to suggest that a colleague place himself in an unduly dangerous situation. No one would have the gall to propose that Armanti do what they themselves wouldn't. But the thought of watching Lieutenant Williams's killers go free, all those months of work rendered useless, would not be appealing. Especially now that Armanti had made his first contact with Tocco.

It went down pretty much as he expected: The detectives and supervisors made their obligatory, halfhearted declarations that the case should be closed to protect Armanti's safety. He sat quietly, while his mind wove wild conspiracy theories, watching each man speak, wondering, *Was this fuck the leak?* He knew Dowd was trustworthy, although Armanti was so shaken that he did wonder—for just an instant—whether his talkative friend might have slipped and revealed the information accidentally. It seemed unthinkable that the two fire marshals would do anything to hurt the case. To them, the attempt to avenge Williams's death was a crusade. The Internal Affairs guys? Armanti had heard a lot of horror stories about them screwing up cases and protecting the department's favored sons. But would they give up an undercover in an organized-crime case? That seemed way beyond what he was prepared to consider, beyond the realm of possibility even for Internal Affairs.

Armanti decided to make it easy on them.

"Why shut it down?" he said. The faces around the table lit up, and he realized they were actually going to let him press on.

After the meeting ended, Armanti and Dowd stopped for a drink. Dowd, who had a wife, a mortgage, and kids, couldn't in good conscience conceive of taking such a risk. He'd already had a street informant turn up dead in this case. He wondered aloud whether they were all being too cavalier with Armanti's life

"Are you sure you want to do this?" Dowd asked. "If you want out, we'll shut it down. We'll find some other way."

"You think I'm gonna stop now?" Armanti said. "I'm going all the way with this one. Fuck the Wrynns. These guys are mine."

EVERYTHING FELT DIFFERENT now, half real, half unreal. He was further out than he had ever been, further away from anything that seemed connected to his real life. He had never walked on ground that seemed so uncertain beneath his feet. The fact that someone—someone supposedly on his side, the side of the law—considered his life something so utterly expendable changed things. Suddenly he was no longer so confident about being the guy they were never going to get. Putting one foot in front of the other and trying to will himself not to think too hard about what he was doing, he returned to the set in Throgs Neck, worried, angry, and driven to find out who in the police department could be so indifferent to the incidental matter of his survival.

Now his mission had new, infinitely complex layers and a lethal edge. Armanti's every glance now filtered through a maze of questions as he searched for threats, weapons, warnings. Having worked at a leisurely rhythm during his first two months, letting things unfold at their own pace, Armanti now felt a grim determination to gather as much evidence as possible—immediately. If he made a case against the Ferrantis quickly, maybe he could save himself. But if he didn't, if this was the case that would end with him gutted in some alley, he wanted to do a favor for himself and his family. Armanti wanted to leave the cops investigating his death ample ammunition. He wanted to give them the chance to arrest or squeeze as many hoods as possible in the search for his killer.

Armanti had always lived by his luck and, so far, had always rolled sevens. But maybe it was his time. He had known men who'd died: Four years after Armanti joined the force, his first mentor, Detective Louis Miller, was shot dead while chasing a burglary suspect in Flatbush. Miller was a former marine who'd chosen Armanti as his driver, had given him Marine Corps belt buckles as gifts, and had refused to take a desk job even after he'd turned sixty. In March 1987, he was training a new crop of recruits when a radio call announced that two armed burglars had fled into a nearby building. Miller led the charge and managed to save a fellow officer by killing a suspect before he was fatally wounded himself. Armanti was devastated by the loss of the man young cops affectionately called "the Commander," but he tried to console himself with the thought that Miller had died in a blaze of glory while protecting the city and the young cops at his side.

The only person who'd ever died on one of Armanti's sets was a dealer who'd opened fire on police officers and took twenty-one shots in return, and even that transpired a few minutes after Armanti's exit. But if this was to be his finale, Armanti knew how he wanted his colleagues to proceed. Undercover detectives don't often discuss death; it's considered bad form and bad luck. But Armanti, no stranger to breaking custom, broached the subject and said his piece. He told his guys he wanted one thing: for them to get the killers. To Armanti, the thought of his murderer escaping justice was the ultimate indignity, like Tommy Williams's killer remaining free, dirtying up a world that was looking filthier every minute. All the hours he had spent trading machismo on city corners made Armanti too revoltingly aware of the glee that some young drug dealer would feel while bragging, "I capped an undercover." It would be an insult—the ultimate kiss-off.

Armanti also agonized that his mother might not have it in her to uphold the mantle of Grieving Police Next of Kin. He had marveled at the graceful way Lieutenant Williams's family had handled the media carnival and the police inquiry. They'd seemed to take real solace from all the efforts to console them. Or they'd at least had the good manners to fake it. Armanti was convinced that if he had been in their place, every fresh honor would have rekindled his rage, reminded him of his loss. He couldn't take the thought of his mother in that kind of pain. If he had to go down, he wanted it over quick.

"Catch the guy who did it, lock him up, and don't go banging on my mother's door every month," he had once ordered two members of his backup team as they drove back from the funeral of an officer killed in the line of duty. "Let her get on with her life. Just leave her alone. And don't go planting any trees in my honor, or so help me God, I'll come back from hell and haunt the fuck out of every one of you."

As Armanti's mind hit red alert, and the unusual hazards of the investigation forced him to take special precautions, he had to concentrate harder than ever to appear nonchalant. He had already fortified his arsenal and hidden a gun and a vest in the trunk of his car, in case of a shoot-out or a running gun battle. He had also thought about carrying a gun with him at all times, but that would be inauthentic—Vinnie Blue Eyes wouldn't risk a parole violation, and an automatic two years in prison, by being armed unnecessarily. So Armanti stuck to the basics: a switchblade in his sock and a few other surprises in concealed spots in his car. He would no longer let anyone sit behind him, for any reason. In a restaurant he'd either sit against the wall or stand. In a car, he would either station himself in the backseat or manufacture some reason to drive separately.

His mind was reeling off a new disaster scenario every second, so he had to keep telling himself to breathe deeply and *slow it down, slow it down*. There was so much happening in his head that at times everyone else seemed to be moving at a completely different speed. During his few hours of decompression, it often felt as if the world had stopped. Just stopped altogether. But his mind kept scanning through scenes from the set. He'd analyze every innocuous word and gesture he'd observed that day to see if they hid some ulterior agenda. When someone asked him along for a day at the beach, was the invitation really just to hang out? Or was it because they knew it was a place where he'd be most vulnerable, because he couldn't conceal a gun? When he was asked to go drinking, was it the same kind of bar as before?

Sleep became elusive. Near his bunk at Fort Totten, Armanti kept a portable alarm clock he'd owned for two years. Now its tick suddenly seemed maddeningly loud. He'd look at the numbers, watching the night slip slowly away. At three A.M., he'd find himself staring at the telephone, thinking about Judith, wondering, *Should I apologize? Should I call her, just to hear her voice, then hang up?* All the caffeine and adrenaline Armanti had used to fuel himself during the day coursed through him all night as he lay sweating in bed, eyes open, trying to figure out who was tipping off John Wrynn. In the morning, there was only one antidote: more coffee, which made Armanti even edgier.

Looking at his haunted face in the mirror one day, Armanti started obsessing over the idea that the unremitting stress was unraveling his disguise. People go into organized crime because they don't want to work long hours in law-abiding jobs, so Armanti had always made sure that his wiseguy characters looked like they slept until noon. But all the commuting, worrying, sleep deprivation, espresso, and Sambuca had left him ashen-faced, with bags under his eyes. As the case dragged on, he started icing down his face and putting hemorrhoid cream on the circles beneath his eyes. He also began carrying a lawn chair in his trunk, so he could sneak in a few minutes of sun worshiping to retain his Sicilian skin tone. On weekends, he'd try to make amends with his body by avoiding alcohol, exercising to sweat out toxins, and eating healthy, low-fat foods. (The only green vegetable he ever seemed to get on the set was broccoli rabe.)

ARMANTI WAS EAGER to speed up the case, but Tocco, unfortunately, had suddenly left town. Dobbs wasn't working either, so Armanti tried to make good use of the time by focusing on Joe Red Bastone, who looked like the weakest link. He was the life of every party, a laugh-a-minute guy. But the minute he stopped joking, Bastone became the punch line. Bad enough that he was a redheaded Italian in a neighborhood where Italians were in perpetual competition with the Irish. But Bastone had the additional misfortune to have some sort of digestive disorder that made him devote an inordinate amount of time to the twin pursuits of eating and relieving himself.

"I think I've got a fucking tapeworm," he'd say as he shuttled between a table full of greasy bar food and the men's room.

"It's more like a fucking snake," Armanti shot back. "You fucking animal."

Worse, Bastone had a skinny build in a crew full of brawlers, as well as a habit that was out of control: his periodic cocaine binges were fodder for endless ridicule, especially from his partner, Carlo Cuzzi. Bastone was a schemer, willing to try credit card scams or delivery-truck stick-ups, but he also seemed the neediest, and the one most buoyed by Armanti's attention. After a few minutes of chatting, Joe Red would want to know if Vinnie felt like shooting pool, and next thing he knew they'd find themselves in a Tremont Avenue social club owned by Tocco's wiseguy cousin Vinny Basciano. On one such occasion on June 10, Joe Red had a question to ask:

"So I saw you with Tocco—what're you two up to?" Joe Red wanted to know.

Armanti laughed. He counted his breaths, careful not to appear anxious.

"Things," he finally said, watching for Joe Red's reaction.

"Things?" Joe Red asked.

Armanti put his fingers up to his nose as if he were snorting imaginary cocaine.

"Don't buy it from that jerkoff," Joe Red said. "I'll get you a better price."

In any investigation, the first drug purchase is a major milestone for the police, and given the perilous state of this case, Armanti was ready to celebrate when he arrived back at headquarters. Dowd, the two fire marshals, and several members of the backup team caught his enthusiasm. But Armanti noticed that the Internal Affairs detectives did not. Later, alone in Lieutenant Shields's office, he found out why.

"Why don't you stay focused?" Shields asked, clearly agitated. "He's not a subject."

"What do you mean?" Armanti shot back. "You gotta buy him."

"We're not here to buy off Joe Red," Shields replied.

Armanti thought Shields might be teasing him, so he tried to stay steady.

"This is my first chance to buy into these guys."

"Your assignment here is to investigate the fire," Shields said. "That means Tocco and Ferranti."

"My assignment is to investigate crime. Why just take down a couple of murders when you can take down a whole neighborhood?" Armanti asked. "If I start buying, it makes me credible. You never know who knows what. People are going to come to me because I'm making money. That's how we'll get the fire. And in the meantime, who knows how many other crimes we can clear? We can take down all of Tremont Avenue!"

Shields wouldn't budge.

"Just keep your focus," he ordered.

Luckily for Armanti, there were units in the NYPD not hemmed in by Internal Affairs. On June 11, two officers from the Forty-fifth Precinct were on routine patrol when they picked up Jack Ferranti for soliciting a prostitute. Even better, while searching his car the officers found a small amount of cocaine and an illegal gun, which upped the charges against him. Ferranti was bailed out in no time, but his weapon, a .22 revolver, was sent to the ballistics lab to see if it matched any unsolved shootings. Two days later, Ferranti's car mysteriously disappeared from the parking lot of the Forty-fifth Precinct, in Throgs Neck. The officers in the precinct said it had been stolen, but the incident gave Armanti and Dowd a whole new universe of police department leaks to fret about. Police precincts are chaotic places where thousands of people pass through each day, many with less-than-legal intentions. But what a coincidence that out of a hundred cars in the parking lot, the one stolen just happened to belong to Jack Ferranti. What were the odds that one of Ferranti's accomplices could nab an auto from right under the NYPD's nose if he didn't have help from inside the department? Especially when Dowd had parked it in the precinct captain's spot. And precisely what was it about the car that Ferranti was desperate to hide? Drugs? Guns? Blood? Maybe evidence linking Jack to Bruce Bailey or the fire and Lieutenant Williams's death?

Armanti and Dowd tried to spin gold from the mystery of Ferranti's missing Lincoln. If the car was off the street, the person who stole it would want to scam some money for it, so Armanti would offer him that opportunity. He got rid of his white Acura and started driving a gray Lincoln, the same year as Ferranti's. For good measure, he also tore out the radio. Ferranti's crew was known to run a chop shop in Harlem, so if someone offered Armanti a replacement radio, the trail might eventually lead to Jack's car.

Nothing happened immediately with the Lincoln, but there were new signs that Vinnie Blue Eyes was earning his bona fides in the neighborhood. Armanti felt the pressure ease a bit. He was starting to believe that, even though members of the Throgs Neck crew were getting tipped off,

they weren't yet suspicious of him. A rumor began circulating that someone had seen him in a park, beating someone's head with a baseball bat.
No one ever directly asked him about it, but Armanti posted no denials;
his status would rise if the Ferrantis thought he had drawn fresh blood.
Sure enough, within days, a member of the crew, a guy called Joey
Scams, struck up a conversation with Vinnie and was soon telling him the
epic tale of how some of the Ferrantis' associates had killed some poor
mope, cut off his dick, then stuffed it in his mouth. It was the first time
someone in Throgs Neck had confided in him about a murder. Vinnie was
touched.

_____

6

THE HUNTER, HUNTED

JUNE 1993

INSPECTOR JAMES PATRICK Wrynn habitually spent balmy spring and summer evenings seated on his front porch, reading a book, and scowling at passersby. And, as spring turned to summer in 1993, he had plenty to brood about. Although he had been a member of the police department for twenty-eight years, and cherished his position in Internal Affairs, Inspector Wrynn, forty-nine years old now, obviously considered himself equipped for loftier endeavors. That intellectual arrogance, along with his righteous reputation as a supercop, made the Inspector a feared and elusive figure to many of the neighbors, who now looked askance at the Inspector's ponytailed son. Often, weeks or months would pass when no one in Throgs Neck would see the man whose stiff, hulking frame and furrowed brow seemed to scream zero tolerance. When he did resurface, his habit of reading on the porch and aiming his guard-dog glare at anyone with the temerity to stroll up Hosmer Avenue further enhanced his reputation as a hard-ass and a bit of an oddball.

To the Inspector, however, bookishness was a trait as deeply ingrained as thrift and obedience. After all, Jim Wrynn had pulled himself up from his humble beginnings with hard work and a keen mind that had little patience for nonsense. His father, an immigrant from Ireland, County Leitrim, had forsaken farming to seek his fortune in New York's unpredictable streets. He'd arrived in 1926, aboard the steamer U.S.S. *Celtic,* and found a job at the Fifth Avenue Bus Company as a porter and elevator operator. Later promoted to driver, for years he drove the Forty-second Street route, coveted because it was short and lively. Even the biggest headache of his occupation, the dance macabre of midtown at rush hour, hadn't soured Big Jimmy Wrynn on his life in the New World.

"Little Jimmy," as the Inspector was known in his youth, was the middle child—a tough kid who tackled each day at school as if it alone would determine whether he would ever amount to anything. After graduating from Fordham Prep, he'd earned his bachelor's degree from Fordham College in 1964. Within a year, he had all the trappings of the middle-class stability he'd dreamed of: a wife, a new job as a New York City police officer, and a baby son named John. The family made do for a few years in a walk-up apartment in the teeming University Heights section of the Bronx, within walking distance of the Fordham campus. In 1968 they moved to Throgs Neck, just eight blocks from where Wrynn's mother and father had considered themselves so lucky to settle. Was it any wonder that Big Jimmy couldn't help but boast about his son?

"My Jimmy just made captain," he once announced to another cop who lived on the block, his brogue swelling with pride. "Don't you like taking those tests?"

Although Little Jimmy's steady march up the ranks certainly qualified him for the title of Local Boy Made Good, the Inspector never really overcame his outsider status on Hosmer Avenue; sometimes, neighbors noted, he parked his car four or five blocks from his home, despite the fact that he had a driveway and plenty of parking spots available nearby. Everyone assumed he was trying to conceal the fact that he was driving an undercover vehicle, but no one dared ask. Wrynn wasn't the kind of fellow you'd expect to confide in anyone. He kept his own counsel and usually traveled alone; no one could have pried out of him the fact that his family and even his prized career were in a state of turmoil.

In the spring and summer of 1993, all four members of the Wrynn family were enmeshed in dramatic personal crises. (Years later, Jane Wrynn would grow pale at the mere mention of "That summer!") Ann Wrynn, the Inspector's daughter, was breaking up with her longtime boyfriend, Sal D'Errico, who lived right around the corner. The Inspector was close with the D'Errico parents, so the end of the romance meant compound aggravation: a heartsick daughter around the house and plenty of awkward social moments with the D'Erricos. But those problems were a minor inconvenience compared to the strain between the Inspector and his wife. After more than a quarter century, their marriage was in its death throes. In less than two months, the Inspector would leave her for good.

Maybe the most wrenching pain of all involved John, whose troubles on the job threatened to not only destroy his own career but sink his father's, too. John was under investigation for allegedly associating with drug dealers, a grave violation of the police department's official regulations and the cops' unwritten moral code. Back during Prohibition, many alcohol bootleggers had been tolerated, even befriended, by cops and civilians, but they were skirting a law many people disagreed with in the first place. During the 1950s and '60s literally thousands of officers from across the city took bribes to protect brothels and bookmaking operations, in a system of payoffs known as "the pad." But bootleggers, even mobsters, were usually careful to confine their murders to their professional rivals. Drug dealers were different. They were ruthless killers, willing not only to sell poison but also to shed the blood of bystanders, children, and innocent civilians. They considered it their own distorted brand of heroism to take out a police officer. In return, the police department developed an aggressively unforgiving attitude toward drug use: Any officer who tested positive for narcotics was immediately fired. No offers of treatment. No second chance. It was over. And anyone facing the allegations leveled at John Wrynn was considered a traitor.

THERE IS NEVER an opportune moment for a police officer to be accused of consorting with drug dealers, particularly if that officer's father is an Internal Affairs commander. But the summer of 1993 was a uniquely difficult time, and the NYPD's Internal Affairs Bureau was under withering scrutiny from all sides: the police commissioner, city hall, the media, the federal government, and the public. For more than twenty years, the NYPD had boasted that its Internal Affairs Bureau was a model for police departments around the globe. By 1993, however, Internal Affairs had been so badly discredited that it was the target of ridicule, and in real danger of being disbanded altogether. If that happened, commanders like Jim Wrynn would almost certainly be forced to retire or cast into professional exile.

The tarnishing of Internal Affairs's once-shining reputation had begun quietly enough. The unit had been formed after Frank Serpico, who'd revealed the existence of the pad in 1971, was shot in the face when his partners failed to back him up during a drug bust. Serpico became a folk hero. His allegations so enraged the public that the city formed a commission, headed by Whitman Knapp, to take a hard look at the dark side of the

NYPD. Two years later, the Knapp Commission documented Serpico's allegations, concluding that a sizable majority of the police department's twenty-seven thousand officers were involved in some kind of low-level corruption. Dozens of police officers were purged, along with their supervisors.

The city was forced to reinvent the department's method of policing itself, and the NYPD's innovations did, indeed, become a model. An independent Special Prosecutor's Office was established to handle police corruption cases and ensure that observers outside of the NYPD could monitor the department's efforts. Internal Affairs got additional equipment and manpower, and also built its own counterintelligence network within the ranks—cops called "field associates" who were selected in the police academy, trained as informants, then sent out to confidentially report on any misconduct in the ranks. Supervisors were warned that they would be held accountable for any corruption that occurred under their watch. Most important, the police commissioner named a no-nonsense commander, Chief John Guido, to oversee Internal Affairs. For fourteen years Guido served like a stern prefect of discipline; he was unflinching but fair in the way he dispensed justice.

By virtually every measure, the effort succeeded. The pad became a thing of the past. Complaints against officers dropped, and the misconduct that was uncovered usually involved small pockets of rogue officers rather than anything large scale. The culture of the department was so thoroughly cleansed that cops felt uncomfortable even joking about payoffs.

In the early 1990s, however, a new generation of corruption problems began to emerge. Chief Guido had retired in 1986, the same year Internal Affairs arrested thirteen officers for shaking down drug dealers in Brooklyn's Seventy-seventh Precinct, the largest police scandal since the Knapp days. The political fallout was immense, and the police commissioner responded by ordering wholesale transfers of officers and supervisors. The shake-up was so drastic—some said draconian—that Internal Affairs commanders began to fear that they themselves might be punished if they delivered more bad news. Chief Guido's successors tried to buff the old squeaky-clean image by cracking down on officers who committed minor infractions—taking a free cup of coffee or wearing white socks with their uniforms. In the late 1980s, an Internal Affairs investigator actually wrote up an officer for accepting a double-dip ice-cream cone when he'd paid for only a single scoop.

But there were signs that the department had lost interest in uncovering more corrosive and embarrassing corruption charges. In March 1990, Governor Mario Cuomo disbanded the Special Prosecutor's Office, promising to divvy up its funding between the five district attorneys' offices. Most of the money pledged to the prosecutors never materialized. The DAs quietly complained that Internal Affairs investigators had grown reluctant to carry out sting operations and often failed to share information with the prosecutors. In 1990, a former Internal Affairs detective, Vincent Murano, even published a book, entitled *Cop Hunter*, that described his ten years as an Internal Affairs undercover and took commanders to task for their timidity. Murano said that Internal Affairs supervisors were so terrified of making political waves that when they found a rogue officer they tried to quietly remove him from the force rather than pressure him to cooperate so they could find out whether he was the tip of a more insidious, widespread problem.

In a different city, in a different time, those warning flares might have piqued at least a small outcry. In the early 1990s, however, New York City was consumed by other distractions: fashion, gossip, high finance, culture, bare-knuckled politics, promiscuity, and racial tension. There was another, uglier, concern as well: An increase in crime incited by the wild popularity, and profitability, of crack cocaine had left a lot of unflappable New Yorkers scared as hell. The number of homicides in New York City had grown from 1,691 in 1987 to an all-time high of 2,245 in 1990. The papers and newscasts told of drug gangs and shoot-outs, gun battles on street corners and in schools, haunting tales of innocent kids spattered by the cross fire. Middle-class and well-to-do New Yorkers saw security bars and bulletproof glass become part of their daily landscape. In city housing projects, automatic weapons spewed so many bullets that in 1990, thirty-nine children aged fifteen or younger were wounded or killed by strays. Some parents actually began tucking their sons and daughters into bed each night beneath bullet-resistant blankets.

On August 30, 1990, both an assistant district attorney and a state assemblyman were shot in separate incidents on the same day. The tabloids seethed. Then, two days later, Brian Watkins—a devout Mormon tourist in from Utah for the U.S. Open tennis tournament—was fatally stabbed while defending his mother from muggers on a Manhattan subway platform. The papers shifted into panic mode. The *New York Post* shoved the burden squarely onto Mayor David Dinkins, demanding, DAVE, DO SOMETHING!

Then *Time* magazine ran a major story about the deadly new urban ills, complete with a cover illustration of a Big Apple infested with hoodlums, gunfire, and worms. The headline: THE ROTTEN APPLE. Dinkins pleaded sensationalism, proclaiming, "This is not Dodge City!" He pledged to hire five thousand new officers, and his plan was considered so crucial that the city's business leaders eagerly agreed to pay increased taxes to fund it. Complaints about the police department's inability to monitor itself rarely managed to be heard above the din rising from New York's deteriorating streets.

In late 1991, *New York Newsday* printed a six-part series describing in detail how Internal Affairs had intentionally botched cases and used a secret filing system—called "the tickler file"—to hide corruption allegations against politically connected chiefs and their cronies. But *Newsday* was the smallest and least influential of the city's four dailies, so Commissioner Lee Brown simply denied the stories, praised the vigilance of Internal Affairs, and reminded city residents that without the valiant sacrifices of the NYPD, the crack dealers would make the city uninhabitable.

Unfortunately for the commissioner, his words did not convince, or transform, the corrupt officers. Crack cocaine was taking its toll, and cops faced dual temptations: the drug itself and the obscene amounts of cash readily available to any officer willing to succumb, for even an instant, to his own darker impulses.

Officer Robert Cabeza didn't resist. In May 1991, Cabeza walked into the Eden Liquor store in Bedford-Stuyvesant, flashed his badge, and asked the clerks to let him behind the bulletproof glass to use the rest room. After he and an accomplice emptied the cash register, Cabeza declared, "They've seen my face, they've got to go," then shot and killed the store owner. His accomplice shot the clerk in the face, rendering him a quadriplegic. Cabeza's actions were atrocious, but the fact that he was still an officer at the time of the shooting was an outrage directly attributable to bungling by Internal Affairs. Two years before he'd walked into the liquor store, Cabeza had been accused of robbing a Nicaraguan man at gunpoint, but Internal Affairs had been unable to locate the eyewitness until May 1990. Then, although the witness identified Cabeza in a photo array, Internal Affairs didn't tell the DA's office about the evidence until August— after the immigrant witness had been deported. The case was dropped, and Cabeza remained on active duty, armed and very dangerous.

But the most infuriating example of Internal Affairs's ineptitude involved Officer Michael Dowd, a cop so blatantly corrupt for so long that he made street-corner crack dealers appear sympathetic by comparison. In May 1992, Dowd (who is not related to Detective Ed Dowd) was arrested by Suffolk County police for selling cocaine in his suburban Long Island neighborhood. And that was just the start; the newspapers reported that Dowd, the subject of fifteen previous complaints to Internal Affairs, had never been reprimanded or even forced to take a drug test. Next came revelations that he'd bought drugs in uniform, while on duty, and had occasionally snorted it off the dashboard of his police cruiser. Like manna from tabloid heaven, the Dowd story seemed self-sustaining. Next came the news that Dowd and six of his NYPD colleagues were paid $8,000 a week to warn a Brooklyn drug gang about possible narcotics raids. They stole cocaine from dealers who wouldn't pay them off. They even helped their underworld employers track down a rival dealer, who was then shot and killed. Dowd, whose take-home salary from the NYPD was $400 a week, owned three homes on Long Island and commuted to the precinct in a $35,000 Corvette.

Even the conservative *New York Post*, a staunch defender of the police, let loose, with headlines dubbing Dowd THE COKE COP and THE DIRTIEST COP EVER. Mike McAlary, the paper's big-name columnist, scored the first interview with Joseph Trimboli, a frontline Internal Affairs investigator who had spent years chasing Dowd, despite his supervisors' best efforts to cut him off. Trimboli became the good guy in the dark saga of Michael Dowd. He also offered a startling glimpse of how Internal Affairs had botched the case—either intentionally or through incompetence or both. When commanders refused to hand over resources, Trimboli pursued Dowd on his own time, using a pair of borrowed binoculars. Once, while Trimboli was begging his commanders to open a full-fledged investigation into Dowd, a supervisor pointed to Trimboli's wristwatch, a fake Rolex he had bought for thirty-five dollars on a street corner, and insinuated that he himself was on the take. In 1990, Trimboli was transferred off the case completely. Dowd remained untouched until the Suffolk County police arrested him two years later for dealing cocaine.

Within the law enforcement community, the Dowd case set shaky fingers pointing in every direction. The police department blamed the Brooklyn district attorney's office for the foul-up. The DA's office blamed the cops. Meanwhile, day after day, the tabloids tried to outdo each other with stories of Dowd's brazenness. Now that the beast of the New York media had been fully awakened to the problems of Internal Affairs, it was ravenous.

As if the stakes weren't already high enough, the upcoming 1993 mayoral election was amplifying the political repercussions. Mayor David Dinkins faced a daunting reelection battle and needed police support, especially with law and order so vital a concern. But Dinkins, who had been elected the city's first African-American mayor in 1989, couldn't afford to alienate the African-American, Latino, and liberal voters who made up his base by failing to react forcefully to police officers rampaging out of control. On June 18, 1992, when one of the papers reported that the FBI was considering opening a corruption inquiry into ten precincts across the city, Dinkins preempted them by launching his own, naming Milton Mollen, a former judge and deputy mayor for public safety, to inspect Internal Affairs.

At Internal Affairs headquarters, this news was welcomed like a ransom note. Internal Affairs commanders figured that the commission had to find *something* wrong in order to justify its existence, appease the department's critics, stave off the feds, and insulate the mayor from charges that he'd whitewashed the situation. Police officials had no choice but to promise cooperation—after all, they answered to the same mayor who'd set it up. But cooperating didn't mean that the NYPD couldn't also attempt to beat the commission to the punch by investigating itself and enacting reforms before Mollen weighed in. That way, when the commission ultimately issued its findings, the NYPD could argue that it had already solved the problem and that Internal Affairs should be allowed to carry on in its new, improved incarnation.

That strategy would save the department the embarrassment of having some outside agency established to monitor corruption. It would spare the police commissioner the loss of face, and power, that would result if all internal investigations fell from his control. So in late 1992, the NYPD set out to rescue Internal Affairs, and one of the crucial players in that crusade was Inspector James P. Wrynn.

IN DECEMBER, BEFORE the Mollen Commission had hired a staff or found office space, the department named three new commanders to upgrade Internal Affairs, including Inspector Wrynn. By bringing back supervisors familiar with the inner workings of Internal Affairs, the

NYPD could quickly enact its own reform plan while the outsiders from the Mollen Commission were still learning their way to the rest room. Wrynn was an obvious choice. He had dedicated his life to the police department and was experienced in internal investigations. He had a solid reputation for personal integrity and was a longtime friend of Al James, the deputy chief brought back to Internal Affairs to lead the effort. A graceful writer by police standards, Wrynn even composed the orders creating the new Internal Affairs, laying out its command structure, operational procedures, and investigative strategies.

Police commanders were also comfortable with Wrynn, who, from his earliest days in the department, had distinguished himself as someone who could tackle difficult, thankless tasks and clean up other cops' messes. His very first assignment out of the police academy had been in the Tactical Patrol Force—an early version of the NYPD's SWAT team. TPF squads were sent to trouble spots, where they'd flood the streets with officers and use any pretense possible to stop and frisk pedestrians. When TPF was called in to quell the Columbia University uprising in 1968, some civil libertarians complained that the unit conducted illegal searches and trampled on the rights of residents in predominantly minority neighborhoods. In time, the unit's tactics were discredited. But so effective was the Tactical Patrol Force that many neighborhood residents eagerly welcomed its arrival, and within the police department, it became a launching pad for scores of ambitious officers.

By 1972 Wrynn was a sergeant, selected to work out of the Fiftieth Precinct in the Bronx, one of five "model precincts" in the city. The program, launched in the wake of the Knapp Commission revelations, was designed to teach impressionable new officers an experimental form of community policing intended to minimize their opportunity for misconduct. Wrynn's record had been so sterling that he was one of a handful of young sergeants entrusted with the job of molding the new breed of cop. In this task, as usual, he received excellent evaluations.

Wrynn's career was defined in various anticorruption units. In 1974, he was assigned to handle corruption cases in Queens, and he later worked for Internal Affairs in the Bronx. By 1980 he'd made captain, and the chief of detectives handpicked Wrynn to head the bureau's anticorruption efforts, which he ran for six years. In 1990, after two Bronx precincts were embarrassed by revelations that officers had been robbing drug dealers and accepting payoffs, Wrynn was dispatched to ride herd over the entire division, which was made up of six precincts.

"There had been a number of derelicts found in the 40th and 44th Precincts and the division commander was removed," he later explained. "And I was sent up there with the mission to try to bring it into line with the rest of the department."

All this experience would be invaluable to Internal Affairs as it tried to beat back the Mollen Commission. But Wrynn also had his own, very personal, reason to be wary of any outside agency snooping through the NYPD's files. Investigators from the commission were preparing to comb through every scrap of paper Internal Affairs had ever produced, and somewhere among those mounds of documents were reports about the Inspector's son. Even if the charges against John were nonsense—and the Inspector insisted that he'd never believed them for an instant—they were potentially devastating. What would be more dramatic than Mollen bringing back the pelt of an Internal Affairs inspector's son? If the charges against John were substantiated, the commission could use them to embarrass the unit. If they were ruled to be unfounded, the commission could concoct an even more sinister spin, accusing Internal Affairs of killing the case simply to help one of its own protect his child.

Years later, Inspector Wrynn would swear, under oath, that no one in Internal Affairs had ever tipped him off to the case against John. He would testify, as well, that he never asked for any special treatment for his son. Many people in the commission and the department consider those assertions implausible, laughable, and demonstrably false. But James Wrynn insisted, under oath, that it wasn't until late September 1992 that he even realized John might be in trouble—and that his friends in Internal Affairs were most definitely not the ones who broke the news.

He said he found out on a Saturday, a brisk afternoon in late fall, when he was home alone, enjoying what was left of the season's sun by washing his cars. Wearing sneakers, a warm shirt, and long pants, he was out on the driveway with a hose in his hand when he heard the telephone ring inside. Realizing that his sneakers were wet from the sudsy water streaming across the pavement, the Inspector considered just letting it ring. But since no one else was home, he decided to hustle inside and pick it up, wet sneakers be damned.

"Hello," Inspector Wrynn said.

"They've got a case on your son," the voice on the phone said.

For a moment, the Inspector thought the caller must have been talking to someone else. There had been no greeting or hello. So abrupt, so startling was the message that Wrynn was simply taken aback.

"Hello," the Inspector said again. "Who is this?"

"He's going to parties where they do drugs."

"Who is this?" Wrynn demanded, jarred by the realization that the call was indeed addressed to him and the message was about John.

"A friend."

The line went dead.

The Inspector was stunned, but livid. His son, doing drugs? Impossible. He knew John, and he felt confident, certain to the very depth of his soul, that he'd raised his boy to know better than to touch that poison. Wrynn was furious that someone would even suggest such a thing, outraged that they'd be too cowardly to say it to his face. He knew how such rumors could cripple a career.

But as the Inspector's flash of anger faded, he gradually began to feel gratitude toward his mysterious caller. After all, the person had taken the time to find his home number and track him down. He'd also felt enough concern for the Inspector to give him a word of warning, so it was unlikely that the caller had lodged the complaint against John or wanted him thrown off the force. There were a hundred questions the Inspector might have asked the caller if he'd only had a chance to talk, most importantly: *Who the hell is saying these things about my son?*

Whoever was to blame, though, the Inspector knew he must warn John fast. His sneakers still soggy, he tried to ring his son's new home up in Pound Ridge, but there was no answer. It was the next day before they talked. Jane was sitting by the Inspector's side as he spoke.

"None of it's true," John insisted, and the Inspector noticed something he hadn't often detected in his son's voice: shame.

"John, it's not true—we know it's not true," the Inspector said.

Even if John was staying clear of drugs, however, there was no guarantee that Internal Affairs or some prosecutor's office wouldn't find cause to nail him on something else. The Inspector had seen enough careers destroyed by "white socks" violations to know that. Placed in the unusual position of defending the target of an Internal Affairs investigation, the Inspector knew precisely what John had to fear.

"You've got to be on the Q's and T's," Inspector Wrynn said. "There's a case on you. When they have a case on you in Internal Affairs, they are looking at you for using drugs—they will catch you taking a two-hour meal period, catch you going home early. You don't do that. You be on your toes."

Despite his many loyal friends on the NYPD, there were plenty of rank-and-file New York City police officers who would have been overjoyed to see Inspector James Wrynn trapped on the worrying end of an investigation. Wrynn's work had made him infamous for his willingness to dole out harsh punishments for the slightest infractions, sometimes on questionable proof. During his first three years on the job, when Wrynn and his young family still rented in University Heights, another cop who lived in their building had a fight with his wife and was startled to find that it had been reported to the department. He couldn't prove it, but he always suspected that Jim Wrynn had turned him in. (More than thirty years later, that officer, who's now retired, was still afraid to have his name published for fear of retaliation.)

In 1986, when Chief Mario Selvaggi found the tires of his car slashed outside the Forty-first Precinct in the Bronx, Wrynn conducted a relentless investigation. Ultimately, the misdeed was pinned on a patrol officer, who was reprimanded and transferred to Brooklyn as punishment. Months later, a criminal picked up on an unrelated charge admitted to vandalizing the car, but by that time it was too late. The officer's reputation had been blemished, his career turned upside down. To exonerate him, Jim Wrynn would have had to do something Internal Affairs investigators are trained to avoid at all costs—admit a mistake.

Even Wrynn's superiors, men who respected and relied on him, sometimes worried that his zealousness made him what the police call a "head hunter." Now that Wrynn's son was the hunted, the Inspector was experiencing, firsthand, the agony of the other side. All the enemies he'd created over the years might view John's predicament as a weakness and move in for the kill. The action might not come for days or months or years, or never at all. You could never tell. The Inspector told John to scrupulously obey all traffic laws, because he was probably under surveillance. If John was stopped for any reason, he was to be courteous. He might even volunteer to take a drug test to prove his innocence, the Inspector suggested.

"They're just doing their job," he told John.

The Wrynns didn't have a large circle of friends outside the department to confide in or turn to for support. Jim Wrynn had long believed that being a police officer sets you apart from your friends because "it makes you something other than them." It was one of the sacrifices that came with the job. You took your oath, got your uniform, and pretty soon your social life began to revolve around the department. Old friends who had problems with cops stayed away. Others just lost touch. Even people who were generally law-abiding began to look at you in a different way.

A lot of people had been looking at Jim Wrynn in a different way recently, and not just because of John. The tawdry details about the breakup of his marriage gave his detractors on the force a windfall of powerful ammunition. Sometime in early 1993, rumors had begun to spread that the Inspector was romantically involved with a lieutenant in the Bronx Sex Crimes Unit, Nancy McLaughlin. Both had worked at the borough headquarters. The contrast between Wrynn's prim wife and his vivacious younger female friend wasn't lost on the other cops, who joked that the Inspector better be careful or he'd end up like former vice president Nelson Rockefeller, who'd suffered a fatal heart attack while cavorting with a woman forty-five years his junior.

As an inspector, however, Jim Wrynn was far too powerful to piss off, a man who had exhibited little sense of humor about anything, especially himself. No one dared make the vaguest reference to his purported dalliance, at least not until his back was turned. Then, a few months after the news about his son, Wrynn began to hear whispers about himself. Word was that he'd been asked to retire—an utter lie, he said, but precisely the sort of vicious gossip that some weasel could use to undermine him.

But even before the Inspector was summoned back to Internal Affairs, there were signs that his friends in high places were still friendly, and still powerful. In February 1992, Internal Affairs chief Robert Beatty had managed to keep investigators from getting anywhere near records of John Wrynn's phone calls, then abruptly declared the case closed. The case folder was deposited in the infamous tickler file. There were other indications that Inspector Wrynn's political muscle wasn't just a thing of the past. In fact, the transfer back to Internal Affairs itself represented an unparalleled chance for Wrynn to advance his career. With a little luck, and lots of thankless work, it wasn't unthinkable that Jim Wrynn might one day be named chief. Maybe he'd even manage to run Internal Affairs or rise to chief of inspectional services—one of the five "superchief" positions that make up the police commissioner's inner circle.

But events intervened. Despite Chief Beatty's decision to grant a pardon to Inspector Wrynn's son, two other police officers launched complaints about John, alleging that the untouchable officer had an inappropriately close relationship with the criminals from his old stomping ground. Then the arson investigation into the death of Lieutenant Williams somehow wound its way from Queens into Throgs Neck, right into the heart of John Wrynn's social circle. Because the arson inquiry involved other agencies—the fire department, the FBI, and the U.S. Attorney's Office—there was no clean and easy way for Internal Affairs to quash the latest accusations.

As he sat on his porch reading through the pleasant nights of June, Inspector James P. Wrynn, part of Internal Affairs's last, best hope to save itself, had unwittingly become part of the case file. Internal Affairs detectives had been assigned to tail John Wrynn, just as the Inspector had warned him, and the surveillance team cruising the neighborhood that month made an odd note of the fact that the subject's father was often seen sitting on his porch, curled up with a good book.

7

9 1 1

J U N E 1 6 – 2 9 , 1 9 9 3

ARMANTI WAS HANGING out in the café when Joe Red invited him to come to Ferry Point Park to "pick up a package." Armanti knew he wasn't talking about a trip to the post office. So he agreed, sensing that the investigation had reached a major threshold. If things went smoothly (as they certainly hadn't been lately) he might actually get a chance to buy cocaine in Throgs Neck before the Ferrantis packed up for a retirement community. But before he and Red got going, Armanti's pager went off. He knew it; the whole thing was too good to be true. With their usual exquisite sense of timing, the IAB detectives were demanding to meet him under the Throgs Neck Bridge.

"It's too dangerous," Armanti was told by Robert Matthiessen, the IAB sergeant. "Don't go." And, astonished at himself, Armanti did as he was told.

The next day, June 17, Armanti got another shot at a score. Passing some time at Sebastian's, he was caught off guard when Dobbs rushed up to him and hugged him.

"Hey, Vinnie, come on with me—I'm going drinking in City Island," Dobbs said.

"Fuck no. Why do I want to go all the way up to City Island?" Armanti shot back. "Let's drink here."

Armanti hated City Island, a rinky-dink Bronx neighborhood of has-been homes and rickety marinas in Eastchester Bay. And despite the hug, something about Dobbs was starting to feel a little flaky, too. Things were moving too fast; besides, Armanti was still so stung by Internal

Affairs stifling the investigation that he wasn't quite ready for another round of rejection.

"Come on!" Dobbs urged him, his excitement stirring Armanti's suspicion. "I want to introduce you to my friend."

"I don't want to meet no friend," Armanti said. The ones he had were trouble enough. Armanti was beginning to feel alarmed, worried that Dobbs might finally be on to him.

"Let's drink here," Armanti insisted.

"Come on, I want you to meet my friend," Dobbs said, undeterred. "John Wrynn. He's a good guy."

Armanti stopped cold. He counted two breaths, careful to slow it down. Then, taking out his cigarette pack, he shook out a smoke.

"Ah, what the hell," he said, taking Dobbs by the arm as his beeper went off in his pocket.

Armanti was so elated at the prospect of meeting Wrynn that it was almost painful. In the sixteen days since their chitchat at Sebastian's, Armanti had learned quite a bit about his fellow detective—some of it intriguing, most of it disheartening. Now that he was set to meet Wrynn in less than an hour, Armanti's biggest worry was resisting the urge to pummel him.

He realized that at some time in the not too distant past he might have appreciated the guy's bad-boy shtick—the ponytail, earring, and motorcycle. He liked rebels, and Wrynn's rep as a smart-ass was something Armanti could definitely identify with. But the two men's defiance came from two completely different mind-sets. Armanti considered his own bravado earned: He could bend the rules because he had worked hard and produced. If he came across as a hotshot, it was because he was confident enough in his abilities to add a few flourishes to keep things interesting.

Wrynn liked to give attitude too, but his status was hardly based on his track record. Formerly a marginal student at the police academy, he had been a mediocre beat cop, and had been promoted to the elite HIDTA drug task force on the basis of his genes and his father's political pull. Inside the Organized Crime Investigation Division, Wrynn complained about the normal annoyances of narcotics work: the paperwork, the beepers, and the irregular hours. He strutted around as if he thought rules were for all the other humps to worry about, that he could do as he pleased because he was who he was. Armanti had seen that kind of arrogance before in countless other cops. Despite the NYPD's size—more than thirty thousand officers in 1993—the department still operated like a very small town, where the right connection was an express ticket. The guys with the hooks always struck Armanti as the most self-important; it was as if they hadn't been bright enough to figure out why they'd gotten all the breaks.

In the ID photo that Internal Affairs supervisors had shown Armanti, Wrynn looked chunky, a little soft. During the fitful nights since Armanti had learned that his reports were being leaked, he had often tried to dream up creative new ways to inflict physical pain upon Wrynn. He wanted to watch that smug, doughy face howl in agony. But not even in his most elaborate fantasy did Armanti think he'd actually get close to Wrynn. Now that their rendezvous was just minutes away, Armanti was aching to get him on tape. He could almost hear the sweet click of handcuffs closing tight around Wrynn's pudgy wrists. But Armanti knew he couldn't be anywhere near where the arrest went down. He was afraid he'd start pounding on Wrynn; if he did, the Inspector's friends in Internal Affairs would be only too happy to fire Armanti for using excessive force.

Meeting Wrynn in the bar would be a clean setup. Clearly, Dobbs and Wrynn had something illicit in mind. If they simply wanted to drink, they could have met at Sebastian's, where their liquor would be free. Armanti couldn't imagine someone with Myron's cocaine habit spending twenty dollars—the price of two perfectly good rocks of crack—on carfare to City Island just to pal around. Maybe Wrynn was going to update the status of Dobbs's pending indictment, or pass on a tip about some other upcoming busts. *How many of my own reports,* Armanti thought, *will I hear repeated back to me tonight?*

Wrynn wouldn't be dumb enough to do anything incriminating in front of someone he barely knew. At some point in the evening, Armanti would head to the men's room so Dobbs and Wrynn could talk freely. But the beauty of the situation was that with Dobbs involved, Armanti didn't even have to coax out the information. Dobbs was a talker, so Armanti knew that during the drive up to the bar, he'd hear a thorough description of his relationship with Wrynn and the purpose for their trip to City Island. On the way home, after a few drinks, there'd be no shutting him up. As they walked toward his car, Armanti charted out the longest possible route to the bar, to be certain there was plenty of time for Dobbs to blather on. Tonight, Armanti's job would be easy: keep his hands on the wheel and make sure the batteries in the tape recorder were fresh. He wanted a nice clear recording, so the department (and one day, hopefully, a jury) could hear exactly what Wrynn had been telling Dobbs.

Armanti was so pumped up that he considered blowing off the call on his beeper. But he noticed that the callback number read *911*. Armanti assumed that the Internal Affairs detectives, listening in, had overheard his plans and wanted him to stall Dobbs so they could set up surveillance vans near the bar on City Island. He told Dobbs not to bother calling the car service, offering to drive them up to meet Wrynn as soon as he returned a phone call. The wiseguys in Sebastian's had warned Armanti that the bar phone might be tapped, so he walked to the public phone on the corner.

Sure enough, it was Internal Affairs, monitoring everything from a van a few blocks away. Sergeant Robert Matthiessen answered, but there was commotion and another voice in the background.

"What's up," Armanti said, his heart pounding.

"Don't go," Matthiessen shot back.

"What do you mean?"

"Go to the café for the rest of the night," Matthiessen said. "Don't go to the bar."

"Are you fucking crazy?" Armanti demanded. "This is it! This is the chance we've been waiting for. If he's the leak, we'll get him."

He could make out one of the voices talking to Matthiessen in the van. It was Lieutenant Shields, screaming, "Don't go! Tell him, Don't go!"

"By authority of Lieutenant Shields, don't go to the bar," Matthiessen said. "Under no circumstances. If you go, you're suspended."

Matthiessen hung up.

Armanti slammed the telephone handset against the metal booth so hard it sounded like an explosion. He charged back into Sebastian's, where Dobbs had been watching from the window. A couple of customers had drifted over and were peering out to see if the bang had been a car wreck or a gunshot.

"Who the hell was that?" Dobbs asked.

"My fucking uncle!" Armanti bellowed. "He's coming by and I gotta wait for him. How about we go another time?"

"Yeah," Dobbs said, looking a bit confused. "What about next Friday?"

Armanti walked to the café fuming, so infuriated that he could barely concentrate on his conversations with Joe Red and the Italians. When Armanti returned to the base a few hours later, Dowd was sitting alone at a desk.

"It gets worse," Dowd said.

RATHER THAN SIMPLY forbid Armanti to meet with Wrynn, Internal Affairs proceeded to completely trash the investigation. They'd gone to City Island themselves. The Internal Affairs van had followed Dobbs to a bar called Rhodes. Then Matthiessen had walked in, his tight jeans and cowboy boots woefully out of place in a bar filled with working-class New Yorkers, and stood next to Dobbs. When Dobbs and a friend started talking about softball, Matthiessen awkwardly barged into their conversation.

Wrynn was nowhere to be found. Having endured a few minutes of excruciating small talk with Matthiessen, Dobbs used the phone, then went to another bar, where he and John Wrynn finally hooked up. A few minutes later who should walk in but Matthiessen, who tried to explain his arrival by saying he'd been stood up by a girlfriend. Matthiessen remained at the bar for a few minutes. With a total stranger standing near them, Dobbs and Wrynn predictably restricted their conversation to trivial matters. Then they left.

The Internal Affairs detectives wrote up the incident and, without the slightest hint of irony, made it appear as though they had carried out a sophisticated sting operation that had, regrettably, failed to yield any useful information.

Dowd and Armanti knew that Internal Affairs couldn't have been more obvious if Matthiessen had worn a neon badge on his chest.

"They completely blew it," Dowd said, aghast. "Internal Affairs fucking blew up the bar!"

A few minutes later, when the IAB detectives entered the office, Dowd and Armanti pounced.

"What the hell was that all about?" Dowd demanded.

"Are you fucking nuts!" Armanti screamed.

The Internal Affairs detectives said nothing. Lieutenant Shields glared.

"That's our investigation with Wrynn, not yours," Shields said, and led his subordinates to the door.

Armanti and Dowd were numbed. Armanti still doubted Internal Affairs would do anything overt to risk his life. But the longer IAB dragged out the investigation by protecting Wrynn, the longer he would have to remain on a set where he could be blown away at any moment. The easy thing to do, the safe thing, would be to just bail. Dowd and the fire marshals wouldn't like it, but they could hardly blame Armanti, who—if he wanted to save face—could just hang back and let the investigation wither on its own. Undercover work is so nuanced that there are unlimited ways to kill an investigation without anyone knowing. A word here, a phrase there, a look—anything to spook a target just enough. With the cost and complexity of this investigation, Armanti knew that all he would need would be a week or two without any progress and Internal Affairs would shut it down. Armanti could return to the safe confines of normal narcotics cases, where only the drug dealers were a danger. IAB would be off his back. Maybe he'd even return to the classroom, track down Judy, and try to reclaim his life. Dowd had offered to go up the chain of command and complain about the interference from Internal Affairs. But they both knew there was little chance their supervisors would prevail. Not when the head of an IAB inspector's son was on the block.

That night, Armanti and Dowd went to a 7-Eleven on Bell Boulevard, bought a six-pack, and sat on the curb drinking a beer. Dowd was beginning to look queasy about the whole thing.

"We've got to watch out, Vin—our careers could go down the drain on this one," Dowd said.

Armanti said nothing.

"I'm telling you, this thing is a career killer," Dowd persisted, waiting to see whether Armanti might be ready to give up on the case.

"This is so fucked up," Armanti said.

"I've got a really bad feeling about this one, Vin," Dowd said.

Armanti looked at him, shaking his head incredulously, until a grin broke across his face.

"What the hell have you gotten me involved with, you prick?" Armanti asked. He cuffed Dowd on the arm, and they both dissolved into laughter.

AFTER THE CITY Island debacle, the Internal Affairs detectives had, incredibly, grown even more blatant in their obstruction of the investigation. After a long weekend, when they all reconvened at the office in the Fort Totten army base, Armanti expected Shields and Matthiessen to be apologetic about what they'd done. At the very least, Armanti figured he'd hear some priceless explanation about why Internal Affairs might possibly have wanted to blow a gift-wrapped opportunity to snare Wrynn. Instead, the first thing that day, Matthiessen and Shields cornered Armanti and Dowd in a hallway to relay a stunning new edict from IAB headquarters. They told Armanti that he was now forbidden, in no uncertain terms, to enter Sebastian's.

The events of the past few weeks had long since convinced him that the higher-ups at Internal Affairs had closed ranks. But he had still held out some hope for John Shields, who Dowd knew from a previous assignment in Brooklyn. As a lowly lieutenant cast away among the overpromoted bosses in IAB, Shields had always seemed to identify with the street investigators, or so Armanti thought. At times, it appeared to him that Shields had seemed hesitant to follow the lead of his bosses. On one or two occasions, Armanti had sensed Shields's sympathy—or was it empathy, or maybe even shame over the whole disgraceful and dangerous charade? So when Armanti calmed down enough to attempt to reason with the IAB detectives over the Sebastian's decision, he addressed himself to Matthiessen, but he stared at Shields, to see whether there was any hope of finding an ally.

"What are you talking about?! You're the ones who told me to go in there," Armanti argued. "It's where Wrynn is. Where everybody hangs out. It's not like you're unaware of this!"

"It's coming from upstairs," Shields said quietly, but with a definite sense of finality, as Armanti studied his expression. He was searching for remorse, ambivalence, some kind of sign that, at some level, the guy disapproved of what was happening. But Shields had turned cold. Either he felt nothing or he had become a better actor than Armanti, who could only assume that the brass had forced the issue and Shields had made his choice. So Armanti tried a different tack, looking to provoke, to stir up a little something, if he could. "What's the matter," he said to the detectives. "Am I getting too close to your boy?"

Shields, finally, seemed slightly embarrassed. He shook his head.

"I keep telling you, you better stay focused," the lieutenant said, taking up the same tired line. "Your job is to buy from Tocco and make the arson case. Period."

Then Shields and Matthiessen turned and walked away.

"You're a fucking mental case," Armanti shouted back as he also turned to go. Then he started back toward them, but Dowd grabbed his arm, trying to keep him from chasing them all the way to the parking lot.

"Like it or not, Wrynn is part of the arson case now!" Armanti screamed at their backs.

"It's an order!" one of the Internal Affairs detectives said, without turning around.

"Fuck your order!" Armanti roared.

Dowd was holding Armanti back by both arms now. "Vin, don't," he said. "We're already fucked. We're fucked."

By the time Armanti strode onto the set an hour later, he knew that each moment on the case might be his last. IAB was clearly searching for any excuse to close him down, and with Sebastian's now off-limits, it was just a matter of time. They'd restrict his movements bit by bit, choking off access to his targets, gradually smothering him. After a month, or a week, or maybe a matter of days, they'd declare that the case had hit a dead end and issue one of their classic bureaucratic postmortems: *Case closed due to inactivity*. It all seemed so obvious that Armanti no longer had time for all the precautionary steps that had protected him in the past. He'd always warned novice narcotics detectives about seeming too hungry, too desperate. But at this juncture, he simply couldn't afford to be laid-back anymore. He needed something tangible—now—or the case would fold. It would be dangerous to escalate the tension with Tocco and Mario, maybe disastrous, but there was simply no alternative.

It wasn't like there had ever been anything conventional about this whole affair. The incomprehensible dynamics of Throgs Neck, where you could never quite be certain who was allied with whom, had already forced Armanti to drastically alter his usual, scrupulously adhered to investigative routine. In most cases where the NYPD worked alongside other law enforcement agencies, investigators tended to close ranks and divide along tribal lines—cops stuck close to cops, fire marshals confided in fire marshals, and nobody trusted the FBI. Armanti knew that he and Dowd would always stand together. But given the Wrynns' network of police contacts in the Bronx, plus their hooks into Internal Affairs, he had by necessity grown wary of anyone else even remotely connected to the NYPD.

Instead, he reached out to the two fire marshals and the FBI agent assigned to the case and asked them to watch out for him. The two marshals, Bobby Thomson and James Desocio, were irrepressibly gung ho about finding Lieutenant Williams's killers. Armanti asked them to stay as close as possible on the set, in case he needed backup and Internal Affairs didn't respond in time. Dowd and Armanti also searched for allies further up the chain of command. Dowd called his supervisor in Queens, but what could a captain in the Queens Detective Bureau do to help them on a case involving an inspector's son? Call Chief Beatty, the head of Internal Affairs? Beatty was Inspector Wrynn's pal and, as Armanti and Dowd would later learn, had already blocked previous attempts to investigate John Wrynn. Dowd's captain offered the only thing he had, a bit of wisdom he'd picked up during his decades on the force: There are certain cases, he said, that aren't worth taking on unless you want to spend the rest of your life assigned to the midnight detail guarding the Fresh Kills landfill. The old-timers called them career killers, and this case was a classic example.

Dowd also begged the federal prosecutor assigned to the case, Assistant U.S. Attorney George Stamboulidis, to help rein in IAB. Stamboulidis tried to follow through, complaining to Internal Affairs supervisors about their interference. But they denied, as he knew they would, doing anything to thwart the investigation.

So by June 22 Armanti needed to try something radical, and knew of only one surefire way to hurry things along: physical aggression. Armanti sat at his usual window table in Café d'Oro, nursing a red wine of questionable vintage and glancing out onto East Tremont Avenue. Joe Red was in the back room taking sports bets on the phone. Armanti, looking for some inspiration, ambled over and started talking, but Red was too preoccupied to broach the topic of cocaine. Next, Armanti tried to engage Carlo Cuzzi in a little conversation. Cuzzi, however, was eager to join the four men huddled around a poker table.

Armanti walked back to his seat, getting a little frantic but feeling in the mood to start improvising something. When one of Joe Red's buddies decided to hang out a few feet from a public phone outside, Armanti headed over to him. He put a quarter in the phone, dialed directory assistance, then launched into a spontaneous ad-libbed tirade, loud and savage enough to attract attention from anyone.

"You tell him he better or I'll cut his fucking head off!" Armanti bellowed. "You hear me? I'll chop him into little pieces just like I did to his fucking brother!"

Joe Red's friend said nothing, just stood there listening like it was poetry. But Armanti could see him watching, and he knew word of his colorful phone declaration would soon start winding its way through the streets. Once that happened, all the serious players in the neighborhood would gravitate toward him, moved by either fear or competitiveness. He had just publicly labeled himself as "Open to Anything." With Internal Affairs encroaching on him every day, Armanti doubted that the murderous boasts would come soon enough to help save the investigation, but it sure beat sitting around idly.

As Armanti headed back to the café, he saw Tocco getting out of his brown Caddy. Armanti sprang out onto the street. He rushed past Tocco without so much as a glance, then kicked the nearest trash can.

"Fucking Joe Red!" Armanti screamed. He pounded the metal can with his foot, sending garbage streaming into the air, then booted it again.

"Fucking motherfucker!"

Tocco watched quietly. Finally he couldn't resist the show.

"What the hell's the matter?" Tocco asked, careful not to move too close.

"Fucking Joe Red! He *fucked* me! That motherfucker was supposed to hook me up and he stiffed me. Made a jerkoff out of me!"

"Calm down," Tocco urged him. "Someone's gonna call the cops."

Armanti gave Tocco a fierce look.

"Motherfucker!"

"What's the matter," Tocco asked. "What are you so pissed about?"

"Joe Red was supposed to take care of me, that prick."

"So calm down," Tocco said. "Calm down. What do you need?"

"What do you mean, what do I need?"

"What do you *need*," Tocco persisted. Armanti eyed Tocco warily as Tocco flashed a nervous smile.

"I can get things," Tocco whispered.

Armanti scoffed.

"What can you get?"

"Whatever you want."

"Yeah?"

"Yeah, I'm telling you . . ."

"You!"

"Yeah, *me*," Tocco insisted.

Armanti gave an evil little chuckle, shook his head, then slowly looked Tocco over.

"How much a gram?"

"Thirty," Tocco said, not missing a beat.

"Well, I need a Big Eight," Armanti said, referring to an eighth of a kilo, or 125 grams, of cocaine.

"I can get whatever you need. *No problem*. I just have to check the price with my supplier."

"You?" Armanti asked.

"Yeah. No problem," Tocco said. "I'll need the money up front, though."

"Yeah, I'm gonna give my money to you," Armanti said angrily.

"I'm telling you, I can get things. I just have to check with my guy."

"You do that. Get me a price, then get back to me, all right?"

Tocco wrote down Vinnie's pager number, promised to call back with prices, and drove off.

Predictably enough, the IAB detectives were spectacularly unexcited by the news that Tocco was once again in play. Armanti and Dowd knew that this could be the last break they were going to get, and the waiting soon became excruciating. One of the fire marshals, Bobby Thomson, tried to lighten up the mood by teasing Armanti about Internal Affairs and its ulterior agenda.

"I saw IAB delivering your reports to Wrynn's father," he said. "It's all very convenient. They just roll around the corner and drop it off at his house. It saves on overtime."

Armanti played along, making sure to laugh a moment or two longer than anyone else, to show what a sport he was. On the set, though, he now felt completely exposed and vulnerable. He spent every moment scanning for an ambush and trying to make sure his hypervigilance wasn't broadcasting itself. The next day, he had to take a deep breath and calm himself as Tocco's Cadillac pulled into view. But Tocco just drove on by, and they waved. No words.

NOT LONG AFTER this latest unsatisfying moment, Armanti decided to stir things up by bringing Cindy Peil, an FBI agent working on the case, onto the set and introducing her as his girlfriend. Vinnie Blue Eyes was brimming with so much testosterone that Armanti had been searching for a way to let Tocco and the Ferrantis know he was getting some action somewhere. But he didn't dare avail himself of any of the women he'd become acquainted with on the set—that would give new meaning to the phrase "unsafe sex." There were several Throgs Neck girls who'd been salivating in Vinnie's direction, but Armanti could never be sure whom any of them might be allied with. Even a little flirting could be hazardous. With a microphone taped to his chest and an electronic transmitter taped near his groin, one playful caress in the wrong place could mean trouble. But by bringing Cindy around, Armanti could not only buff up his image but also try to rev up the investigation.

Of all the strange alliances Armanti had entered into during his crazy days in Throgs Neck, the oddest by far was his relationship with Peil. In the past, Armanti had had no time for federal agents; he'd considered

them paper pushers, not true-blue cops. They were usually midwestern-
ers, guys with starched shirts and sharp elbows who twanged their way
around New York without getting a clue about what made the city tick.
Yet once the arrests came down, they always managed to somehow Big-
foot the local cops out of the credit they deserved. Peil was different. Sincere and smart, she was a team player and seemed totally committed to
taking the Lieutenant Williams case as far as it would go. Armanti also
thought Peil was quite attractive, although the good-girl type didn't usually get his blood flowing.

But the real reason he wanted her on the case had nothing to do with
aesthetics or hormones; it was his instinct for self-preservation. Peil might
have looked unapologetically Middle American, like someone who'd just
walked off the pages of *Martha Stewart Living* magazine, but anyone
who'd ever seen her at the shooting range knew she was more a candidate
for a spread in *Guns & Ammo*. Peil was a deadly shot, far more accurate
than Armanti himself or anyone else on the case. In the catty world of law
enforcement, news of such talent quickly spreads through the grapevine,
especially when the shooter wears a size-five dress.

To transform her into Vinnie's girl, Armanti had to nudge Peil a few
degrees higher up the hottie scale, but Peil's girl-next-door demeanor
would clash with any overtly sexual outfit. Armanti's first instinct was to
tart her up, add tight pants, a low-cut blouse, and enough heavy-duty hair-
spray to shellac a trawler. But the more he tried to envision her as some
Avenue U *bracciole,* the more Armanti realized this was never going to happen. It would take a Hollywood makeup artist to give Cindy a believable
veneer of Bensonhurst, and she'd never pull off the accent or get the lingo
of Armanti's gangster turf.

In the end, he knew that the only choice was to let Cindy be herself
and get creative with her cover story. Armanti and Peil decided that
Cindy would play the wife of some Wall Street type who was dallying with
Vinnie because she was exasperated by her workaholic husband. Tocco
and the Ferrantis, who managed to see themselves as downtrodden even
as they trampled on the downtrodden, would love the thought of Vinnie—
someone like *them*—getting over on some Wall Street prick's wife. And
they'd never expect that inside her understated little handbag, or
beneath that smart silk blouse, she was strapped with a nine-millimeter
automatic she could use to pick them all off in a heartbeat. Cindy seemed
jazzed by the prospect of entering the set undercover, although she was,

not surprisingly, a bit wary. Armanti wondered if his reputation as a wild man might have intimidated her. So he tried to put her at ease.

"You know, I'm not some kind of degenerate or anything, but you're supposed to be my girlfriend," he explained. "If I kiss you on the cheek or something, you don't have to worry. I'm not gonna ram my tongue down your throat or anything. I'll be respectful."

Peil laughed.

"If something goes wrong in there, it's all on your shoulders," Armanti warned her.

Peil responded without missing a beat.

"Fine," she said, totally cool.

Beneath her calm exterior, however, Peil was all jitters. Although she was thirty, Peil had joined the FBI only two years earlier, after her job in banking became just too mundane to stomach. She had been raised in small-town western New Jersey, had attended a small college in Podunk, Pennsylvania, and if her parents were concerned by her decision to become an agent, they were terrified when she was assigned to the New York City office and the organized-crime unit. Her first two years in the bureau were spent in glorified training sessions—doing surveillance, document research, and other low-priority jobs far from the front lines.

In March 1993, when her supervisor informed her that she had been assigned to work with Dowd and the fire marshals on the Lieutenant Williams investigation, she felt the sinking sensation of someone shoved off a cliff and ordered to soar. It was Peil's first real case, and it had enough complications to consume an investigator's entire career: a tangle of law enforcement agencies, suspects capable of unlimited and creative forms of homicide, evidence of police corruption, and shaky, circumstantial evidence. *Couldn't they have let me cut my teeth on some simple gambling case?* she'd thought. *Something where no one's life was at stake?*

To make matters worse, her bosses suggested that they wouldn't mind if she lived up to the FBI's reputation for poaching by maneuvering the investigation as far as possible away from the NYPD and the fire marshals. So, on the day she first met with Dowd and his entourage, Peil felt as if she herself were the suspect. She opened the office door and walked in to find some unsociable, burly detectives and fire marshals, accompanied by their bosses, with boxes of evidence in tow. During her first two months working alongside Dowd and the fire marshals, Peil had begun to feel a bit less intimidated. But when Armanti asked her to join him on the set, any fleeting sense of comfort instantly vaporized. Peil wasn't sure who made her more uncomfortable: Tocco and the Ferrantis or Armanti, who had given her the kind of welcome usually reserved for tax auditors. He had grunted hello, then slowly stared her up and down. If he had checked her out that thoroughly at a bar, she might have been tempted to toss a drink at him. Beyond the sexist innuendo, there was an additional layer of offensiveness to his careful scrutiny. The macho, streetwise undercover shot her such a skeptical look that Peil felt self-conscious about her inex-perience and unfamiliarity with the city, as if she were Elly May Clampett from *The Beverly Hillbillies*.

But from the moment of their grand entrance, Armanti and Peil were more like something from *My Fair Lady*, and their pairing in the barroom was an instant hit. Peil's bourgeois glow was such a stunning contrast to Vinnie's outer-borough attitude that she immediately elevated him in the eyes of the café crowd. The surest measure of their success, catcalls from Vinnie's associates, began at once.

"What's a nice girl like you doing with a guy like him?"

Cindy smiled, rolled her eyes, and squeezed Vinnie's arm a little tighter. Armanti just laughed along, relieved. As the night went on, Armanti was impressed by Cindy's performance, how well she seemed to internalize her new uptown persona. Best of all, she knew when to keep quiet. In the past, Armanti had worked with female undercovers who'd talked too much and inadvertently contradicted him. But when Peil was asked anything unscripted, she gave a knowing smile and just said, "Ask Vinnie." To the patrons of the café, her coyness was interpreted as a sign that she was completely aware of her date's dark history. To Armanti, Peil's cautiousness was a sign that she was unlikely to say anything that might get them both shot.

Peil even got a peek at Tocco during her brief stint at the café when the Torch walked past.

"You get those prices?" Vinnie asked him.

"I'll get them," Tocco said, without stopping.

Armanti had hoped that Tocco would be ready to consummate the sale, and his delays were growing a bit unnerving. But now Armanti knew he was free to bring Peil along for backup in case things got tense later. So pleased was he with his new partner that Armanti kept his tongue where it belonged—though as he walked out of the bar with his arm around

Cindy's waist, it occurred to him that it had been months since he'd felt such soft curves.

And it had been longer, a lot longer, since he'd been so intrigued by a woman that he studied her every move. When they were on the set together, Armanti noticed that nothing seemed to get past Peil. She walked to the jukebox and played Eddie Money's "Two Tickets to Paradise" and a few make-out songs by heavy-breathing soul artist Barry White. When the napkin under his drink got soggy, Peil picked it up, swabbed the bar, and replaced it with a dry one. She didn't say much during her forty-five minutes in the café, but her rendition of the restless suburban housewife was pitch perfect: She gave the impression that Vinnie's dangerous lifestyle didn't frighten her; it turned her on.

Peil just seemed so totally *there*. Since combustible Judith, and all the strays and princesses and ne'er-do-wells he'd tussled with before her, Armanti had come to assume that every relationship was just turmoil. He had made his peace with the chaos by acting out, playing the madman on the street, the smart aleck in the office. And then he'd let his personal life atrophy because, frankly, he had no idea how to make sense of it all. But Peil seemed just the opposite; she radiated tranquillity. She was the first person he'd met in law enforcement who wasn't disgruntled, drunk, disenfranchised, or disgusted. Was it possible he could end up with a woman who was so together? Someone with such smarts, good manners, common sense, and calm?

Nah, Armanti thought, *I'm too fucked up.*

DAYS PASSED, AND the longer Tocco delayed, the more time Armanti had to torture himself with suspicions. When Tocco disappeared for four days, Armanti spent every minute inventing an endless loop of bloody endings, and straining to create an exit strategy for each one. It wasn't Tocco himself that concerned Armanti. The Torch didn't have the nerve to take on Vinnie; Armanti was sure of that, and it was probably a good thing for both of them. If it came down to guns, Armanti figured that Tocco was so incompetent he'd end up shooting himself.

The Ferrantis were another matter altogether. Mario had bragged to his friends that he was the butcher who had sawed off Bruce Bailey's hands. Armanti had seen Mario only a handful of times on the set, but it was clear by the way he carried himself that the guy was a degenerate. As a teenager he had threatened his neighborhood peers and their parents alike.

When Mario was about fifteen, a woman from the neighborhood, Carol Gross, had looked out her window and seen him pinning a much smaller boy to the ground, grinding his genitals into the kid's face. She'd raced out and scolded Mario. He'd stopped, but he'd shot back a frightening scowl. A few months later, the Gross family had returned from a vacation to find that their home had been burglarized, emptied of virtually everything of value. Word had quickly spread around Throgs Neck that Mario was responsible.

Mario had continued to instigate erotic wrestling matches with younger boys in the neighborhood. Even members of Mario's own family were embarrassed by Mario's uninvited advances. According to one police report, Mario once made uninvited sexual advances on his niece's fifteen-year-old boyfriend. The boy ultimately decided against pursuing the matter in court, but the incident enhanced Mario's reputation for preying on underaged boys. But Mario was quite capable of mixing it up with the tough guys as well. He was a vicious brawler, and his slight build had lulled many bigger men into the painful mistake of underestimating him. He also carried himself with the air of someone who wouldn't think twice about taking a life. In the marines, the NYPD, and the streets, Armanti had met men who had killed for an assortment of reasons. There were servicemen who did it out of duty, patriotism, or self-preservation; scared teenage muggers who killed out of pure panic; desperate drug addicts; gang members who killed to prove their loyalty or improve their status; hit men who viewed it as their craft. He'd seen fellow cops, forced by circumstance to kill a suspect, who'd then agonized for years, replaying the fatal moment again and again, trying to divine whether they might somehow have avoided taking another human's life. Never before, though, had Armanti met someone like Mario, someone who spoke as though he found a sheer, sadistic joy in it.

On the set, Armanti kept up the usual routine: selling swag, slapping backs, buying drinks, working the room like an underworld ward heeler. All the while, though, he waited for the Ferrantis to come at him. Armanti had been forced to push this case so much faster than usual that he wasn't certain whether he was being incredibly efficient or a fool. If haste somehow made him sloppy and tipped off Tocco or the Ferrantis, they wouldn't think twice about murdering him. And if they did, it would be Mario who made the move.

The longer they waited for Tocco to finally set up the sale, the more the other detectives teased Armanti about the Wrynns, trying to lighten the tense mood. But as things dragged on, their jokes grew stale. Finally, on June 29, a week after he'd first discussed a possible deal, Tocco walked into the café and asked Vinnie to step outside. Armanti followed Tocco onto the street, searching in vain for any sign that Mario might be in the area. Then Tocco laid out the conditions of the sale: The price was $2,000 and the money had to be paid up front. Tocco also said that he had no transportation, so he'd need a ride to his supplier's safe house.

It was all surprisingly businesslike, and as they said their good-byes, Armanti couldn't help but think that Tocco had simply been reciting lines written by the Ferrantis. Armanti spent a sleepless night trying to figure out why Tocco would want him to drive. Tocco certainly had his own car, and also had access to a half dozen vehicles owned by the Ferrantis. So why would he want Armanti to drive? No drug dealer wants a customer to know his suppliers, for fear of being cut out of deals in the future. And no self-respecting supplier would allow an underling to bring a customer anywhere near him, as a simple matter of precaution. Armanti could only assume that the Ferrantis wanted him to be distracted by the chore of driving because it would make him an easier target.

The next day, as Vinnie bided his time in the café, Tocco returned— this time, with Mario in tow. Mario hardly said a word, but he watched, with a vaguely conspiratorial look, as Tocco leaned toward Vinnie.

"I didn't forget our conversation," he whispered. "Beep me tomorrow at four-thirty, and at six I'll have Mario drive me downtown to get it. But I need the money up front."

The instant he heard the words, Armanti knew he wouldn't be able to sleep until the deal was completed. Back at the base, Armanti and the other detectives worked frantically for hours, reviewing their plans for the buy over and over. They had to arrange for backup teams, record the serial numbers of each hundred-dollar bill Armanti would use, and prepare fallback plans for any of a hundred possible emergencies. Five months after the undercover operation had begun, a year and a half after Lieutenant Williams had died, they finally had a chance to get their hooks into Tocco. At one point in the frenzy of preparation, Armanti looked up at Dowd and the fire marshals.

"We're either going to get him tomorrow, or you guys are going to a funeral." Then he fixed Dowd with his stare. "And it's gonna be your fault, you fuck, for getting me involved."

8

FIRST BUY

JULY 1, 1993

THE SQUAT, BRICK homes on Tommy Tocco's section of Revere Avenue are squeezed together tightly enough to allow someone to travel from one end of the block to the other by walking roof to roof. The nondescript, two-story 1950s row houses call to mind the gritty South Philly of *Rocky* rather than the rest of the Bronx, with its apartment buildings and war-torn housing projects. Yet amid the uniformity, there are enough personal touches to distinguish most homes from one another: A patch of black-eyed Susans. A trellis or two of roses. A window sticker proudly display-ing the flag of Ireland or Italy. A religious shrine of the Virgin Mary standing within a shell-like grotto, known colloquially as "Mary on the Half Shell."

The outside of Tocco's home, 244 Revere, was adorned only with the white security bars across its windows. Nothing else divulged the slight-est detail about its occupant. Only after the door opened into Tocco's basement apartment could one begin to get a sense of the true, inner man, and as Armanti stood in the doorway and surveyed the squalor, he knew that he had not underestimated the Torch. He saw dog food on the floor, dirty clothes and old newspapers scattered across the couch and tables. A sour, fetid aroma like spoiled milk filled the air, as if the apart-ment hadn't been scrubbed since before the Torch had taken up resi-dence. Armanti scanned the pit looking for Mario, but he caught no sign. Not yet.

This, Armanti thought, would be a depressing place to die.

Tocco had been so jumpy in the days since they'd first discussed the sale that Armanti considered it an accomplishment to have even made it into his living room. Armanti had arrived on the set at 6:20 P.M. and paged Tocco from the pay phone outside the café. After fifteen minutes, he was startled by a brown van with Tocco hailing him from the passenger seat. As it got closer, Armanti winced: Mario was driving.

Tocco got out and, with an unsettling absence of small talk, laid out his terms. But, not surprisingly, he screwed it up. Tocco said he'd bought sixty-five grams and was prepared to sell sixty-two grams, which should have cost $1,800. But he mistakenly quoted the price for two ounces, which is fifty-six grams and cost just $1,580. Armanti fetched his car, which had been equipped with a transmitter, and invited Tocco inside. He pulled out $1,600 and made sure he counted it out loud, so the microphone would pick it up. Then he coaxed Tocco into double checking, counting out each hundred-dollar bill, just to impress the eventual target audience, the ladies and gentlemen of the jury. Tocco drove off to pick up the product, but after twenty minutes or so he finally figured out his mistake. He returned, a bit embarrassed, and Armanti handed him the extra $200.

Then came the big wait.

Thirty minutes crawled by. Then half an hour more, still with no sign of Tocco. Eventually, the brown van pulled up—this time with no Tocco, only Mario.

"You know where Tommy is?" Mario asked.

"No," Armanti said, glad he had strapped a nine-millimeter to his ankle.

"He should be back," Mario said. "I'll go to his house to see if he's there."

Armanti nodded, watched Mario drive off. Something told him he would probably be seeing Mario again before the night was over.

Tocco finally arrived, this time with Mario nowhere in sight.

"Hop in," he said. "We're going to my house."

Armanti had opened the car door, scanned the back seat to be sure Mario wasn't hidden there, and climbed in front. Tocco turned, shot Armanti a glance, and off they went. Even under the best of circumstances, Tocco wasn't deft at repartee, but on this night, with his life hanging in the balance, Armanti felt so much edginess that the three-block drive seemed like a haul across the desert.

Tocco parked the car in the driveway in front of his house. As Armanti strode toward the front door, he reminded himself that there was at least one strategically important reason Tocco wanted the sale to take place in his home. And probably two. An informant had warned the police that

Tocco had rigged up a bug-sweeping device above his doorway. It was a small electronic mechanism—purchased at one of those spy stores that sell high-tech gizmos to James Bond fans, paranoid executives, and crooks—designed to detect any transmitter or listening device within ten feet. In an uncharacteristic burst of ingenuity, Tocco had reportedly hooked his up to the illuminated exit sign above the door. If someone entered wearing a wire, the light flashed. Armanti reached deep into his pocket, where he'd wired a shutoff switch to his transmitter, which he had taped rather uncomfortably under his crotch, and disabled the device a few feet before he reached the front stoop.

As the door swung open and Vinnie surveyed the ratty little hellhole, he had concentrated on the second likely reason Tocco wanted to deal here: home-field advantage. By bringing Vinnie into his empty apartment on this quiet street, Tocco and Mario could control virtually every variable. There was little chance of an unexpected passerby or, God forbid, a cop. If they were planning to rip Vinnie off, or if they had been tipped off about Armanti's true identity, Mario would have the upper hand.

Now, Armanti scanned the breadth of the place, trying to figure where he might hide if he were about to kill an undercover. The apartment was unnaturally quiet. All he heard was the faint shush of traffic far off in the distance. No television, stereo, or radio—odd, because Tocco had mentioned hanging out at home earlier, and he seemed so slovenly that Armanti couldn't imagine him actually bothering to switch anything off before heading out. Unless it was a special occasion.

Tocco pulled the bag out of his pocket and placed it on the table.

"I'll go get the scale," he said, heading to the closet.

Why is Tocco narrating? Armanti thought. *Is it some kind of code for Mario to spring out of hiding?*

Armanti bent down to tie his shoe, so the gun under his pant leg was within easy reach. With Tocco facing away from him, rummaging through the closet, Armanti eased back toward the kitchen, hoping to find cover behind the island separating the two rooms. When Tocco carried the scale back to the table—and Mario didn't pop out—Armanti joined him. Tocco poured the white powder onto the tabletop and started to take out the three grams he'd bought himself. The instant it fell from the bag, Armanti could see its crystalline, "fish-scale" look. It was genuine. Of course, that didn't stop Vinnie from driving a hard bargain.

"This looks a little bit banged up," he grunted. "What'd you cut it with?"

"This is how the guy gave it to me. I came straight to you with it," Tocco shot back. "I didn't fuck with it."

"Then he's making a jerkoff out of you, and you're making a jerkoff out of me."

Tocco poured Vinnie's cocaine into a plastic bag, then handed it to him. Armanti looked around the room and placed the bag in his pocket. Tocco was now facing twenty-five years, Armanti thought, still on the lookout for Mario.

Tocco returned the scale to the closet, then turned and asked a question that made Armanti's heart jump.

"You're not wearing a wire on me, are you?" Tocco asked.

There is nothing quite as staggering as someone asking whether you're wearing a wire. Especially when you are. Armanti knew he had to respond forcefully.

"No. What?" Armanti growled. "What are you, some kind of fucking clown?"

"No, no, no," Tocco explained, slightly apologetic. "My best friend wore a wire."

"What do you mean, your best friend wore a wire? Where is he now?"

"He's gone. I couldn't even go to the funeral," Tocco said, shaking his head. "They killed him. He's dead."

Armanti knew immediately that Tocco was talking about Eric Mergenthal. The night had gone better than Armanti had ever imagined—not only had he made his first drug buy, he'd also gathered evidence about a possible homicide. Now all he had to do was make sure he lived to see the morning.

Tocco drove back to the café. Armanti waited a few minutes, then called Dowd.

"It's a positive buy," Armanti announced. "I just fucked him in the ass."

When Armanti brought the evidence back to the office, Desocio, one of the fire marshals, had tears in his eyes. Dowd gave him a hug. No one had really believed Armanti would be able to make a buy from Tocco, not when he knew there was an undercover roaming around Throgs Neck. The Internal Affairs detectives hurried out of the building with hardly a word.

"Did you see their faces!" said Thomson, the other fire marshal. "Didn't they seem pissed?"

Armanti just smiled. He didn't have long to savor his victory, however. The next day, he learned that IAB had somehow failed to tape most of the sale, and had nothing at all about Mergenthal's death. The next week, he got an even bigger surprise. Armanti's supervisor called from Brooklyn to pass on a message from Internal Affairs. The department's allegedly random system for choosing which officers had to undergo drug tests, the one that Detective Wrynn had ridiculed, had come out with its weekly list of names. Armanti was ordered to report to the health-services office in Lefrak City, Queens, for a urine test.

9

"THERE'S GONNA BE TROUBLE!"

JULY 9, 1993

DETECTIVE SIXTO SANTIAGO was leafing through a file folder on his desk in room 127 of Internal Affairs headquarters when he heard the footsteps. Santiago wasn't the type to be easily rattled, not after twelve years on the force, including four in Internal Affairs. But he was entwined in the kind of top-secret investigation that makes every creaky floorboard seem sinister. So even before he looked up to see who was approaching, Santiago felt dread.

Room 127 was the new home of the IAB Special Projects Unit, one of those dismal government offices with linoleum floors so scuffed and blurred and furnishings so nondescript that the place seemed overcast even on the Fourth of July. From above, the lurid glow of fluorescent lights gave the room the sickly appearance and unsettling buzz of a hospital waiting room. The nature of the work only amplified the oppressiveness: IAB special projects investigated highly sensitive corruption cases against police commanders or employees of Internal Affairs. A few of Santiago's colleagues were scattered around the office, working quietly, but even when you were alone in room 127, there was always the sense that somebody was looking over your shoulder.

As Santiago closed his case file and looked up, he instantly sensed someone approaching. An imposing, heavyset man, his forceful intensity seeming to precede him, had somehow made it through the locked doorway and was moving toward the inner office where Sergeant Matthiessen was at work.

The special projects team's new office space had been designed to prevent precisely this kind of unannounced entrance. In a police department that prided itself on keeping secrets safe, IAB's special projects was supposed to be impenetrable. Less than two weeks earlier, the entire Internal Affairs operation had been moved from Brooklyn Heights to an obscure location on Hudson Street in SoHo, a Manhattan neighborhood clustered with art galleries and high-end shops where few off-duty cops were likely to happen by. Inside that enclave, special projects was tucked at the end of a corridor, not far from the chief's office, an area where no one dared venture without clearance. Although it was on the third floor, special projects was inexplicably given the room number 127, and it had no sign outside to distinguish it from a broom closet or storage room. Its door was also secured by a special electronic lock, restricting access to only those issued the secret pass code.

Yet the man who stormed past Santiago's desk had breached the security without even breaking his stride.

For months, Santiago had been among the unfortunates assigned to the John Wrynn investigation. Experience had taught Santiago that any case involving IAB bosses was an ulcer waiting to perforate. A year or so earlier he had been part of the team that had investigated Al James, an IAB deputy chief who was, coincidentally, a friend of Inspector Wrynn's. The whole thing was like a high-wire act with a gun at your temple: One wrong move and your career got splattered across the floor. Within IAB, loyalties remained unseen and motives were often ulterior; there was no way to know which commanders might have spies. Or who might be offended by the most innocuous word or implication.

Detectives on every shift felt burdened by pressure—seen, unseen, and sometimes imagined. Despite the evidence they had gathered against James, Santiago was disheartened that no disciplinary action was taken against him. Just the same, those who worked on the case would spend the rest of their careers wondering whether they'd one day be punished because some superior had decided they'd failed to exhibit the proper deference to Chief James's decades of service.

The Wrynn family affair was even more troubling because Internal Affairs was no longer being left alone to do its work. The Mollen Commission was breathing down every neck, searching. The only thing that would make the commission members happier than nailing an IAB inspector's son would be to show that IAB had purposely tanked the investigation. So the bosses would have to be exceedingly careful about justifying their actions in the case.

The big decisions would ultimately be made by someone far above Santiago's rank. But before the chiefs could convene to figure out whether or not to pursue charges against Wrynn, they had to invest enough manpower and resources and generate enough paperwork to create the impression of a thorough investigation. The thankless task assigned to Santiago and the others in special projects was to tail John Wrynn, as if he were any other criminal suspect, and gather as many facts as possible. Or at least as many as their superiors would allow them to.

From the very beginning, Santiago had had a bad feeling. When it had all started, with the allegation that Wrynn had been using drugs with his neighborhood buddies, Santiago and his partner had been sent to conduct surveillance on Sebastian's, where Wrynn routinely partied a few times week. But suddenly Wrynn had lost interest in his old hangout. Night after night, the detectives would roll by in unmarked cars, and send in undercovers. Night after night, Wrynn stayed away. During six months of surveillance, IAB saw Wrynn set foot in Sebastian's only once, briefly, and he made little contact with Myron Dobbs or any of the crew members who moved drugs out of the location.

After months of this charade, detectives in any other unit would have grown restless. Not in IAB. Santiago knew better than to mention the obvious fact that their confidentiality had been burnt; you never knew what got repeated, what could cause real repercussions. In the warped world of Internal Affairs, it would be heresy to actually acknowledge that an investigation was pointless, because pointlessness was the entire point. Santiago knew someone had tipped off Wrynn, and it was likely that the tip came from within Internal Affairs. Yet they pressed on, going through the motions, generating paperwork, without actually gathering evidence.

When Dobbs had invited Armanti to meet with Wrynn on City Island, IAB commanders had made the outrageous decision to prevent the meeting from taking place. Instead they'd sent Matthiessen in, to carry out his pathetic farce of a sting. You might be able to devise a more obvious way to undermine an investigation. But you'd have to think pretty hard.

After Armanti made his first buy from Tocco, who could give them information about Wrynn, it looked like the Inspector had abandoned even the pretense of legitimacy. It was all incredibly delicate: An undercover was in the field; surveillance teams were risking their lives each night by circling around mobsters and drug dealers. And now, eight days after the big buy, who should head right into the center of the investigation in room 127 but Inspector Wrynn himself. Unauthorized. Shook up. Moving like a gale-force wind toward the office where Matthiessen was trying to concentrate.

Santiago recognized the Inspector immediately, and instinctively glanced away. Although they had never been formally introduced, every peon knew who Wrynn was. They also knew he was someone to be feared. Santiago stared at the cover of his closed file folder, then stole a glance at Al Ramirez, another special projects detective sitting behind a desk a few feet away. The stricken look on Ramirez's face said it all. Santiago's first impulse was to hide what he had been doing. Call it naïveté, but until that afternoon, Santiago had tried to convince himself that perhaps, just maybe, Inspector Wrynn didn't know that special projects was watching his boy. One look at the Inspector's furious face dispelled any doubts.

Although Wrynn was one of the highest-ranking commanders in Internal Affairs, there was no other reason he would have been in special projects. Assigned to work out of a field office in Queens, he also had a desk in IAB headquarters, but he had no business here in special projects. He wasn't friendly with anyone in the unit, so there would have been no reason for a social visit. In fact, the Inspector was not among those who had the security code, so Santiago couldn't figure out how he'd managed to get past the locked door.

Unnerved, Santiago knew to keep his mouth shut. In the NYPD's paramilitary culture, even subtle challenges were considered an act of insubordination. So the words that might have accurately described Santiago's reaction to the Inspector's visit—"What the fuck are *you* doing here!"—would definitely be out-of-bounds. And the Inspector didn't look like he was in the mood to be bothered. He just went straight ahead, past the filing cabinet where the evidence against his son was accumulating in audiotapes, surveillance videos, and work sheets. Then he slammed into the inner office.

JAMES WRYNN HAD plenty of reasons to seem agitated, reasons beyond his son's troubles on the job. At home in the Bronx, Wrynn had finally made the break with his wife just a few weeks earlier. Then he'd packed his belongings, left the home where they'd spent a quarter century, and moved in with his mother and sister, a few blocks away. The Wrynns had been such a solid couple, for so long, that the neighbors were dumbfounded.

Once the shock subsided, many quietly said that it was a blessing that a woman as good-natured as Jane Wrynn had been liberated from a man so dour and condescending. They also expressed a bit of glee that a man as sanctimonious as Jimmy Wrynn would have to endure the humiliation of moving back in with his momma, not to mention the shame of being known as a home wrecker who had ditched his faithful wife for some younger woman.

John Wrynn was apparently stunned and dismayed by his parents' separation. For years he had bragged to friends that his parents' marriage, cranky though it might be at times, was the gold standard of family stability. The notion that his father was destroying their home left him shattered.

John had been shaken further in early July 1993, when he'd heard more mind-bending gossip about his father. A friend in the department told him that a police wiretap had picked up information about Inspector Wrynn's possible involvement with members of the Luchese crime family. Jimmy Wrynn, Mr. By-the-Book? A year or two earlier, John would have actually laughed. But if someone had asked him a year earlier whether his father, Steady Jimmy Wrynn, was going to heave-ho his wife, he would have laughed that off, too.

So John had decided not to let this one drop. He had to find out for himself what his father was up to—whether the old man was in trouble and, if so, whether he needed John's help. If the Inspector was going to brush the whole thing off, John still needed to hear it for himself. He had never been comfortable confronting his father, but on something this important John decided to do it face-to-face, to look straight into his father's eyes.

John approached him in early July, when the Inspector was washing his car in his mother's driveway. Immediately the Inspector noticed that his son—his macho, distant son—was on the verge of tears.

"I'm hearing there's a case on you," John said, "having to do with the Luchese family."

The Inspector was blindsided. He scoffed, then let out a curse or two.

"John, I wouldn't know a member of the Luchese family," he had said.

The Inspector was skilled at using his rage to end uncomfortable conversations, but this time it would take more than one bellow to persuade John.

"Dad, I'm living out of the house, I don't know what you're doing. What are you doing? Are you all right?"

"What are you talking about?" the Inspector said.

"I am getting information that they have a case on you. For the Luchese family."

"John, I wouldn't know a member of the Luchese family."

John persisted, telling the Inspector that "a little bird had whispered into my ear" about a police wiretap.

"John, are you out of your mind?" the Inspector shot back. "What do you think I am? You know me. I work, I read history, I play paddleball, I pay taxes. What are we talking about? I raised you. You've known me all your life."

They tried to calm each other down. Once the Inspector's shock subsided, he began to worry that the pressure of being investigated might be making his son paranoid. The Inspector had seen it happen before, strong men so overwhelmed by a protracted Internal Affairs investigation that they lost control and, in the indelicate phrasing of police parlance, ate their guns.

It was ironic, and a bit absurd, that John might expend energy worrying about his father's career when his own had been receiving even closer scrutiny. Ever since Internal Affairs had refused to let Armanti meet with Wrynn on City Island, there had been heavy static. Dowd's supervisor had complained to the chief of detectives. The U.S. attorney had complained to Internal Affairs. There was speculation that the feds might take IAB off of the case completely.

It was within a week of his conversation with John that the Inspector could hold back no longer. He barreled straight into the special projects commander's office, where Robert Matthiessen—one of Armanti's IAB sparring partners from Throgs Neck—was sitting and the most sensitive files were kept.

Once the Inspector could no longer see them, Santiago and Ramirez exchanged astonished looks. They strained to hear what Matthiessen might say. There was no one less welcome in special projects, but would Matthiessen have the courage to confront someone of higher rank? They craned their necks and breathed as quietly as they could, afraid that the Inspector might catch them listening. A few minutes passed, with no audible sounds other than footsteps and rustling paper. Then the Inspector's voice boomed out of the office, so loud it made Ramirez and Santiago nearly jump.

"There's gonna be trouble!" he roared.

The Inspector stormed out of the office and down the hall. Santiago ducked his head down as the Inspector blew by him. He and Ramirez sat motionless until they heard him leave, slamming the door. Then all their pent-up anxiety exploded. Ramirez shot up from his desk. Santiago moved toward the inner office, shocked. Before he reached the door, Matthiessen appeared, looking dyspeptic.

He gave only curt, fuzzy answers to their inquiries. When they pressed him, asking what Inspector Wrynn had been doing in there, Matthiessen seemed unwilling to answer directly. When they asked him what Inspector Wrynn was referring to when he warned that there was going to be trouble, Matthiessen's answer was perplexing.

"I thought he was talking to you," Matthiessen said.

Later that day they discussed the incident with their immediate supervisors, but no one complained to the police commissioner or the Mollen Commission.

That night, however, outside the confines of Internal Affairs, Matthiessen apparently felt more forthcoming. Inside Fort Totten, where the detectives prepared for each night's work, Matthiessen stared at Armanti, who had just returned from taking a drug test and was getting ready to enter the set and put his life at risk yet again. Matthiessen looked physically ill, so Armanti asked him what was the matter.

"The old man was at my desk," Matthiessen said. "Looking through the file. We're fucking dead."

10

ARE YOU HOT?

JULY 10–16, 1993

THERE WAS ONE sound Armanti always longed to hear during the tense, off-duty hours that punctuated his undercover operations, three simple words that meant he might, just for an instant, find some peace. He'd be sitting in some sleepy bistro, far outside the city limits, when some waitress or total stranger would innocuously utter the phrase "Excuse me, sir."

Not *suh*, like some gum-snapping waitress in a mobbed-up Coney Island coffee shop. Not *suh!* like an ambitious Gambino soldier or some kiss-ass detective flattering a lieutenant. But "Excuse me, sir," the way people pronounce it in the real world, in places where he wasn't expected to act as live bait to attract killers. That was what he was always looking to hear. Just a little courtesy.

The moment Armanti heard those words, that soothing pronunciation that suggested genuine manners and respect, he would smile. Suddenly his exhausting attempts to relax might at least have a slim chance of succeeding. His mind might wander, then return from some daydream elated. *My God, I actually avoided thinking about Vinnie Blue Eyes for three minutes.*

But most of the time, whether he was on the job or off duty, Armanti's thoughts never really left the set where the NYPD's treachery had made the pressure inescapable. When he was in character, everything was magnified; everything was of possible concern. If a car drove up with a catchy tune blasting from its radio, Armanti never even heard the music—he was too busy trying to memorize the license plate.

Once his marathon shift ended, he'd head home, which before Throgs Neck had meant that Judith would try to provide a diversion—or at least force him to pretend. But now that his house was empty, all that free time just brought him back to the case. *Had he made any mistakes that might have blown his cover? Was he missing any obvious signs of trouble?* The Fort Totten army base was so close to Throgs Neck that Armanti often slept on a cot there to save himself the hour-long commute. He'd go home once or twice a week to fetch a few changes of clothes, try to convince friends— who might, if he was really clicking, believe he was paying them some sort of attention—to join him for a drink out in Jersey or up in Westchester, where there was little chance that anyone might recognize him.

Yet in some ways, the oddest time of all was the interval between the intensity of his undercover hours and the slow burn of the personal life he'd walked away from—the hours when Armanti found himself in the purgatory of the office. Each time he left the set, Armanti was still flying on such an adrenaline rush that his high-octane personality seemed turbocharged. He joked and cursed even more incessantly than usual, leaving Dowd and the fire marshals wondering whether he was coming unhinged, and making Armanti feel as if he were somehow in a different time zone or on a different planet.

To Armanti's surprise, the person who made him feel most comfortable was Agent Peil. She'd help him type his daily reports when he was too wired to sit still, and her naïveté and enthusiasm were a warm counterpoint to the jaded abruptness of Dowd and the fire marshals. Her accent, attitude, and earnestness seemed to come from a place where they still said "Excuse me, sir."

As the investigation intensified, Armanti began to treat Peil like the kid sister he'd never had—wrestling with her in the office, teasing her about her accent and her inexperience as an agent. Armanti also began to joke about the culture clash between their backgrounds. "So you gonna finally take me home to meet your parents this weekend?" he said one Friday.

Peil rolled her eyes. "If I walked into the house with something like you, my parents would have a heart attack," she said, smiling as she walked out the door.

Dowd had endured endless teasing from Armanti about his conventional lifestyle—the wife, the ever-expanding flock of kids, the Detective Who Lived in a Shoe—and despite their friendship, he seemed to see Armanti as a creature beyond the possibility of conventional domestication. "Forget about it, Vin," Dowd said one day in early July.

"What do you mean?"

"You're not her type."

"What are you talking about," Armanti said. "I'm just joking around."

"I'll bet you anything you couldn't get a girl like that," Dowd said.

Armanti scoffed, uncertain whether Dowd was ribbing him and hoping he hadn't flirted too obviously.

"Save your money."

"Ahhh, listen to you," Dowd said. "Come on, then. Bet me."

"Get out of here."

"Bet!"

"Save your money," Armanti said. "You've got like, a hundred and fifty kids at home to support."

"How about dinner at Embers?" Dowd said, referring to Armanti's favorite steakhouse in Brooklyn.

Armanti laughed.

"So, bet!" Dowd taunted him.

"Embers," Armanti said. "All right. You've got it."

But the moment Armanti learned about Inspector Wrynn raiding the special projects office, the jokes and other thoughts of distraction all ended. Until that moment, Armanti had somehow managed to view the Wrynns as near abstractions. He had gathered evidence out of a sense of duty, momentum, and self-preservation. When Detective Wrynn had first emerged as a possible leak, Armanti had felt the same visceral disgust he had for every dirty cop. But the instant he heard that Inspector Wrynn had threatened the detectives in special projects, it all became intensely personal. John Wrynn might have been acting on impulse or out of habit when he'd first started tipping off Tocco; and on some level, Armanti could understand the Inspector's instinctive desire to take care of his son. But by this point in the case, Armanti was certain that the Wrynns knew how deeply the Ferrantis—the vicious Ferrantis—were wrapped up in it. Inspector Wrynn also had to know the risk he was taking by interfering with an investigation involving an undercover in the field. By now, Armanti figured, the Wrynns knew that it wasn't just some nameless, faceless undercover moving through Throgs Neck. It was he, Vincent Armanti. It was almost certain that, by now, the Inspector knew Armanti's real name, address, maybe even his phone number.

This was no longer about any nebulous investigation, anonymous adversaries, or veiled threats. It was about survival. The Inspector, a powerful man in the most brutally powerful unit of the police department, had granted his son an official indulgence for his actions. If anyone dared to challenge him, they might well be destroyed. Inspector Wrynn never mentioned any names when he promised trouble, but Armanti had to assume the first casualty would be him.

Anyone who had crossed Inspector Wrynn in the past knew that he wasn't the type to make idle threats. Sure enough, a few days after his rampage through the special projects office, IAB took Matthiessen off the case and replaced him with Lieutenant Michael Gagliardi, who was renowned within IAB for his unquestioning loyalty to the chiefs. The boys were making their move, Armanti thought.

Only two choices remained. Armanti could do the prudent thing: solve the Lieutenant Williams case, forget about the Wrynns, and most likely enjoy a happy, lengthy career. Or he could press ahead, go where the evidence took him, and run the risk that IAB would either endanger his career or somehow allow the Ferrantis to endanger his life. There were more murmurings that IAB might shut down the operation any day. Shortly after Tocco had made his first sale to Armanti, Shields had confided in Dowd that he was taking a vacation, and he'd suggested that Dowd take a week off, too. Dowd figured they were trying to create a lull so they'd have an excuse to kill the investigation once and for all.

But Armanti suspected that there was a more sinister motive behind IAB's sudden, uncharacteristic interest in Ed Dowd's vacation plans. With his friend Eddie out of the way, the one person whom Armanti knew he could rely on for anything, they could set him up. There were any number of ways to do it. Leak his identity to Mario Ferranti. Try to goad Armanti into firing a shot at someone, so he could be charged with attempted murder. Or they might try to end the investigation by threatening his job. The day the police department tested him for drug use, Armanti went to visit Bob Masci, a narcotics sergeant he would trust with his life. With two witnesses observing, Armanti produced another urine sample, which he placed in a sealed evidence container, then tucked in the back of a precinct refrigerator where the sergeant stored his lunch. Just in case the police lab tried to tamper with his drug test and claim he'd tested positive, Armanti would have his own sample to prove that he'd been clean.

He also began planning various disaster scenarios in his head, in the event that Internal Affairs did manage to force a violent endgame. When

Armanti was learning the intricacies of undercover work, his mentor taught him one important rule to remember if death appeared imminent: *Think about the blaze*. Killings in public places are far more likely to be solved than quiet shots to the head in back alleys or basements. If Armanti sensed that his own time was coming, he would try to run into a busy street corner or shop. Maybe the confusion would allow him to escape, or shoot his pursuers before they got him. (If Armanti had to go, he at least wanted to take a few people with him.) If enough potential witnesses were around, his would-be killers might wait for a more opportune moment. At the very least, someone might see who shot him and help the poor detective forced to investigate.

In the past, whenever the case had approached some surreal new low point, Dowd had been the voice of reason, dutifully urging Armanti not to let his adrenaline and testosterone overpower his common sense. Dowd was far more even-keeled, and because he wasn't directly on the set, it was his duty to remind the undercover of any looming danger. But this time Dowd felt different, too. Even before he had learned of the Inspector's threats against the Special Projects Unit, Dowd had been smoldering to find out who'd helped Tocco and the Ferrantis destroy his informant Eric Mergenthal.

Like most police officers, Dowd thought of informants as something akin to a prostate exam: a necessary evil, and an unpleasant one at that. Unlike most informants, however, Mergenthal had actually been a likable guy, a harmless, good-hearted heroin addict who reminded Dowd of a childhood friend who had been felled by a drug problem. But even if Mergenthal had been as worthless as other informants, he was Dowd's informant. Dowd had lured Mergenthal into the case, had bullied him a bit when he'd gotten cold feet, and had given him grief when Tocco had inexplicably walked away from the deal. Dowd already felt responsible for putting Mergenthal in harm's way. And to think that Wrynn, or anyone else in the NYPD, might have leaked Mergenthal's identity, and cost him his life, made Ed Dowd just furious. The other investigators teased Dowd mercilessly, hoping to ease his guilt with a bit of macabre police humor. Jimmy Desocio would occasionally call Dowd at the office, disguising his voice.

"You killed me," Desocio would say in his best junkie growl.

"Who the fuck is this?!" Dowd would scream into the phone.

"It's me," Desocio would groan. "Eric. You killed me!"

Dowd would laugh. A little. As a father, though, Dowd felt obligated to Mergenthal's parents to determine exactly what had caused their boy's death and to nail whoever was to blame. And he didn't want to see anyone else die. He recognized that Armanti's situation in Throgs Neck had just become immensely more treacherous. The low-level IAB guys had been busy for months interfering with the investigation, but they were inept, and at least they were out in the open, where Armanti and Dowd could keep an eye on them. Once Inspector Wrynn and the higher-ups joined the hunt, there was no telling what back-room maneuver they might use to cut Armanti's legs out from under him, and there'd be no warning when they did. Dowd had used his friendship to lure Armanti into this case; it would destroy him to see Armanti get out of it the same way Mergenthal had. Eager as he was to nail the Wrynns, Dowd forced himself to offer Armanti an out.

"So," Dowd asked, careful to sound sincere, "what do you want to do?"

"Fuck you!" Armanti shot back. "We're not stopping."

Dowd spared them both the charade of a lengthy argument. Rather than back off, Dowd and Armanti decided to turn their investigation up another notch and solve Eric Mergenthal's murder.

OF ALL JOHN WRYNN'S troubled friends, Eric Mergenthal had seemed the last guy anyone would want to murder. He was, undoubtedly, the most harmless. As a boy, Eric had struggled in school and had been teased for being a bit slow-witted, so he'd compensated with his sense of humor and kindheartedness. During his teenage years, Eric's long, curly blond hair and his good-time attitude helped him win the hearts of girls who should have known better. Eric stood out by going to extremes. The neighborhood kids formed a rock band, and in the hard-rock era of wild-men drummers like Led Zeppelin's John Bonham and the Who's Keith Moon, Eric played the part of the hyperkinetic percussionist perfectly. Occasionally neighbors would complain about Turuk and Eric getting drunk while playing hooky, then throwing bottles at kids on their way home from school. Usually, though, when Eric caused trouble, he inflicted it upon himself.

It wasn't surprising that Mergenthal had been dragged into the case by Steve Turuk, who had always managed to manipulate his neighborhood peers into doing things they shouldn't. Dowd and the fire marshals had been led to Turuk's door five months after Lieutenant Williams died, when they were desperately searching for a break in the case and Armanti had not yet entered the scene. After they arrested Turuk for threatening to burn his father's house down, he was more than willing to provide information about Wrynn. But Tocco didn't trust Turuk enough to commit a crime with him, and Dowd and Fire Marshal Bobby Thomson weren't about to let Turuk go that easily. They kept calling Turuk's house, driving by, threatening to lock him up on another drug charge. Eventually, to get rid of them, he offered up Eric Mergenthal—an inspired choice, because Tocco and Eric had been friends for decades. Mergenthal even seemed to enjoy being an informant at first. He wanted to help. The money wasn't particularly good, but when you've got a heroin habit, every little bit helps. He lived in the basement of his parents' house, and he'd sneak the detectives inside as if he were playing a game of cops and robbers. In early November, however, when Tocco complained that he suspected a police informant was loose in the neighborhood, Mergenthal began to realize just how high the stakes were. He told Dowd and Thomson that he wanted out.

Dowd and Thomson refused to let him leave. With no other leads in the neighborhood, they couldn't afford to. They showed Mergenthal the photos of Bruce Bailey's dismembered corpse and threatened to tell Ferranti that Eric was an informant.

Mergenthal put the wire back on, but his enthusiasm was gone. So, to be certain Mergenthal didn't try to drop out again, Dowd and Thomson would drive past his house in a white van decked out with flashy high-tech gizmos. It was mostly cheesy Radio Shack equipment, but it was enough to convince someone as naive as Mergenthal that he was under constant surveillance. One day his mother asked Eric why he seemed so upset, and he put a finger to his lips, asking her to be silent. Mergenthal then gave her a piece of paper and a pencil.

Do you think this house is bugged? she wrote.

Yes, he wrote back.

Why?

I'm working with the police, Eric scrawled on the paper. *I CAN'T GET OUT!!!*

Eric's addiction had already dragged Millie Mergenthal through endless indignities, but this was more than even she could bear. She had driven him to rehab clinics only to watch him slide back into abuse. She'd invested money, time, and tears trying to help him find a way out. She'd lied to friends and neighbors about the problem, tried asking doctors, priests, anyone for advice. To think that she and her child were unable to speak in their own home because the police had latched on to him was infuriating. Millie's father had been a police officer, so she knew well the disdain most detectives had for informants. She begged Eric to get out, and she promised to get a lawyer to help him keep the police away.

But Eric couldn't face the thought of jail. On November 10, wearing a wire, he asked Tocco if he'd sell a weapon to his cousin. Tocco seemed eager to do the deal, bragging that he could get automatics, revolvers, even bazookas. A few days later, Mergenthal introduced Tocco to an undercover detective from the firearms task force who was posing as his cousin. Tocco was paid $750 for a gun.

Dowd could barely wait. If Tocco sold the weapon, he'd be facing heavy time, and Dowd and the fire marshals were certain they could strong-arm him into giving up Jack Ferranti's role in the fire.

But instead of producing the gun, Tocco brought back only excuses. He said he was busy and was having trouble with his new supplier. Finally, on November 23, Tocco told Mergenthal that the deal was off. The undercover confronted Tocco, demanding his money back. But Tocco refused, and they almost came to blows. Tocco later called Mergenthal, furious, and said he wanted nothing to do with his "cousin."

"Don't bring him around here anymore," Tocco ordered.

In the days that followed, Tocco didn't seem angry at Mergenthal. In fact, he never gave Eric the slightest indication that he knew Eric had been setting him up. He'd apparently just changed his mind. Dowd's arson investigation was back to square one, because Tocco had obviously grown cold.

Eric went on with his life. He took another try at rehab and once again started talking to his mother about looking for a steady job. On March 19, Eric went out to celebrate his twenty-eighth birthday with Steve Turuk. Mergenthal's brother, who had pushed Eric to enter rehab, nagged him about hanging out with his old drug buddies, but Eric said he and Steve were just going out for a few drinks. At about 11:30 P.M., Millie Mergenthal heard Steve drop Eric off, then drive away. Less than an hour later, she heard a loud thump that sounded like it had come from the basement, near Eric's room, but she figured that a large pile of snow had just fallen off the roof.

She called downstairs to Eric, asking if he knew what had happened. When he didn't respond, she walked downstairs and knocked on his door. Still no response, so Mille pushed open the door and saw Eric kneeling on the floor, his face slumped on his bed. She bent down, tried to rouse him, but Eric was cold. His breathing and pulse had stopped. One hand was still clutching a needle.

"Oh my God!" she cried. "My Eric! Please help my Eric!"

Her husband called their next-door neighbor, a retired police officer. He ran over through the snow and tried to revive Eric, but it was clear that it was too late. The ghastly procession began. The ambulance, the flashing lights, the coroner, the detectives. They carried Eric out of the house covered with a sheet as a handful of neighbors looked on, crying and shaking their heads.

Millie Mergenthal had seen an autopsy in nursing school and, in her grief, she had no intention of allowing her boy's body to endure that. With no autopsy and Eric's long history of drug abuse, the detectives from the Forty-fifth Precinct proclaimed the death an accidental overdose.

At the funeral, Millie Mergenthal's official explanation was that Eric had died of asthma. Her friends, neighbors, and relatives nodded in agreement as they clasped her hands or hugged her. No one had the heart to call her on such an obvious falsehood. Among the mourners was one of Eric's boyhood chums, John Wrynn, who sought out Millie and expressed his regrets. Months later, as he drove around the neighborhood, Wrynn, still shaken by Eric's death, told a friend: "A lot of the people I grew up with are either dead or in jail."

The thought that Wrynn had had the gall to show up at the funeral made Dowd boil. The instant Tocco had first mentioned to Armanti that he'd been tipped off about an informant, Dowd had begun formulating a plan to determine whether the leak had originated with Wrynn. But now that Internal Affairs was liable to end the case at any moment, Dowd and Armanti had no more time to spare.

ON JULY 16, one week after Inspector Wrynn warned that trouble was on its way, Armanti went back on the set, beeped Tocco, and tried to arrange another cocaine deal.

"I'm a little worried about something," Armanti said, as he and Tocco sat in his car.

"Sure."

"This thing's been driving me nuts," Armanti said. "You ain't hot, are you?"

"No! Why?" Tocco said. "Who says I'm hot?"

"It's just something you said. Fucking shook me up. I was fucking sick."

"What'd I say?"

"Somebody wore a wire on you."

"Oh, it was back then, it was a long time ago," Tocco explained. "Narcotics set me up, and it was for a gun, but the deal never went through."

Then Tocco turned deadly serious. He turned to Armanti.

"You wearing a wire?" Tocco asked.

Armanti had taped a recorder to his ankle and a microphone behind his calf. Suddenly they felt as big and obvious as a jukebox. He scoffed, trying to buy time and figure out a way to distract Tocco. Had the Wrynns tipped him off? Everything began to move slowly. Armanti smiled, then unbuckled his belt and quickly ripped his jeans and underwear down to his knees.

"Yeah, I'm wearing a wire," Armanti said.

Tocco was startled by the sight of Armanti's naked crotch, but Armanti wasn't taking any chances. He grabbed his penis, wagged it at Tocco, and thrust his hips upward.

"Wanna speak into the mike?"

Tocco flashed a nervous grin, and they both broke into laughter.

Then Armanti waved his hand up and down, motioning for Tocco to prove he wasn't wired either. Tocco sheepishly unbuckled his belt and dropped his pants.

Armanti laughed.

"Jesus, if the cops come by they're gonna think we're blowing each other," he said.

Tocco chuckled and quickly zipped up.

"You just scared the fuck out of me," Armanti said.

Tocco was so disarmed he tried to put Armanti's mind at ease.

"It happened several months ago," Tocco said, referring to the aborted setup. "The guy died."

Armanti sensed that his own uneasiness was making Tocco talkative, so he tried to keep up the pressure.

"I mean, you understand, there's other shit going on and I don't need no fucking feds coming down, you know, interfering in other shit."

Tocco laughed nervously, afraid that Armanti's jumpiness might cost him a sale. He was anxious to end the talk about wires and get on with business. But Armanti delayed, holding out for more reassurance. Exasperated, Tocco finally told the whole story of setting up a gun deal, accepting money, and backing out at the last minute. As part of his rant, Tocco also gave an indication of where the leak had come from.

"The reason why I found out, I have a friend on the force," Tocco said. "He told me. He goes, 'It's a good thing.' He told me a month later. He goes, 'You almost went through with a deal? And you backed out?' I go, 'Yeah.' 'Good thing you didn't, you were being set up.' I said I had a feeling I was, that's why I stopped."

Tocco also assured Armanti, whose wire was getting the whole story for posterity, that the informant was no longer a threat because he had died.

"They made it look like an overdose," Tocco said, flashing a smirk.

Now that he had what he'd come for, Armanti arranged to make another buy from Tocco the following day. Although Tocco hadn't named either Wrynn or Mergenthal, it was clear whom he was referring to. The case had taken a quantum leap: Wrynn's leaks hadn't just endangered Armanti; they had most likely cost Eric Mergenthal his life.

Back at the office, Armanti, Dowd, Peil, and the fire marshals jumped into action to plan their next move. Dowd decided to call the medical examiner's office the next day to see what tests had been performed. They began formulating follow-up scripts, to see if there was a way to coax Tocco into giving up the name of his source.

Their enthusiasm wasn't shared by the Internal Affairs detectives. The night Tocco made his admission to Armanti, Dowd heard Lieutenant Shields phone the chief of IAB and say, "Yep, it's the son." Later in the week, when Dowd and Armanti suggested exhuming Mergenthal, Lieutenant Shields reacted angrily.

"Mind your own business, and stay focused on Tocco," he snapped.

"I am focused!" Armanti shot back. "If this is true, I've got Wrynn on conspiracy to commit murder."

11

" A ROCK AND A HARD PLACE "

JULY 22 – AUGUST 3, 1993

THIS TIME, TOMMY TOCCO wasn't going to just sit back and take it. He was down in his hovel of an apartment again, haggling his way through another drug deal. Only this time he had a fully loaded .32-caliber revolver tucked into his pants and would not hesitate to use it. Less than a week had passed since Tocco had made his incriminating admissions about Mergenthal's death, and the Torch was busy trying to move more narcotics. But today Tocco and his would-be customer, a small-time dealer named Fahed Bashdar, started arguing about prices, and their dispute spiraled into a vicious brawl. Bashdar drew his gun, but Tocco sprung at him before he could fire, pounding him with his fists and grabbing the weapon.

Tocco opened fire, and as Bashdar ran for his life, two bullets entered his left leg, sending spurts of blood onto the trash strewn across Tocco's floor. Tocco squeezed out several more shots as Bashdar scrambled out the door, screaming for help. Afterward, Tocco scurried around the house, gathering his drugs and as much other illegal merchandise as he could carry. By the time the police arrived, he had already told the tenant upstairs to distract them. Meanwhile, Tocco escaped by climbing out the back window. Later, he bragged that he and Mario had cleaned all the drugs out of the place before the police arrived, but they'd still left some interesting hardware behind. After forcing their way in, officers from the Forty-fifth Precinct found a 12-gauge Beretta automatic and a Remington .30-06 shotgun. Also on hand was a Ruger 10/22 carbine, a leather ammunition belt loaded with seven shotgun shells, assorted ammunition clips, and boxes of shells for shotguns. There was even a cache of hollow-point bullets, known on the street as "cop killers."

Incredibly, Armanti wasn't notified about all this until two days later; and oddly enough, it was Mario Ferranti who delivered the news. On the set, Armanti had phoned Tocco's pager and Mario returned the call, gleefully providing a blow-by-blow account of the gunfire. Armanti was staggered that no one from the NYPD had bothered to tell him. The NYPD's channels of communication were efficient enough to allow Myron Dobbs to recite the contents of Armanti's top-secret reports soon after they were written. But somehow, the staff of the Forty-fifth Precinct had never told the investigators on the Lieutenant Williams case, easily one of the highest-priority investigations in the Bronx, that their prime target had been arrested.

Even before the shooting, Tocco's suggestive remarks about Eric Mergenthal's death had set off furious arguments among the investigators. But Armanti had forged straight ahead, grilling the medical examiner who had handled Mergenthal's case: Were there any indications of a struggle? Was it possible that someone else might have injected Mergenthal with the fatal dose? Could someone have waited for the drugs to render him defenseless, then used a pillow to finish him off? Given that Eric lived most of his life on the verge of nodding off, it wouldn't have taken much for Turuk, Tocco, or Mario to subdue him. So Armanti pressed the coroner for information from Mergenthal's postmortem toxicology report about the mix of drugs in his system. When he learned that no complete autopsy had been performed, the next step seemed too obvious.

"So let's dig him up, do it right," Armanti said, eager to sustain the momentum.

Exhuming a body can be an involved legal ordeal, but when Dowd took the phone from Armanti and had a calmer discussion with the medical examiner, she said she'd be willing to consider it. But she warned that they'd better hurry. If Mergenthal had been given a "hot load" of tainted heroin and then smothered, they'd have to examine his lungs and each passing day made it more unlikely that they would still be intact.

Dowd knew that Mergenthal's family was still furious at the police and would fight any effort to dig Eric up. Millie Mergenthal had made it clear that she considered Dowd and the other detectives to blame for using her son and getting him killed. Why should she help them now?

Under certain circumstances, the medical examiner can order an autopsy over the family's objections, but only if there was enough clear evidence to declare a killing a homicide. For that, though, they'd need something more direct than Tocco's suggestive but elliptical statements. Dowd had no doubt they could get it—if they could keep Internal Affairs out of the way.

The mounting suspicions of murder certainly weren't lost on Assistant U.S. Attorney George Stamboulidis, an organized-crime prosecutor who had agreed to take on the Lieutenant Williams investigation only out of pity. He was already caught up in one of the city's wildest investigations, the Colombo family mob war, which would run for five years, leaving twelve mobsters dead and dozens wounded, decimating the Colombos, and forcing Stamboulidis to tangle with two of the day's most infamous wiseguys: Vincent "the Chin" Gigante (the Genovese family boss who wandered the streets in a bathrobe, feigning insanity) and Sammy "the Bull" Gravano, John Gotti's hit man and the underboss of the Gambino family. But when Stamboulidis's supervisor had told him a few stories about Tommy Williams's career and family, how could he say no? Stamboulidis vowed to find some way to squeeze the case in.

As the IAB's foot-dragging grew more blatant, however, Stamboulidis found more time. He was outraged by the Inspector's rampage through the Special Projects Unit, and his threats against the IAB underlings. How could any police official attempt to undermine an investigation so flagrantly? Stamboulidis started talking obstruction of justice, but IAB commanders insisted that Wrynn, just a concerned father, had done nothing to chill the investigation into his son. Stamboulidis considered Williams's killers his first priority and he knew that the IAB investigators who'd witnessed the Inspector's transgressions would not be eager to testify. So he decided to deal with that aspect of the investigation once the Ferrantis were locked up.

As a mob prosecutor, Stamboulidis was familiar with the ugly methods used to muzzle witnesses and eliminate informants. He also knew that in many cases, the cover-up was easier to prove than the crime. So he huddled with Armanti and Dowd to devise a sting operation that would lead back to the NYPD. It would work something like this: Armanti would ask Tocco to have his "friend on the force" run a license-plate number. If Tocco came back with the information, Stamboulidis could check the NYPD computer and trace whether Wrynn had been the leak. But the timing made things tricky. With the city awash in police corruption investigations, no one wanted another public relations nightmare involving dirty cops and informants headed for the morgue. But baby-faced

Stamboulidis—whose tongue-twisting Greek name reminded Armanti of President Clinton's former aide George Stephanopoulos—was determined to follow the evidence wherever it might go.

IN THE DAYS following Tocco's assault on Fahed Bashdar, Armanti was also shaken by his own miscalculation about the man he had been observing up close for months. Armanti made his living, and preserved his own life, using his ability to accurately assess characters as bizarre as Tocco. It was jarring to the undercover, who figured he had at least a sixth sense about such things, to realize how badly he had underestimated Tocco's viciousness. Yet Tocco's arrest offered an opportunity. With Tocco sidelined, Armanti could draw Mario Ferranti, who was much higher up the food chain of the Ferranti organization, into the action. If Armanti could work his way into Mario's confidence, he might be able to finally gather some hard facts about the Williams fire. And who knew? Since Mario was always so determined to one-up Vinnie Blue Eyes, he might acknowledge killing Mergenthal just to get the style points.

Doing business one-on-one with Mario was potentially far grislier than dealing with Tocco, but the upside was greater, too. Luckily, Mario seemed game. For months, he and Armanti had played cat and mouse, as Armanti had watched the sociopath's never-ending effort to prove his manhood in the most repugnant ways possible. One day when an unsuspecting patron walked into the café and someone suggested that he might be an undercover, Mario didn't miss a beat. "I'll find out where he lives and blow up him and his whole family," he sneered.

The guy was all charm. When the subject of Sebastian's bar was raised, Mario became so enraged about being thrown out of the place that he said he planned to drive a truck through the front window. If a group of fellows were hanging out on a street corner, Mario's trademark entrance was sneaking up and belting one of his close buddies in the back or arm, so hard that it wasn't uncommon to see the guy doubled over in pain.

Armanti saw how Mario used his strength and reputation as a sexual predator to cow those around him. Armanti knew that he had to avoid appearing intimidated at all costs. He constantly braced himself for a physical challenge from Mario where he would have to respond instantly with massive force. The battle might escalate to a knife fight or a shootout. If things got really bad and Mario lost face, maybe he'd go looking for

Turuk's Sawzall again. But Armanti simply couldn't let Mario get over on him, or else he would never respect him enough to do business.

Armanti had become so combative with Mario—edging into his personal space, flashing his serial-killer gaze—that Mario didn't know quite how to react. But the longer Armanti remained the sole person Mario never slugged, the edgier Mario got. He was always desperate to assert his dominance, and Armanti was the new kid, someone who everyone else in the Ferranti crew seemed to fear, or at least respect. Even when things appeared relaxed, every meeting between Armanti and Mario had the undercurrent of a stare-down.

As Mario described Tocco's arrest, Armanti had hung on each syllable, wondering if he was playing Mario or Mario was playing him. Armanti had repeatedly told Dowd that Mario was such a degenerate that he wasn't sure whether the sociopath intended to drug him, kill him, or rape him. If Mario found out Armanti was an undercover, he'd probably do all three, in that order. So Armanti tried to use Mario's cell-block libido against him. It was summer, after all, so who would think twice about Vinnie's showing up in a muscle shirt or tight tank top? Every so often, when the weather was steamy enough, Armanti would glance away, slowly peel off his shirt, and silently count to two or three. Then he'd quickly turn back, catch Mario eyeing his chest or biceps, and shoot him a look that screamed, "What are *you* looking at?" It made Armanti's skin crawl to think that somewhere in the recesses of that imagination there were sweaty little fantasies starring Vinnie Blue Eyes as Mario's bitch and next victim. But the beefcake show worked. Within ten days of Tocco's arrest, Mario was smitten enough to talk about his various crimes in vivid detail. He bragged about how he'd taken care of Tocco's case and how the legal problems would soon be going away.

"Everything is taken care of, and that kid he shot isn't going to show up to testify," Mario told Armanti. "And if he does, he's gonna have problems."

Mario hadn't yet offered to sell Vinnie drugs, but on August 3, however, he did begin going on about his drug connections in Harlem, which he considered the perfect place for a Bronx guy to do business. It was far enough away from home that his suppliers wouldn't know too much about his affairs. Besides, Mario added, Harlem's major drug dealers welcomed him because he had a source inside the NYPD who tipped him off about upcoming drug raids.

"They take care of me and give me good prices because I let them know when the cops are gonna hit," Mario said. "I let them know, and they do the right thing by me."

The next day, Tocco made his first public appearance on the Throgs Neck scene since the arrest and was greeted like a conquering hero. Clearly pleased that his status had been elevated by the gunplay, he ridiculed the police officers. Best of all, Tocco boasted, the guy he'd shot was almost certain to drop the charges. It would all be over in a week, Tocco promised.

The Torch seemed so pleased with himself that Armanti took a risk and asked if Tocco's cop friend could run a license-plate number for him. It was pushy, even audacious, considering that Tocco still had an open case. But with IAB ready to end the investigation, Armanti had no room to breathe.

"I don't think so. I don't want him to know my business," Tocco said. "A cop's a cop, no matter who he is."

Armanti forced the issue, but Tocco held firm.

"When he has information, he gives it to me," he said.

DESPITE THIS, WITH both Mario and the newly triumphant Tommy Tocco now competing for his attention, Armanti found himself being swept faster and deeper into the Ferranti crew. Mario couldn't resist rhapsodizing about a building on 146th Street that the Ferrantis owned, a lair with a secret, secluded subbasement. Only he knew whether he was suggesting the spot for a romantic rendezvous or as a convenient venue for a hasty dismemberment. But it was an important admission, because the Ferrantis were believed to have sliced up Bruce Bailey in such a place, letting his blood run down a metal drain in the floor, as if they had been dressing a deer. The police had searched a basement on 146th Street and found nothing. Now they knew there was another level below.

"You could do things down there," Mario said, with one of his lurid smiles.

As the days since his arrest passed, Tocco got more relaxed, promising he'd resume cocaine sales again as soon as his court case was over. Until then, he tried to keep himself relevant by talking big. For the first time, he made references to the Luchese family conducting "sit-downs"— meetings to settle disputes among its various thugs. On the night of

August 5, a Thursday, Tocco even invited Armanti to join him for drinks at a wiseguy bar, but Lieutenant Shields once again said he wouldn't allow it.

Armanti spent the entire weekend fuming, wondering if Internal Affairs had blown yet another chance for him to meet up with Wrynn. When he returned to work the following Monday, Armanti couldn't stand it anymore. He waited for Shields to walk out of the office, then followed him into the parking lot.

"What the fuck!" Armanti demanded. "Are you trying to *do* me?"

"No, no, no," Shields shouted, trying to wave Armanti off and climb into his car.

"You're trying to do me!"

"You don't understand!" Shields cried. "You don't understand. I'm between a rock and a hard place."

"What the fuck does that mean?"

"You don't understand," Shields pleaded, ducking into his car so quickly he banged his head on the door frame.

He sped away, tires spraying gravel across the parking lot.

The next day, August 10, Shields ordered Dowd, Peil, and one of the fire marshals into his office. Once Lieutenant Shields opened his mouth, it became clear why Armanti hadn't been invited. IAB wanted to start building a case to have the undercover taken off the investigation: He was out of control and wouldn't take direction. Dowd and the others defended Armanti, arguing that he had made incredible progress. But Shields wouldn't hear of it, throwing around wild allegations that Armanti seemed more like a gangster than a detective.

Dowd, flabbergasted, tried to fight back, assuring Shields that as high maintenance as Armanti might sometimes be, his dedication and effectiveness were beyond question. Countering, Shields threw out another theory IAB had been kicking around: Armanti was so enthralled by playing the gangster, maybe he didn't want to give up his double life. Maybe, Shields said, the real leak was Armanti himself.

The instant the meeting ended, Dowd and Peil found Armanti and filled him in. Armanti just laughed, strapped on his microphone, and headed out to the set.

At the café that night, Tocco was still balking at Vinnie's request to run a plate number, but Mario was eager to please. He introduced Armanti to a friend, Anthony, who offered to check a license-plate number through a contact on the force. It was clear by the description of the officer's assignment—the Bronx Task Force—that it was not Wrynn, but the U.S. attorney had asked for Armanti to have a plate number run, so he did. He had a hunch that if Mario's friend managed to get him a plate number, Tocco would feel pressured to get him another, courtesy of John Wrynn.

So much for out of control, Armanti thought to himself.

Armanti still needed more, something promising enough so that IAB wouldn't dare dream of stopping the case. So two days later he played his last card: the car. When Jack Ferranti's Lincoln Town Car had been seized by the police back in June, then stolen from the Forty-fifth Precinct parking lot, it had been a clear sign to Armanti and Dowd that the Ferrantis were getting help from within the station house. Armanti had started driving a similar car (the same make, model, and year), waiting for the chance to use it. On August 12 he told Tocco that his radio had been stolen. Did he know of any chop shop where Armanti could buy a replacement?

Tocco smiled.

"I'll sell you the whole car," he said.

Armanti smiled back and arranged for delivery the next night. Jack Ferranti's pilfered Lincoln was on its way.

Losing focus? Armanti thought.

But the night was still young. So Armanti chatted up Mario, who explained how the Ferrantis had fixed the shooting case against Tocco. They fixed cases all the time, Mario bragged, and one of the people who helped them was a guy down the block; his name was "Joey Wrynn."

Armanti's heart skipped a beat.

A few minutes later, Mario invited Armanti to a barbecue at his house the following Saturday. The whole family would be there, Mario said.

Armanti spent days formulating his approach, perfecting his outfit, preparing for any possibility. So far, Mario was facing only a weak A-1 felony, for his part in the drug deal. But Armanti was convinced that if he brought up a crazy tale about a homicide, Mario wouldn't be able to resist trading stories. He had been invited to a barbecue with a family of killers—the perfect place to eat, drink, and compare notes.

On Friday, the day before the big event, Armanti arrived at the office early so he could review his scripts a few last times before the backup team arrived. But Internal Affairs never showed up. An hour after the

IAB detectives had been scheduled to appear, Lieutenant Shields returned Dowd's twenty calls to his pager.

"We're not gonna be there," Shields said.

Armanti, although desperate to preserve his credibility with Mario and Tocco, couldn't go to the party without backup. That would make it too easy for Shields to suspend him for insubordination. Instead, he drove past the café, honked his horn, and stuck his head out the window.

"I gotta go somewhere with my uncle," he told Mario's friends. "Tell Mario I'm sorry I can't make it tomorrow, but I'll see him Monday."

A FEW miles south of the Bronx, inside the HIDTA narcotics office in northern Manhattan, Detective John Wrynn encountered no such interference. Internal Affairs detectives were keeping him under surveillance, but they were so obvious and amateurish that Wrynn often joked to friends about them. During work hours, he had access to the same weapons and confidential police department information as any other narcotics detective.

Within the HIDTA unit, which was composed of some of the most seasoned investigators in the department, Wrynn was affable and well liked, but because of his thin résumé and lax work ethic, many of his colleagues considered him a lightweight. Still, the other investigators, who spoke respectfully about John's father, calling him "the old man," were careful not to tease the younger Wrynn too harshly about his family connections. Wrynn's standing in the unit was best summed up by his nickname, "Ponyboy." Beyond its obvious reference to Wrynn's ponytail, the name was also an allusion to a character in *The Outsiders*, a novel about teenage gang members written by S. E. Hinton. Ponyboy wasn't the toughest or smartest or best-looking member of the gang—he was the sensitive guy, the kid with the good heart and amiable disposition, the one who wasn't quite bad enough or serious enough to tangle with the Big Boys.

Fittingly, John Wrynn was relegated to menial work at HIDTA—delivering copies of surveillance tapes or wiretap transcripts to the prosecutor's office. During the week of August 16, 1993, two days after Armanti was prevented from attending the barbecue, one of those gofer jobs involved researching arrests records and search warrants, so Wrynn traveled to police headquarters, where he was allowed to peruse one of the most top-secret documents in the department, the Drug Enforcement Coordination System book. The DECS book contains information about

every confidential drug investigation in the entire city; it is a log so sensitive that it is kept under lock and key. Every time the police make a
major buy, the name and address of each suspect is listed in the book, to
ensure that different narcotics units don't inadvertently interfere with
each other's investigations. Sometime in the spring of 1993, the names
Tommy Tocco and Mario Ferranti were entered into the DECS logbook,
along with the locations they worked out of, Sebastian's Sports Pub and
Café d'Oro.

Several months later, John Wrynn was spotted leafing through its pages
by the integrity patrol officer in the unit. A secretary in the office also saw
Wrynn studying the contents of the book. But no one thought to ask why
he was lingering there.

It would be weeks before anyone told Armanti and Dowd about
Wrynn's latest, potentially deadly, breach of department security. In just
a few days, however, the entire tenor of the investigation would change,
quite drastically, for the worse.

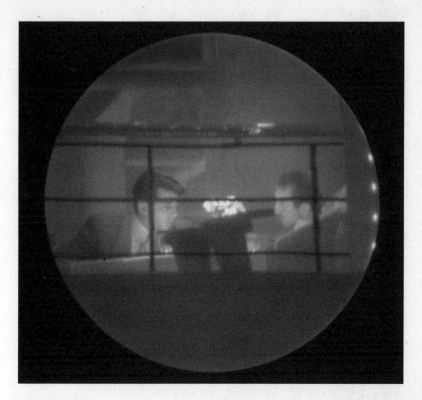

During his fifteen years as an undercover detective Vincent Armanti posed as a mobster on countless occasions and was responsible for helping take more than $100 million in narcotics drugs off the streets. In this photograph, taken in 1992, Armanti (left) negotiates with a Turkish criminal who sold him $2 million in heroin and asked him to assassinate a Turkish politician in exchange for two extra kilos. No photographs in this section reveal Armanti's face because he is still in danger from those he helped bring to justice.

Armanti is seen working undercover in Borough Park, Brooklyn, using the pseudonym Vincent Penisi, which he also made use of in Throgs Neck. Disguised in sunglasses and a Hugo Boss suit, he helps a suspect into a Cadillac where they will negotiate a drug deal.

Driving to an undercover assignment in Sunset Park, Brooklyn, in 1989, Armanti found himself in the middle of a drug-related shoot-out. He is seen at left, firing at his would-be assassin.

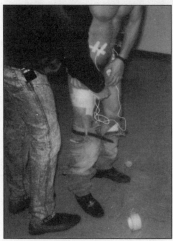

ABOVE: To build a case against a drug-dealing hit man in 1999, Armanti and his backup team designed and built their own social club in Queens called Charlie's Barbershop. Once the suspect was lured inside, Armanti charmed him into reenacting the fatal shooting of an off-duty New York City police officer.

LEFT: Before heading out onto the set each day, Armanti was wired with a hidden tape recorder on his thigh and a microphone under his shirt.

With a bookie working from the backroom and a clientele that included an assortment of police officers and criminals, Sebastian's bar on East Tremont Avenue in Throgs Neck was a challenge for Armanti to infiltrate. Once inside, Armanti realized that his top-secret police reports were being leaked to the criminals, and his life was in grave danger.

LEFT: Before it was set ablaze on February 24, 1992, the Today's Styles clothing store had so little business that its owner, mob associate Jack Ferranti, threatened to burn it down and cash in on the insurance.

RIGHT: On the night of the fire, FDNY Lieutenant Thomas A. Williams was searching for victims trapped in the smoke and flames when he leaped to his death through this window.

Tommy "the Torch" Tocco, who set the deadly blaze, was known for using his Doberman as a weapon.

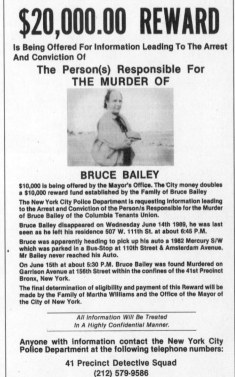

ABOVE LEFT: Jack Ferranti earned impressive underworld notoriety. In addition to terrorizing his tenants with threats and vicious dogs, Ferranti was suspected of ordering the murder/dismemberment of rent activist Bruce Bailey.

ABOVE TOP RIGHT: Jack Ferranti strolls through Throgs Neck.

ABOVE LOWER RIGHT: Jack Ferranti meeting with one of his compatriots.

RIGHT: Bruce Bailey disappeared after meeting with the superintendent of one of Jack Ferranti's buildings.

BELOW: Bailey's body was discovered on a deserted street in the Bronx. Other body parts were discovered in plastic bags.

$20,000.00 REWARD

Is Being Offered For Information Leading To The Arrest And Conviction Of

The Person(s) Responsible For
THE MURDER OF

BRUCE BAILEY

$10,000 is being offered by the Mayor's Office. The City money doubles a $10,000 reward fund established by the Family of Bruce Bailey

The New York City Police Department is requesting information leading to the Arrest and Conviction of the Person/s Responsible for the Murder of Bruce Bailey of the Columbia Tenants Union.

Bruce Bailey disappeared on Wednesday June 14th 1989, he was last seen as he left his residence 507 W. 111th St. at about 6:45 P.M.

Bruce was apparently heading to pick up his auto a 1982 Mercury S/W which was parked in a Bus-Stop at 110th Street & Amsterdam Avenue. Mr Bailey never reached his Auto.

On June 15th at about 5:30 P.M. Bruce Bailey was found Murdered on Garrison Avenue at 156th Street within the confines of the 41st Precinct Bronx, New York.

The final determination of eligibility and payment of this Reward will be made by the Family of Martha Williams and the Office of the Mayor of the City of New York.

All Information Will Be Treated
In A Highly Confidential Manner.

Anyone with information contact the New York City Police Department at the following telephone numbers:

41 Precinct Detective Squad
(212) 579-9586

ABOVE LEFT: Growing up in Throgs Neck, Tommy Tocco (third from right) and Eric Mergenthal (fourth from right) frequently played together on the docks behind the Mergenthals' home.

ABOVE RIGHT: Angelique Montemurro, who socialized with John Wrynn, Eric Mergenthal, and Tommy Tocco during high school, married a neighborhood friend Tommy Gross. She later married Tocco.

A teenage Tommy Tocco (second from left) on the docks behind the Mergenthal home, near the Throgs Neck Bridge.

FAR LEFT: John Wrynn hugging his boyhood friend Eric Mergenthal at Angelique Montemurro's wedding. Years later, police investigated whether Wrynn's leaks to criminals may have cost Mergenthal his life.

LEFT: John Wrynn in a photograph taken for his sixth-grade yearbook.

ABOVE: John Wrynn in a photograph taken for the New York Police Department.

BELOW: Before he retired and moved to the Jersey shore, Inspector James Wrynn was known as a powerhouse in Internal Affairs.

Patrick Kelleher (center) was an NYPD inspector in 1990 when he totaled his department car in an off-duty accident in the wee hours of a Saturday morning. Inspector James Wrynn was involved in the investigation that cleared Kelleher of any wrongdoing. Later, Kelleher was promoted to chief of Internal Affairs and then to first deputy commissioner—the second highest post in the entire NYPD.

Howard Safir (far left) was New York City fire commissioner on the night this photograph was taken at a Fire Foundation dinner. At the time, Safir told Armanti that he was troubled by the NYPD's handling of the Wrynn investigation, saying, "It's a shame what they've done to you, son." When Safir later became NYPD commissioner, Armanti wrote him a letter asking for help in the case and Safir did not respond. Also pictured, from left to right, are: Fire Marshal James Desocio, Armanti, and Fire Marshal Bobby Thomson. FBI Agent Cindy Peil is seated in front of Desocio.

BELOW LEFT: Cindy Peil had worked for the FBI for only three years before being sent to Throgs Neck. The case was her first major investigation. A former bank executive, she was wary but willing when asked to accompany Armanti onto the set and pose as his girlfriend.

BELOW RIGHT: In the months before Armanti became involved in the case, Ed Dowd (far left) became so engrossed in the investigation of Lieutenant Thomas Williams's death that he used his own time and money to search for leads. He later referred to the investigation as the "case that ruined my career."

12

"COMING FROM THE TOP"

AUGUST 18, 1993

THE INSTANT ARMANTI set foot in Café d'Oro on that hot summer night, he could feel the strands of the investigation beginning to unravel. A half dozen of the café's usual suspects sat nervously around the poker table, but there was no card game going or music playing, just edginess heating up the place. Mixed into the crowd were three or four brutes Armanti had never seen before, a sure sign of trouble. Carlo Cuzzi, who was both a police cooperator and a suspect in a double murder, stood with his burly arms crossed—not exactly a harbinger of peace.

"Up against the wall, Vin," Cuzzi demanded, sounding grim. "I've got to search you."

Fear flooded through Armanti's body in a fast, hot wave. His first instinct was to laugh the whole thing off and order a drink. But the tense look on Cuzzi's face told him this was not cocktail time. Glancing around the room, Armanti saw anxious men peering at him with the steady gaze of a firing squad. He headed over to the wall and slowly turned to face it.

"Drop your pants," Cuzzi ordered. "Full search."

Armanti let out a pissed-off sigh and glanced over his shoulder to gauge whether a *Whaddaya, queer?* joke might defuse the situation and help him avert a search. The audience was none too giggly, so he grabbed reluctantly for his belt.

"Sorry, Vin, I gotta do it," Cuzzi said, patting down Armanti's shoulders. "Walter flipped, so everyone gets searched."

Walter was a recently arrested Gambino family associate who was reportedly cooperating with the authorities. No one could be certain who or what he'd give up, so anyone who'd ever known him was forced to flash back through the years and wonder whether he'd be exposed. Also, because defections often happen in waves, there was some concern that one rat might beget another. Everyone was suspected of working with the police until proven otherwise.

Armanti lowered his trousers, his nerves crackling and mind spinning frantically. Less than an hour earlier he'd been fully wired—tape recorder strapped to his belly, cord winding up to a microphone near his chest. A search would have earned him three quick shots to the back of the head. But the weather was so muggy that he had ignored his backup team and removed the gear in his car before hitting the café. His big fear, as Cuzzi patted down his legs and checked under his silk boxer shorts, was a radio transmitter inside the box of Newport Light cigarettes that were visibly tucked beneath the strap of Armanti's muscle T-shirt.

Still, a knowing eye could tell that Armanti had been wired. The peeled off surgical tape used to hold down the microphone and cord had left red marks and traces of adhesive. Armanti could only pray that the dim lights would provide some cover.

He knew he was a security threat to Cuzzi, from whom he'd weaseled some highly incriminating secrets. When Armanti had first arrived on the set, Cuzzi had played it cool, eyeballing clowns like Tocco as they strutted and showboated to impress the new thug on the block. Then one day in early July, when Armanti had ambled into the café, Cuzzi had stunned him by pulling the metal security gate down over the window. As the lock clicked shut, Armanti felt powerless, trapped. This time, he thought, he was leaving in pieces—stuffed into an assortment of suitcases.

"Are you a federal agent?" Cuzzi had demanded.

"No," he replied, without flinching, as Cuzzi looked for any sign of uncertainty. Armanti made it out alive, but he still felt blindsided and started to obsess over whether Cuzzi had been getting information from John Wrynn.

As time passed, Armanti had pounced on every opportunity to schmooze Cuzzi, turning himself into a mirror, a ruse he'd perfected long ago. Cuzzi was a bodybuilder and a ladies' man, so Armanti brought up weight lifting and the art of seduction. Cuzzi was a slick dresser—he favored silk jogging suits, gold chains, and Italian loafers—so Armanti flattered him about his clothes. Cuzzi was also a serious earner, so Armanti gradually diverted discussions toward his own off-the-books business ventures. By mid-July, Cuzzi was so enamored that he asked Armanti to carry out a hit. Cuzzi and some bookies were trying to connive their way out of paying a $21,000 debt. After a sit-down with one of the made men who controlled Tremont Avenue, Cuzzi had been ordered to pay up, an order it would be unwise to blow off. But that didn't stop Cuzzi and Joe Red from asking Armanti to kill and rob the guy a few minutes after the cash changed hands. Armanti was elated but politely declined, saying that he didn't do fellow wiseguys unless the hit had been sanctioned by a Luchese boss. Cuzzi had taken it in stride.

"If you ever need a piece of work done," Joe Red added in his best neighborly fashion, "I could do it."

Now, spread-eagled against the wall, Armanti reeled off plausible excuses for those tape marks, trying to occupy his mind and hoping to avoid becoming someone's piece of work himself. Holding up his sleeveless silk T-shirt for Cuzzi, he felt a strong wave of desire for more body hair. As Cuzzi examined his chest, Armanti wracked his brain for a cover story. Would they believe it if he told them he'd just had an EKG?

But Cuzzi squinted, then looked up and smiled.

"Sorry, Vin," he said, giving Armanti a friendly cuff on the shoulder. "It's just business, you know? Things are getting crazy."

Armanti dropped his shirt and laughed.

"No problem," he said, pulling up his drawers. "I want to find this rat. That's one piece of work I'll do for nothing."

Having passed the security check, Armanti was quickly thrust into the role of debugger; he, Cuzzi, and the rest of the crew spent the rest of the night peering up under the acoustical ceiling tiles, checking beneath chairs and counters and posters on the wall. Every minute they cursed Walter for his betrayal. Armanti should have felt euphoric, but the outbreak of paranoia on the set was just a trivial inconvenience compared to the flak he'd been taking from IAB. Since Mario's barbecue, the IAB detectives had grown more obstinate, and now that Throgs Neck was on alert, Armanti's chances of gathering more evidence had vanished.

The IAB detectives were still going through the busywork necessary to fill out their daily work sheets. But the investigation had spun in circles. On August 19, the day after Armanti was frisked, Lieutenant Shields ordered Armanti to buy the stolen Lincoln from Tocco. But a week had passed since Tocco had offered to sell it, and the car had already been sold. Still, the Internal Affairs detectives could write on their reports that they had, quite sensibly, instructed Armanti to buy the vehicle.

Armanti saw the case as a dysfunctional gang free-for-all. But as the warfare dragged on, he came to understand that the IAB chiefs couldn't ignore the larger audience now tuning in to this sad little show. The Mollen Commission and the city's prosecutors had spent more than a year examining allegations of police corruption that IAB had been incapable or unwilling to investigate. The dirt they'd unearthed was staggering. In the Seventy-third Precinct, in Brooklyn, the commission had found more than a dozen officers who'd systematically robbed drug dealers and accepted payoffs. (The self-described "Morgue Boys" met at an old coroner's office to divvy up their loot.) In precincts in lower Manhattan and the Bronx, prosecutors found entire shifts of officers shaking down dealers. In Staten Island, an NYPD inspector was forced to resign after news reports that he'd stymied a murder investigation that had been targeting his best friend's son.

Police officials insisted that IAB was newly reformed and now completely state-of-the-art. But by midsummer at least thirty-five police officers faced arrest for a startling variety of crimes committed right under the bureau's newly scrubbed nose. The "Coke Cop" himself, Michael Dowd, agreed to testify at the commission's televised public hearings to offer a dramatic inside look at NYPD corruption and IAB's ineffectiveness. Ratcheting the political stakes higher, the commission announced hearings to begin as September faded, just five weeks before the mayoral election.

Armanti was so crazed that he passed up the papers, and the TV news made him squirm. But early in the summer, a commission investigator had contacted one of Armanti's former supervisors, to see whether he'd testify about the Wrynn case. Armanti had immediately jettisoned the commission's phone number. For months he'd been risking his life while being undercut by IAB yet no one at police headquarters had stepped forward to protect him. If he couldn't count on his top bosses, how could he trust a bunch of lawyers and politicians whose commission would be dissolved in six months? What would happen if Armanti agreed to testify under oath at the hearings? Internal Affairs could manufacture phony evidence and accuse him of perjury. Who'd be there for him then?

From the very beginning, IAB commanders had regarded the commission's investigation as an attempted coup. And they weren't about to make it an assisted suicide. At first, IAB stonewalled, refusing to turn over records until ordered to by the police commissioner and city hall. Later, when commission investigators arrived at IAB for a meeting, the commanders in the room stood up and walked out en masse. By late summer, Deputy Chief Al James was urging his troops to never fear and delivered stern words about the police officers who were helping the commission—some of whom were in that very room. "We all know the people who are testifying—they're a bunch of miscreants, malcontents, and psychopaths," James said. "And they will be dealt with once this is over."

At the same time the commission and the NYPD were publicly bemoaning the "Blue Wall of Silence," here was the deputy chief of Internal Affairs warning honest officers that they had better not dare come forward with information.

By late August, with the hearings just six weeks away, the hysteria coursing through the halls of IAB headquarters was so uncontrollable that its reverberations even reached Armanti on the street. On the afternoon of August 20, as Armanti lay, unseen, underneath his car's dashboard checking its concealed recorder, Lieutenant Shields and one of his IAB detectives leaned against the auto and chatted about the case.

"Chief Beatty's afraid the Mollen Commission's going to nail him to the wall over this case," Shields said.

Armanti dropped his pliers and sprang up from under the dashboard.

"Really!" he said, glaring at Shields.

Shields slapped his forehead in disbelief, then turned away.

ARMANTI KNEW THAT, despite the controversy, his crusade was over unless he brought back more evidence. Now. But on the set, things had grown ominously inactive. On August 26, Armanti saw Tocco and Mario driving down Tremont Avenue. Flagging them down, he asked his onetime pals to join him for a drink. Tocco, clearly uncomfortable, sputtered and said he was too frazzled. Then he hit the gas. It was the coldest reception Armanti ever received from Tocco and Mario. When he left the set a few hours later, one of the other detectives told him that Mario had been gesturing to Tocco, as if to say *Don't go near him!*

"Those motherfuckers finally did it," Armanti said to Dowd. "They burned us."

In the next few days, Armanti called Tocco three or four times a night but got no response. Mario was missing in action. Cuzzi was so obviously skittish that a chat about business would have been dangerous. The IAB detectives just gloated, smugly, silently, as the lull threatened to put everyone to sleep. Armanti was now flatly refusing their orders, which gave Internal Affairs one more excuse for slamming the case shut.

On September 3, after fuming through weeks of futility, Armanti saw Tocco walking down the street—and charged.

"Where have you been!" Armanti laid it on thick, saying that he had customers waiting and needed to talk business.

Tocco had a strange look on his face, part annoyed, part amused.

"I'm not doing that stuff anymore," he said.

Armanti noticed that Tocco was wearing a T-shirt with a Forty-seventh Precinct logo.

"What, are you gonna bust me?" he asked.

"Yeah, for A-1," Tocco said, using police jargon for the most serious type of felony.

When Armanti left the set later that night, his fury was so obvious that the Internal Affairs detectives didn't dare smirk. Armanti called the U.S. attorney, demanding to be allowed to stay on. Even if Tocco and Ferranti had made him, he could goad them into revealing something. If he pushed hard enough, maybe one of the crew members would slip and blurt out Wrynn's name by mistake. If Armanti was inflammatory enough, Tocco or Ferranti might take a shot at him, and give him the justification to shoot back.

But each day, the pressure to shut the case down intensified. Even the commanders began pressuring Dowd, Armanti, and their immediate supervisors. On September 7, three weeks before the Mollen Commission's public hearings, Internal Affairs rolled out its top gun: Chief Robert Beatty, who asked the U.S. attorney for a status conference on the case. At a meeting between the two men, Stamboulidis told Beatty he didn't see the need to rush.

Beatty wasn't about to back off. He told Stamboulidis that on several occasions Armanti and the fire marshals had been seen drinking beer outside their base at Fort Totten after their shifts had ended. Beatty said the undercover was interested in prolonging the investigation only so that he could continue drinking on the job. Stamboulidis thanked Beatty but made no promises. As soon as the meeting was over, Stamboulidis called Armanti to fill him in.

"We'll keep it going," Stamboulidis assured him.

Internal Affairs kept up its pressure. Three days later, Dowd and Armanti met Agent Peil to buy her a drink for her birthday. Looking uncharacteristically morose, Peil tried to just toss off the news that she'd been at a meeting the previous day—a summit conference that Dowd and Armanti hadn't been invited to. Her FBI supervisors had decided to end the undercover phase of the operation and bring Detective Wrynn in for questioning. Peil said that Wrynn had written a letter, denying that he'd shared anything more than a few harmless conversations with his neighborhood friends and complaining that the pressure of the investigation was unbearable.

"They're afraid he's going to kill himself," Peil said.

"Who gives a fuck!" Dowd shot back. "I hope he does."

"Someone from the PD got to you people, didn't they?" Armanti said. "They cut some kind of deal, didn't they?"

Peil didn't have the heart to tell Dowd and Armanti that it wouldn't have taken any outside pressure for the FBI to abandon the case. Her bosses had always considered the Lieutenant Williams case an afterthought. She had the distinct impression that they had assigned her to the arson investigation only to prevent her from making her rookie mistakes on the organized-crime cases they considered more important. But she had been denied even the basics, like buy money, and had often found herself in the humiliating position of begging other agents for their cars.

"I'm sorry," Peil said. "There was nothing I could do."

"And you just laid down?" Armanti said. "You turn on me and I'll fucking ruin you."

"I'd never turn on you!" she said. "I'm as committed to this case as you are—I'm just scared. There's nothing I can do. If my boss says it's over, it's over."

"What the hell do you have to lose?" Armanti shouted. "What were you before this, the president of a bank? You lose your job, you go back to a legitimate job. I go back to driving a goddamned truck!"

Armanti could see tears in her eyes.

"Take it easy on her," Dowd said. "What are you doing?"

"Fuck her too!" Armanti said, storming out of the bar.

Internal Affairs soon fired again. The next Monday morning, Lieutenant Frank Pooley, a supervisor from the NYPD's Organized Crime Investigation Division, called to inform Dowd that Detective Wrynn was going in for questioning. "We need more time," Dowd pleaded. "Just let Vinnie take it slow. Please. The more people he talks to out there, the more he gets."

"This isn't me talking—it's coming from up above," Pooley said.

Dowd assumed he was referring to the chief of the Organized Crime Control Bureau, but Pooley informed him otherwise. "It's higher than my guy—this is coming from the top," Pooley said. "I just got back from Kelly's office."

Kelly was Ray Kelly, the police commissioner. Pooley paused so Dowd could feel the full weight of what he was about to say.

"Kelly was there," Pooley said. "He wants this shut down. They're afraid the kid's gonna kill himself. He can't have that happen."

He went on to say that Wrynn had been spotted several weeks earlier looking through the Drug Enforcement Coordination System book. "He has to have told everyone that Vinnie's hot. Vinnie's gonna get hurt up there."

"We're not shutting it down!" Dowd said. "I've got a dead fireman."

Then he slammed down the receiver.

IF THE police commissioner truly was backing IAB, Armanti was cornered. He fought to stay on the set a few days longer, hoping for a miracle that would make his case against Tocco, the Ferrantis, and the Wrynns. He began wearing a second tape recorder, to make sure he'd have an independent record of every conversation he had on the set. Armanti knew he had to prepare himself for the day Internal Affairs came after him. It was dangerous, almost reckless, for him to load himself down with extra equipment so soon after being frisked by Cuzzi. But he had as much to fear from the police officials as he did from the mopes on the street.

But now there was nothing left to record. Tocco and Ferranti treated Armanti as if he were radioactive. He spent a few nights on the set drinking Sambuca, choking down his rage, praying for an opening. By mid-September, the bosses had held another round of meetings, and Internal Affairs got its way. Every unit involved would make one final trip up to Throgs Neck. Armanti would be given one last chance to engage Tocco, by springing on him at his home. Then the investigation would be shut down.

To Dowd, it was as if the bosses were writing their own ending to the case—and an unhappy one, at that. He stalled, hoping he could interest the Bronx DA's office or some other prosecutor to keep the case alive. Two days before the final assault was scheduled to begin, he urged Armanti to simply refuse to go.

"Don't do this," Dowd said. "We don't have to do this! You're the under-cover. They can't go up there without you."

Armanti shook his head. He had no doubt that he was burnt, and that Tocco was finished with Vinnie Blue Eyes. But he still thought there was a chance he could jar something loose. Mario Ferranti had already threatened to blow up the house of one suspected undercover, so Armanti assumed that there was now a contract on his life anyway. Catching Tocco at home, descending on him with unmitigated fury, Armanti could try to force the moment. Maybe Tocco would get flustered and give up Wrynn to save himself. Better yet, maybe he'd draw his gun.

Armanti had always believed that the biggest, most tragic mistake an undercover could make was to force the moment. But after four months of fending off ambushes from IAB and weeks of watching Tocco slip through his grasp like smoke, he didn't see how a little drama could make matters any worse.

"I'm going," Armanti said. "But it's gonna be a shoot-out."

13

"ONE SHOT, ONE KILL"

SEPTEMBER 28, 1993

FOR HIS SHOWDOWN with Tocco, Armanti would need more than just an extra tape recorder—he'd need an extra gun, too. Standing near his locker in the empty dressing room at Fort Totten, he stowed his nine-millimeter service pistol in his ankle holster. Next, he strapped a belly band around his waist, tucking a .380 near his left hip—the most convenient spot for a quick draw—and smoothed his shirt over it. Then he reached into his right pocket to be sure his rosary beads were there, but even they didn't give him much comfort. So he drew his nine-millimeter, to check that it was packed with bullets and the firing chamber hadn't jammed. He pulled out the .380 and looked it over, then checked the nine-millimeter again. Dowd came in and, seeing Armanti's half-crazed smile, became increasingly dismayed.

"You don't have to do this," he said. "Let's just not do it."

Armanti acted as if he hadn't heard. He called the fire marshals over and told them that if the situation erupted, he wanted them to stand back.

"If it starts to go, let it go," Armanti said. "Just give me a little time."

Jimmy Desocio grabbed Armanti's shoulder, massaging him like a corner man at a prizefight, trying to break the tension.

"Make sure you get the first shot in," he said. "Don't panic. Make sure you shoot straight. And don't waste any rounds. You're a marine, remember? One shot, one kill."

Armanti couldn't muster much in the way of false optimism. He took the clip out of his gun again. In the days leading up to the operation, he had pored over the details of Tocco's recent shooting arrest. Once the drug deal in his basement had gone bad, Tocco had handled the situation like a pro. He had wrestled the gun away from his would-be assailant, then pumped two shots into his victim and escaped unscathed. Impressive moves for someone who everyone in Throgs Neck, including Armanti himself, had once written off as lightweight. It was clear to Armanti that if he was going to draw his gun, he'd better fire quickly, because it was going to happen—Tocco was certain to open fire himself.

He checked the clip on his .380 again and looked up at the clock, eager to get started on a mission that was beginning to feel like a grave mistake. Then Armanti walked into a storage room, where he could have a few moments to himself.

A FEW MILES south, just outside the ornate, oak-paneled auditorium of the City Bar Association, Detective Joseph Trimboli sat picking at his lunch like it was an enemy. The Internal Affairs investigator, who had fended off his bosses for four years to hunt down "Coke Cop" Michael Dowd, was the day's star witness at the Mollen Commission's televised hearings. Since first setting eyes on Dowd in 1986, Trimboli had longed for this—his moment—when he could finally speak his mind. But now that he had the city's attention riveted upon him, Trimboli was edgy. After three hours of testimony, he had the unmistakable sense that the commissioners were trying to deny him the opportunity to tell the world exactly who had allowed Michael Dowd to rampage through the city streets for years.

Trimboli had always been skeptical of the commissioners' motivations; his wariness had intensified on the first day of the hearings, as he'd watched Michael Dowd take the stand without being asked to take an oath. After seven years of outwitting Internal Affairs and the city DAs, Dowd proved that he hadn't lost his skills as a negotiator or a storyteller. Sporting a business suit and a slick new haircut, he delivered a gripping performance as the latest incarnation of the bad-boy cop. He explained that when he had begun ripping off drug dealers he'd viewed it as a "kind of tax" on their business. But as his greed, drinking, and cocaine use had grown, the payments had evolved into an enterprise that netted him $8,000 a week in cash. He described the crafty way he'd tested new, possibly corruptible recruits on the force before inviting them to join his ranks. Dowd talked of supervisors who looked away while their men

looted, brutalized, and stole; entire precincts left unguarded while officers held secret rendezvous to plan their stings; and secret codes the
bosses would transmit over the radio to warn their men to lie low because
there might be honest cops or federal agents in the area. Dowd described
the perverse subculture of corrupt officers, among whom the phrase
"good cop" meant someone who would never report the misconduct of a
fellow officer, no matter how depraved.

His words offered a jolting look at police officers who had adopted the
moral code of the drug dealers they were supposed to despise. But
through it all, Dowd never apologized, never gave up another officer. He
described rogue cops as victims, entitled to live by their own rules
because they didn't get the support they deserved from the politicians,
the media, the public.

"It's us against them out there," Dowd sang. "*Us* is the police officers,
them is the public. . . . Cops don't turn in other cops. Cops don't want to
be labeled as rats. Cops have to depend on each other for survival."

Trimboli, up next, was to be the commission's angel of hope. In the sixteen months since the Dowd case had first burst, he had been canonized
by the city newspapers and on TV. Inside the police department, though,
he had it rough. The NYPD's official analysis of the Dowd case—a 161-
page exercise in obfuscation written by Ray Kelly before he was promoted to the department's top job—somehow neglected to name the IAB
supervisors who had sabotaged Trimboli. But, incredibly, Kelly had criti-
cized Trimboli's work, citing "ineffective investigative techniques" and
"ambiguous" phrases in his reports.

By the time Trimboli sat down on the morning of September 28,
beneath the glare of klieg lights and the unblinking eyes of television
cameras, he was desperate. He wanted to tell the public the real lesson of
Dowd's case: that atrocities like this don't just happen; people allow them
to happen. People with names, who still held incredibly powerful positions in the NYPD and were angling for even more power. People whose
ambition and eagerness to placate their superiors made them forget their
duty to protect the public and abandon the honest cops who depended on
them. Trimboli wanted, once and for all, to sound the truth.

But like a diamond or a lump of coal, the truth has many facets. And the
lawyers who ran the Mollen festivities were highly discerning about the
ones Trimboli was invited to illuminate. The commissioners encouraged
Trimboli to catalog Dowd's many sins. When it came time to talk about

the people who'd prevented Trimboli from nailing Dowd, the commission's lawyers had no hunger for detail. The questions were so generic that Trimboli himself often sounded like a bureaucrat.

"I believe, based upon my experience, there was a lack of resolve to go after these individuals . . . because it would be a tremendous embarrassment to the New York City Police Department," Trimboli said. "They did not want this investigation to exist."

When it came to the specifics, accountability, the commissioners seemed reluctant to ask the follow-up questions that might have allowed Trimboli to name names.

By lunch, Trimboli was beginning to fear that he had made a terrible mistake by agreeing to testify at all. Then Joseph Armao, the lead counsel of the commission, approached him.

"Will you play ball?" Armao asked.

"What?" Trimboli said.

"Will you say that we need a permanent outside monitor?"

Trimboli was shaken. Both he and Armao knew perfectly well that there had been a Special Prosecutor's Office when Michael Dowd was running circles around IAB. And they knew it had changed nothing. But it was clear from the leaks to the newspapers that the commissioners had decided to seek a new outside monitor's office. That symbolic achievement would allow them to declare political victory, break for a few photo ops, and leave the field. So what choice did Trimboli really have?

After lunch, Trimboli gave the commissioners the endorsement they so desperately wanted, saying that an outside monitor might help improve IAB. Then the commissioners thanked Trimboli and sent him on his way.

As he exited the room, flanked by reporters and television cameras, Trimboli ended his day in the spotlight with a surprise announcement: He'd decided to put in his retirement papers.

ARMANTI WAS FOUR doors away from Tocco's house when he saw the first warning sign. Driving slowly up Tocco's street, he had intended to turn into the driveway and pull up close to Tocco's front door. That way, he could take cover behind the car once the shooting started. But for some odd reason Tocco had parked at the street end of the concrete driveway. That left Armanti no place to take cover. No safe place at all. *Why would he change his routine today?* Armanti thought. *Had he been warned?*

Armanti tried to rid his mind of a particularly vivid memory of one previous undercover operation that ended in gunfire. Years ago, he'd been driving through a set in Sunset Part, Brooklyn, when he'd heard *Bang! Bang! Bang!* and found himself in the middle of a drug rip-off involving five armed dealers. One of the gunmen ran to Armanti's car and shoved a nine-millimeter in his face. Armanti ducked under the steering wheel, then forced his way out of the car and chased the dealer. A few instants later, the gunman took aim at Armanti, who raised his .380 automatic, squeezed the trigger, and heard gunfire, then a sickening *Click!* of a gun jamming. It all happened so fast Armanti wasn't sure whose gun had misfired, so he dove to the ground to take cover and ripped open his shirt to see whether he'd been hit. Then he scrambled to his feet, realizing that his gun had jammed. He pointed his weapon at the gunmen, praying they didn't realize it was inoperable, then leaped over the hood of a car and zigzagged along Ninth Avenue, somehow escaping unscathed. But as he parked his car a few doors from Tocco's house, Armanti could still hear that *click*.

The fireworks had been scheduled for the afternoon—a time when Tocco was usually home and few pedestrians would be endangered if things turned violent. At Fort Totten, Armanti had barely listened as the bosses from the FBI, the fire department, Internal Affairs, and the Organized Crime Control Bureau set up their tactical plan and script for the day. He knew, whatever they said, that there was only one approach that stood even the faintest chance of success: pure fury. He'd accuse Tocco of being the rat, say he'd heard something on the street, then barrel in, demanding an explanation. If Tocco suspected that Armanti was a police informant, he'd most likely open fire on the spot. If the Wrynns' leaks had gone all the way, and Tocco had learned that Armanti was an undercover, he might think twice about shooting a cop. But Tocco's temper was so combustible, there was no telling what he'd do if he was armed, riled, and face-to-face with Armanti.

Armanti rushed up Tocco's driveway, his fists clenched and face twisted into the full serial-killer look. Tocco's curtains were drawn, even though it was the middle of the day, so Armanti scanned from window to window, waiting to see whether Tocco or Mario would show. Finally, Armanti pounded on the front door so hard that his knocks sounded like punches.

"Tough guy, get out here!" Armanti demanded.

Armanti gave the door a thunderous kick, then ran to the side of the house, found a window, and began banging and screaming.

"Tommy! Get the fuck out here! Tough guy!"

The door cracked open. Armanti was greeted by the terrified blue eyes of Angelique Montemurro, the mobster's daughter who'd grown up with Tocco and the Wrynns. Armanti was startled. Tocco had lured a woman inside his cesspool?

"Get Tommy, now!" Armanti growled. "You tell him Vinnie's here."

Angelique backed away silently as Armanti searched for a suitable defensive position. Jamming his body against a wall to the left of the door frame, he waited, ready to spring out and grab Tocco's gun before it fired. At the sound of a faint rustling from inside, Armanti reminded himself to pivot and come at Tocco sideways, so that the full force of any shot would first strike his arm or shoulder rather than his chest or gut. Peering through the crack of the door, Armanti saw Tocco strolling toward him wearing basketball shorts, a T-shirt, and sneakers with no socks. The Torch also wore a coy expression: a little intimidated, but so cocky. Tocco pushed the door open with his right hand, and when Armanti saw that his left hand was empty, he took two quick steps forward, meeting him at the threshold. Surprised, Tocco backed up—allowing Armanti to step forward, in Tocco's face, his hand near his gun, waiting for Tocco to draw.

Instead, Tocco flashed something more devastating: his cheap, dingy smile.

The instant Armanti saw it, it was clear he was burnt. No other explanation. A criminal in Tocco's position would have come out pumped, demanding to know who the hell was banging at his house. Tocco was a portrait of schooled restraint, his eyes amused and knowing.

Armanti ran through all his moves, trying every inflammatory line he could think of—challenging Tocco's manhood, taunting, calling him a rat, punk, fool, fuck. Tocco just smiled. It was obvious that he had a tactical plan, too. Armanti accused Tocco of wearing a wire and demanded that he explain himself. Tocco's words came back as if they'd been written by Wrynn himself.

"I know nothing," Tocco insisted. "I know nothing. I go to work. I work for a living."

Armanti spit.

"You think I'm a rat?" Tocco asked.

"I don't know. You tell me."

"You got—"

"I'm just asking," Armanti said.

"You got the wrong person," Tocco replied.

Nothing left to lose, Armanti tried to pry Wrynn's name out of Tocco.

"Maybe your fucking cop buddy told you," he said.

"My cop buddy?" Tocco said, glaring. "Your cop buddy."

"No, no," Armanti said, infuriated that leaks from within his own department had allowed an imbecile like Tocco to taunt him. "I never said anything about a fucking cop."

"Your cop buddy," Tocco insisted, sounding pleased with himself.

"No!" Armanti said. "No cop buddy ever came out of my mouth."

"No cop buddy ever came out of my mouth," Tocco said, content to play this game all afternoon.

Armanti could barely resist the urge to give Tocco a horrific beating. After all the pain Tocco had caused, his arrogant smile should be shattered by a fist. But Armanti thought about the smile that would light up the Internal Affairs detectives' faces as they arrested him for excessive force. He turned, shaking his head in disgust, and walked away.

"It's over," he said to Dowd through his body mike.

TWO DAYS LATER, the U.S. attorney called a meeting to formally confront the IAB detectives. George Stamboulidis, the assistant U.S. attorney, brought in commanders from all the NYPD and FBI units involved in the Lieutenant Williams investigation and laid out his complaints. The IAB supervisors offered excuses, saying that the files on John Wrynn were locked away and inaccessible to Inspector Wrynn. They also said it was unfair to assume that the Wrynns were responsible for the leaks; there had been so many other units involved.

Then Stamboulidis sprang his trap. Stamboulidis had armed one of the detectives on the case, Bill Clark, with all the evidence against IAB. When Stamboulidis gave the cue, Clark confronted them with the fact that Sergeant Robert Matthiessen and the other IAB investigators had admitted to seeing Inspector Wrynn barge into the office and read through the confidential reports about his son. As IAB's detectives tried to respond, Stamboulidis, who had been raised a *Honeymooners* fan, could think only of Jackie Gleason caught in a desperate spot and jabbering, *Humma-na, humma-na, humma-na, humma-na . . .*

As soon as the meeting ended, Stamboulidis phoned Walter Mack, the former U.S. attorney whom Ray Kelly had called in to oversee IAB. Stamboulidis officially demanded that IAB be thrown off the case. Mack didn't argue; he agreed to order his men to box up their files and send them to the U.S. attorney's office.

Armanti was long gone before the meeting had even taken place. The morning after his confrontation with Tocco, Armanti had driven off without telling a soul where he was headed. With the investigation pronounced dead, he feared that the Mollen Commission would try to drag him into the hearings. But he had no intention of being anybody's prop.

He rented a room at a bed-and-breakfast in Spring Lake, New Jersey, a beachfront town where he'd once stayed with an ex-girlfriend. After nine months of living the case, he needed to decompress—to sleep late, run, swim, fall asleep on the beach. He looked up an old flame, had a few relaxing dinners, and, for a few moments, the city, the investigation, the department, and the Wrynns all seemed blown away by the breeze. Armanti's room at the bed-and-breakfast had an old photo of an elderly man walking hand in hand with a boy, and every time he looked at it he would think back to his own childhood, when his grandpa Joe, "Joe Bananas," would walk him down to the pier on Shore Road in Bay Ridge to watch the fishermen. Back when things were simple.

Each day, though, Armanti found himself drawn to a newsstand to buy the New York City newspapers, or sneaking into his car to listen to radio reports about the commission's hearings. It made him furious to hear how the commission had taken on a small number of corrupt officers and demoralized every honest cop on the force.

There were tales about officers too high on cocaine to respond to calls, about degenerate officers who specialized in beatings and rapes. There were precincts with such widespread criminality that the entire shift would report to a secret location to divvy up their drug money. Through it all, there was endless lofty talk about accountability, but few examples of any commanders ever being held accountable.

Armanti was relieved that he'd never let himself be lured to the stand. But sometimes he fantasized about barging into the hearings unannounced, grabbing a microphone from some white-hair, and hijacking the entire proceedings. He'd even roughed out a draft of a speech in his head. "You want to know the truth?" he imagined beginning. "I'll tell you the goddamned truth. These people are supposed to be fighting against killers and degenerates and they're worse than the people we lock up. You want to hear a story about believing? About how they tore my heart out and destroyed the only thing I ever believed in? Us against them? I'll tell you about us against them. *Us* is the public, the people trying to live their lives, and all the good cops out there every day trying to keep them safe. *Them* are the dirty cops, and all the bosses and politicians who are too busy thinking about themselves and their careers to do anything to stop them."

But watching the hearings play out, Armanti came to regard them as a political theater, a carefully scripted exhibition designed to shock the public just enough to justify taking a baby step. The commissioners talked tough to a handful of rogue officers. They roughed up a low-level sergeant who answered phones in Internal Affairs. But their lawyers seemed to develop a fear of heights as they scaled the chain of command, becoming more deferential and indulgent the higher they went. Chief Beatty was slapped around a bit in front of the cameras, but there was no mention of firing him. His predecessor at IAB, retired Chief Daniel Sullivan, seemed befuddled and pathetic as he explained his reluctance to report a major scandal to city hall or the police commissioner's office. "When I brought them bad news, it felt like they were going to shoot me," he said.

Incredibly, the commission never called Lee Brown, the police commissioner who had brushed aside the news reports about the failures of Internal Affairs. Brown had since left to become President Clinton's drug czar. With a Democratic mayor running for reelection, there was little chance that the commission would upset a Democratic president by publicly humiliating one of his prominent appointees. Brooklyn District Attorney Charles "Joe" Hynes was given a pass too, even though he'd had two chances to stop Michael Dowd—once as special prosecutor for police corruption, the other as Brooklyn DA—and had failed both times. Hynes sent word that he'd like to attend, but his busy schedule prevented him; the commission, which had subpoena power, chose not to antagonize someone of his stature by compelling him to testify.

Police Commissioner Ray Kelly was masterful at handling the hearings. During the first few days he played the victim as he observed the goings-on, often complaining to the press that the proceedings seemed one-sided. Then, as the days passed, the litany of police abuses demanded a different tack. With an election just a few weeks away, it seemed inevitable that the mayor would have to propose the creation of an outside monitor. So Kelly changed course, showering Trimboli with praise, promising him a promotion, and convincing him to postpone his retirement. Kelly also threw the commission a bone by reversing himself and announcing on a TV news show that he would be willing to accept an outside monitor—as long as the police commissioner would still have some say in the discipline process. When Kelly took the stand, the Mollen commissioners seemed so delighted that he'd endorsed the concept of an outside monitor that they questioned him with all the ferocity of animals at a petting zoo.

On October 4, six days after Armanti's undercover investigation had effectively been ended, it looked for a moment as if the commission might finally get around to mentioning the Wrynn case. The commission spent part of the day's hearings talking about the tickler file, the secret filing system used to tank corruption allegations against high-ranking police officials and their relatives, including the Wrynns. But Wrynn's name was never actually said out loud.

In Armanti's opinion, the hearings were most remarkable for what they failed to address. Eric Mergenthal was dead. The people responsible for killing Lieutenant Williams were still free. Armanti had been forced to spend months operating under the danger caused by Wrynn's leaks. Yet IAB had managed to prevent Armanti, the U.S. attorney's office, or anyone else from building a case against them. John Wrynn was still in the drug unit, with access to sensitive details about hundreds of other narcotics cases. Inspector Wrynn was free to roam the highest reaches of Internal Affairs, where he wielded the power to destroy anyone in the department who got in his way.

The day Armanti packed his bags and returned to the city, he called Dowd, who had convinced the Bronx DA to pick up the case and wanted Armanti to try a few more days on the set in Throgs Neck. Armanti agreed, out of loyalty to his friend, but his real target now was somewhere in police headquarters.

"This is when the real war begins," Armanti said.

PART II

THE REAL WAR

14

" A HEADS UP "

JANUARY – APRIL 1994

THE CALL WAS no surprise. John Wrynn had been just waiting for the FBI to make his day. Early on January 11, 1994, at a time when most people were still dreading the light of morning, Wrynn was with his girlfriend, Melissa Paradiso, at her apartment on East Tremont Avenue in the Bronx. The phone rang. He roused himself. A few uh-huhs later, he was at the door, promising, "I'll be back in a few minutes." The way he strutted out the door, it was as if he were stepping out for cigarettes. Outside, an unmarked car with two police officials streaked through the streets and pulled up at the curb. After Wrynn got in, they took off to HIDTA headquarters in Manhattan, the building where he worked. The room Wrynn wound up in was normally used for monitoring wiretaps. Today the agenda was different. They were looking to crack him.

During the three months since the undercover operation had tumbled down on Tocco's shaky stoop, Armanti and Dowd had alternately ranted and prayed, fearing that the cops and the FBI would never make a move on Wrynn. Things didn't look encouraging. Shortly after the Mollen hearings were shuttered, Mayor Dinkins, who had created the commission, lost his reelection bid so the commission's mandate evaporated. Mayor-elect Rudolph W. Giuliani's promise to support an outside monitor for IAB had sounded great on the campaign trail. Yet once Rudy actually ascended, it was anybody's guess how much capital he'd invest in a crusade begun by a predecessor considered a lightweight. Giuliani's career as a prosecutor had been defined by his aggressiveness—and propelled by his eye for photo opportunities. On his charge toward Gracie Mansion, he'd locked up Mafia dons, Wall Street icons, drug dealers, and dirty cops with a zeal that made him look like Superman—at least on television, where no one could hear his colleagues curse his grandstanding. But Giuliani also deftly ingratiated himself with the pugnacious NYPD unions: At one point, the ambitious mayor-to-be had led a frenzied, obscenity-laced police demonstration on the Brooklyn Bridge that ended with some officers storming half-cocked into City Hall, where they'd heckled Dinkins, referring to him as a "washroom attendant."

Now Mayor Giuliani had to make good on his impassioned promises to tame the city's wild streets. Could he really risk chilling his warm relationship with the cops by taking up the anticorruption cause? Armanti was slightly relieved when Giuliani replaced Police Commissioner Ray Kelly, a man whom they felt would shield his IAB buddies until his heart beat its last. (After the Mollen hearings, Kelly had finally bowed to public pressure and replaced IAB Chief Beatty, but only after creating a cushy new command where Beatty could be transferred.) Giuliani's choice to succeed Kelly was William Bratton, whose ego made even the mayor look like a model of humility. Together, these two high-voltage politicians promised the public that they would cleanse the force. But no one knew how far they'd actually go. All Dowd and Armanti could do was sit tight and hope that neither city officials nor the public lost their appetite for ending police corruption.

On the morning of his interrogation, John Wrynn sat tight, too, looking as if this were the start of a day on the Throgs Neck waterfront during some vaguely remembered summertime. During the Mollen investigation, the younger Wrynn had routinely ridiculed the commission as a "political witch-hunt," predicting that the festivities would end with a whimper. He'd joked with friends about being targeted by IAB. Wrynn bragged about being able to spot the Internal Affairs surveillance teams the second they came near. In a conversation with his father, John howled about the time he and Melissa, in separate cars, had stopped at the house on Hosmer Avenue to pick up a plastic police union card for her windshield, to ward off parking tickets. Walking out of his family's home with the PBA card, John immediately noticed the IAB detectives trying to look covert.

"John, you realize . . . what they must have thought," the Inspector had said, assuming the detectives suspected that his son had just sold the girl a packet of coke.

Inspector Wrynn continually warned John to strictly observe even the most picayune department guidelines. He lectured him repeatedly that, if stopped for questioning, he should mind his manners. John swore to play it safe. But out in the field during the months before his interrogation, he had still felt invulnerable enough to nose around narcotics investigations involving some of Throgs Neck's other illustrious residents. As early as the winter of 1993, John had begun quizzing another detective about a case called Operation Big Shot, one of the biggest cocaine investigations going on in the city at the time. He asked the detective, Elizabeth Rye, if any of the suspects involved were from the Bronx, inquiring specifically about Tommy Tocco and another local named Marcos Ciao. Wrynn seemed to know a lot about the Ciao family, Rye thought; he was up to speed enough to ask if the target was Marcos (the son) or Sal (the father). Days later, when the arrest teams moved in, the Ciaos, who had been seen recently in the neighborhood, had vanished.

Later in 1993, Linda Nelson, the assistant DA Wrynn had dated, noticed that her charming lover was becoming increasingly inquisitive about her work. One night when Nelson was on warrant duty, preparing affidavits and search warrants, Wrynn called to ask about any upcoming raids in the works in his old neighborhood. Nelson said she'd just sworn out an affidavit for a DEA case in the Bronx, and when she told him the address, it turned out that Wrynn was familiar with the place. He explained that a friend owned the building in question and had been concerned about a tenant who had been selling drugs.

By November 1993, Wrynn's game face was showing signs of strain. He was making a very public show of attempting to clean up his act and polish up his slipshod work ethic. The ponytail was history; one day Wrynn reported to work with a haircut that wouldn't have shamed a stock broker. He also began vowing to colleagues and supervisors that he would try to be more serious about his job, even the paperwork, which he'd always whined about. But his conversion came too late: He couldn't escape the wrath of his supervisor at the Organized Crime Investigation Division, Lieutenant James Hall. On November 13, Hall was ordered to call Wrynn in to inform him of a written reprimand issued for his repeatedly failing to file daily reports punctually. Hall also blasted Wrynn for what the NYPD labeled his "poor performance." More serious disciplinary action was threatened *if* the detective didn't adjust his attitude.

Wrynn made a feeble bid for some sympathy. He told Hall he had been disoriented by his parents' serious marital problems—even though he was twenty-eight years old and lived on his own. He promised to try to catch up with all the unfinished reports piling up on his desk. Pointing to his newly shorn hair, he spoke of "turning over a new leaf." Wasn't it great?

Ponytail or no ponytail, Hall wasn't about to be patronized. He asked Wrynn if there might be some other problems weighing on him. Something, perhaps, having to do with his job. At this point, Wrynn had seemed to realize that dancing around the real issue was futile. He said he was aware that he'd been under investigation for more than a year, because his name had been mentioned during a conversation wiretapped by officers investigating organized crime. Hall demanded to know just how Wrynn had learned that he was the target of an IAB inquiry meant to be confidential.

"I'd rather not say," Wrynn replied.

Wrynn did volunteer that his father's name had also been overheard on the wiretap. He said he suspected that some building contractors who had performed a recent cement job at the Inspector's home might have had mob connections. But Wrynn insisted that he and his father were innocent victims of some personal vendetta. As proof, he pointed to the fact that their anonymous enemy had somehow managed to have the complaint sent directly to the chief of Internal Affairs.

"Someone has it in for me and my father," Wrynn said.

If he had intended to intimidate Hall by mentioning the Inspector, Wrynn found out quickly that playing that particular card was no genius move. Hall curtly told John that if he simply did his job and stayed out of trouble, he'd have nothing to fear. When Wrynn called his immediate supervisor too demanding and "too serious," Hall—a man with a blunt approach to problem solving—suggested that Wrynn consider transferring into a position with less exacting standards. Hall ended the meeting by informing Wrynn that if he needed to talk about family problems, the NYPD had a counseling unit. The shrinks were on duty around the clock.

Some men might have been chastened, even humbled. Not John Wrynn. He started filing his reports sooner, but clearly he wasn't too rattled. In fact, in early January, when Wrynn bumped into a friend from the Joint Drug Task Force (run by the NYPD and FBI), he asked about openings. He thought he might be able to swing a transfer.

NOTHING HAD CHANGED by the time the FBI arrived to question Wrynn on January 11. He seemed unruffled, even though the stakes had clearly been raised. As it happened, among Wrynn's interrogators was none other than Cindy Peil. It was her first major interrogation, and she had prepared like a law school student cramming for the bar, devouring every shred of paper about Wrynn, studying the tapes involving Tocco and the informants, and poring over Wrynn's personnel file and the assorted intelligence. To try to unnerve Wrynn, Peil brought along Richard Rudolph, an FBI veteran who had never set foot in Throgs Neck, but had the crusty appearance of someone who'd beaten confessions out of plenty of stouthearted men. Peil had also boned up on a few of the mind games she'd learned at the FBI Academy in Quantico. She stapled Wrynn's photograph inside the case file to make him feel like a perp; she had stuffed hundreds of pages of unrelated paper into the folder to make it appear chock-full of evidence. Finally, she had checked off several of the pre-printed boxes on the cover of the file: "Armed and Dangerous," "Escape Risk," "Suicidal."

Wrynn didn't appear fazed. Standing up to shake hands with Peil and Rudolph, he flashed a confident, cooperative smile. Moments later, rocking back slowly in his chair, he acted calm and in control, as if he were the one in charge. After a minute or two of small talk, Peil began the interview. When asked about the last time he'd spoken to Tocco, Wrynn responded in a friendly tone.

"I haven't spoken to him on the phone in two years," he said.

"I didn't ask about the phone," Peil snapped. "I said when did you speak to him. *Period.*"

"I don't know," Wrynn said, exhaling very loudly over his failed maneuver. "Probably this past summer."

He described this chat as pure coincidence. Driving in the neighborhood, he'd spotted Tocco on the corner of East Tremont and Sampson Avenues, outside Sebastian's, so he'd pulled over. Ten or fifteen minutes they chatted, Wrynn said. Just catching up. "You know," Wrynn emphasized. "We've known each other since we were ten years old."

Wrynn was minding his manners, just as the Inspector had advised. But already Peil detected a subtle modulation in the tone of his voice. When she asked for more details about his dealings with Tocco and Mario Ferranti, she noticed Wrynn taking a deep, deep breath and looking slightly put-upon. Still, he restrained himself, brushing aside the suggestion that he'd had any interactions with them in recent years. They were guys from the neighborhood, Wrynn said innocently. He'd known them in high school. He'd briefly worked with Mario doing odd jobs at his brother Jack's buildings in Harlem—but that was back in the day. Wrynn emphasized that he had always kept his distance from Mario, who was "demented" and "a pervert." Once John had joined the police force in 1986, they'd all gone their separate ways.

"I've hardly had anything to do with them since then," he said, crossing his arms and cocking his formidable V-shaped eyebrows.

"Are you sure?" Peil asked.

Wrynn was rocking more quickly now.

"Yeah," he said. *"Positive."*

"Really," she asked, locking onto his eyes with her own.

"Really," he said, his voice smooth but his eyes showing the first sign of something resembling concern.

Peil reached into her bag and pulled out a tape recorder. As she set it up, she heard Wrynn take another breath.

"I'd like you to listen to this tape," she said, slipping in a recording of Tommy Tocco telling Armanti that a "friend on the force" had tipped him off about Eric Mergenthal working as an informant. "See if this refreshes your memory."

She played a section of the tape with Tommy Tocco's grating voice, then paused the tape and asked, "Do you recognize who's speaking?" She realized she was straining not to appear excited.

After waiting a few seconds, Wrynn nodded his head yes.

"And who would that be," Peil said.

"Tocco," Wrynn said, suddenly deflated.

Peil clicked the tape recorder back on, but a few seconds later, Wrynn threw up his hands and stretched his neck. He said he couldn't make out what Tocco and Armanti were saying. Stopping the tape, Peil reached into her folder, making certain that Wrynn could see his photo stapled inside like a child molester's mug shot. She then pulled out a written transcript of Tocco's statements.

"This should help you follow along," she said.

Wrynn took the transcript and started reading. Peil clicked the tape on again, and when Tocco began talking about the source of his leak, she couldn't resist adding some dramatic flair: She stopped the tape, rewound it, and played it over and over and over.

"A cop told me"—*click, whirr*—"A cop told me"—*click, whirr*—"A cop told me—"

When the tape ended, she turned off the recorder. She let five or ten seconds of silence weigh down on Wrynn before speaking.

"So," she said. "Who do you think he might be talking about?"

"I don't know," he replied quietly. "I knew Eric Mergenthal."

Wrynn appeared saddened as he spoke about Mergenthal. But if it had dawned on him that he had cost his friend his life, he didn't let on. Wrynn claimed he knew that Mergenthal had OD'd but said he had no idea that Eric had been involved in any gun deal. Someone had told him that Mergenthal had shot up so much heroin that he'd suffocated. Wrynn was speaking more slowly now, almost as if he were thinking out loud. He mentioned, for no particular reason, that he didn't recall having seen Tocco or Mario Ferranti at the funeral.

"Were you the one who told Tocco?" she asked.

Wrynn shook his head over and over.

"Not me," he said.

Peil saw that Wrynn was reeling at the mention of his late friend. Maybe he had never really allowed himself to think very hard about Mergenthal or his death. But now that she had drawn him into her trap, it was time to spring. Opening her folder, she took out another piece of paper, but this time she didn't bother to close the folder. Wrynn's photo just stared up at him.

Peil read him a statement the FBI had taken from Terry O'Madden, the undercover who had tried to buy the gun from Tocco in November 1992. O'Madden had told the FBI that he'd bumped into Wrynn a week or so before the deal went bad and had asked for background information about Tocco. O'Madden had told the FBI that he'd made it clear that Tocco was a target of the Lieutenant Williams investigation and that the police were trying to catch him selling an illegal gun.

Wrynn had now abandoned any pretense of appearing cool. He was outraged.

"You guys are making me sound like a criminal," he said. "I just gave a heads up to someone in the neighborhood!"

"A heads up?" Peil questioned.

"Yeah," he said. "*A heads up.* I told him, Watch who you're talking to, clean up your act, watch your back, and keep your nose clean."

"And you think that's okay?" Peil said.

Wrynn glared at her.

"We've got to stop now," Wrynn said. "I want my union delegate."

Rudolph, mostly silent throughout the questioning, was stunned by Wrynn's bizarre defiance.

"Delegate?" he said incredulously. "You're gonna need a *lawyer!*"

Peil agreed to a short break, so Wrynn could call his union. Leaving the room, she was breathless. "They're not supposed to just admit it like that!" she said to Rudolph. "I thought that only happened on *Law and Order*."

Wrynn returned without a lawyer or delegate, his attitude more belligerent. He denied ever having asked his former girlfriend, the Bronx ADA, about cases. He insisted he'd never given any information to neighborhood friends. When told that a police officer had accused him of prying into Operation Big Shot, he said he couldn't recall anything.

Peil already had gotten more out of Wrynn than she'd ever dared hope for. But as long as he was willing to keep on talking, she figured she'd see if he'd give up his father.

"How did you know you were under investigation?" Peil asked.

Wrynn played dumb, asked what she meant. Peil shuffled through her folder once again, pulling out another piece of paper. When she told Wrynn she had a copy of the statement he'd made to Lieutenant Hall two months earlier, he threw his head back and closed his eyes.

"Who told you you were under investigation?" Peil demanded. "Was it your father?"

At the first mention of his father, Wrynn seemed ready to explode.

"My father had *nothing* to do with *anything*," he said.

"Then how did you know?"

"Look, it's one thing to ask me about Tocco and these guys from the neighborhood," Wrynn said, livid. "But now you're talking about my dad!"

Peil kept prodding, but Wrynn had finally, belatedly, decided to keep his mouth shut. By the time Peil and Rudolph wound up the two hours of tense questioning, she was drained. The next day, she would find out just how rattled Wrynn had been. Wrynn's two supervisors had driven him home to Pound Ridge after the ordeal. They reported that he had remained silent, sighing and sulking—most of the way. But at one point during the trip he shook his head and blurted out, "That woman sure did her homework."

BY ACKNOWLEDGING THAT he had been the one to leak information to Tocco, Wrynn had provided a devastating link between himself and Mergenthal's death.

"We got him!" Armanti screamed when he heard the news. "We've got him on conspiracy to murder! He's *ours!*"

Dowd smiled as Armanti gave him an embrace, but he knew they'd still need a lot more evidence before they could seek criminal charges. And he couldn't help wondering why Wrynn had folded. Was it because he didn't understand what he was up against? Or because he knew his father's Internal Affairs connections would allow him to float far above the fray?

Wrynn's admissions were the first boost for Dowd or Armanti in months. Usually after an undercover operation, Armanti would find himself feeling relieved, elated, and let down, all at once. He'd go somewhere, take a few weeks to unwind, and then get edgy waiting for the next assignment. But when he'd returned to headquarters with Lieutenant Williams's killers still on the loose and the case pulling on him like a whirlpool, his anger at being betrayed had been surpassed only by his eagerness to find anyone and everyone who'd been part of what had happened.

Long before Armanti had returned to the Special Projects Unit office at One Police Plaza, word had begun to filter back about the ordeal he'd been put through on the street. Narcotics detectives and undercovers considered it sacrilege. Armanti was greeted with handshakes, high fives, and offers to do anything to help him avenge himself. Deputy Chief Frank Biehler, head of all the NYPD's narcotics units, had called Armanti in to welcome him home. "I heard about what they did to you," Biehler said. The chief also invited Armanti to sit next to him at his weekly executive staff meeting, at the head of the conference table. When the background chatter died down, Biehler began the meeting by clasping Armanti's shoulder.

"This guy here is a hero," Biehler said.

Not long after, Armanti's warm welcome turned chilly. A lieutenant from narcotics stopped him in the hallway, shook his hand, and gave him an envelope. Inside was a command discipline—a written reprimand. He hadn't been wearing a department-authorized holster in a shoot-out eighteen months earlier.

"You're fucking kidding me, right?" Armanti said

"Well, it's not me," said the lieutenant. "It's coming from above."

"You are fucking kidding me!" Armanti said.

As he drove home that night, Armanti couldn't help but dwell on the fact that Biehler, a powerful figure, had never even mentioned the prospect that the Wrynns might be forced to pay for what they'd done. During his first week back at headquarters, Armanti had already recognized something disturbing: Armanti's colleagues in special projects wanted vengeance and promised to do anything they could to make the

Wrynns pay. But the higher-ups warned him to let the whole thing drop. Armanti's bosses in narcotics were old-timers, men who'd seen the department operate for decades; they knew that the tough men who ran it had their own ways of handling things—hard, determined, uncompromising ways. If someone pushed them too much, even someone who had been wronged outrageously, he ran the risk of offending, becoming the enemy. *You've got a long career ahead of you,* Armanti was told again and again. *You're not going to win this one.*

After weeks with no clue about how to proceed, Armanti began to consider just moving on. But his uncertainty vaporized on the day that Stamboulidis finally succeeded in forcing IAB to turn its files over to the U.S. Attorney's Office. When Armanti, Dowd, Peil, and the fire marshals gathered in the assistant U.S. attorney's office to review the paperwork, they were astounded to find that IAB's double-dealing had been even more blatant than they'd imagined.

Tucked away in the boxes was a note written by Chief Beatty, denying a request for Wrynn's telephone records. The note had been written in 1992—long before Eric Mergenthal's death, long before Armanti had ever set foot on the set. There was also evidence that Internal Affairs had withheld vital information from Armanti and Dowd. On the night of July 1, for instance, just minutes before Armanti made his first buy from Tocco, IAB had spotted Wrynn at a pay phone outside a restaurant just five blocks away, holding a brown paper bag. But the IAB detectives hadn't seen fit to mention this to anyone working on the undercover operation.

Most appalling of all was a photograph. Leafing through the IAB folders, Armanti found an old photo of himself wearing an NYPD uniform— something he hadn't done in a decade. Armanti stared at the face in the photo, so young and idealistic. The camera had even captured the glint of the badge he had kept so carefully polished. Looking at the picture, Armanti remembered his pride at having come so much further in the world than he had expected would be possible. Now, with the folder open in front of him, he looked too stricken to speak.

When Peil saw the photo, she gasped. "Oh my God," she whispered, realizing that it may have been used to identify Armanti to the criminals.

Sometime in February 1994 Armanti first learned that the Detectives Endowment Association was providing Wrynn with a lawyer free of charge. Armanti was rendered speechless by the fact that his dues to the organization might somehow be protecting the man who had endangered his life. He called his union delegate, but was told that the union's policy was to provide legal representation to any member. He demanded to speak to the DEA president. Granted a meeting with the vice president, Jack Healy, Armanti pounced the instant he entered the man's office.

"I hear you're giving legal coverage to John Wrynn," Armanti announced, scorn radiating from his eyes.

"Yeah," Healy replied nonchalantly. "He's a friend of mine."

"He gave me up!" Armanti shot back, surprised at how loudly his voice echoed. "He left me out there to get murdered. How can you give him representation?"

"He's a good friend of mine," Healy said, on the defensive. "His father's a good guy."

Armanti sprang up from his seat, jabbing his finger toward Healy. "I'm gonna walk out that door and we're gonna start over," he said. And he did, barreling out of the office and then returning.

"Jaaaaaack," Armanti said, his smile saccharine as he extended a hand toward Healy. "Do you know your friend is a *scumbag*?"

"What are you, a fucking joker?" Healy shouted.

"No, but you are," Armanti said, lunging at Healy.

The union delegate who had accompanied Armanti tried to hold him back and herd him to the door. Healy's assistant grabbed Armanti, too.

"What is this!" Armanti screamed. "The fucking Irish Mafia?"

DOWD WAS NAVIGATING through his own obstacle course in the Lieutenant Williams case, which Dowd had convinced the Bronx DA's office to resuscitate. But the longer he flailed about in search of clues, the more frustrated Dowd grew. Facing the fire marshals each day, the men who called Williams their "brother," Dowd was bewildered at the NYPD. He kept thinking of Williams, his family, Bruce Bailey's widow and child, the Mergenthals—all these innocent people whose lives had been ripped apart—and meanwhile the police department was busy covering its ass.

Tommy Tocco had been arrested on cocaine charges on January 11, 1994 (the same day Wrynn had been questioned). Briefly, it had seemed that he might actually give up the Ferrantis. Along with Bill Clark, one of the NYPD's most fabled interrogators, Dowd attempted, for more than twenty-four hours, to goad a confession out of the Torch—haranguing him, threatening him, cudgeling, and cajoling. They promised to drop the drug charges if he'd testify about the Ferrantis' role in the fire. They warned that he'd do fifty years for the cocaine sale: The next time he walked the streets he'd need a cane. At several points, Dowd thought he saw tears welling up in Tocco's eyes and, by the second day, the Torch had grown punchy and despondent.

"Give me my lawyer," he said. "Give me my lawyer, and I'll tell you everything."

When the lawyer arrived, he, too, urged Tocco to take the deal and testify. Then Tocco asked to use the phone to call his father. When he came back, the tide had turned.

"*Fuck you,*" Tocco scoffed, his voice even more gravelly than usual. "I'm not telling you a fucking thing."

Next, Dowd decided to look up Joey Ferranti, the heroin addict who'd given him his first lead two years earlier. Joey was locked up again on drug charges, and a week after Wrynn and Tocco were questioned, Dowd and Peil went to visit him in prison. Joey's story infuriated Dowd, confirming his worst suspicions without actually offering enough firsthand evidence to charge anyone. Word on the street was that Eric's death had indeed been a murder, Joey said. Mario had somehow been involved in passing him the tainted drugs.

Armanti badgered Dowd into asking the U.S. Attorney's Office to exhume Mergenthal, but Stamboulidis said he'd need more solid evidence before trying to take the drastic step of disinterring Eric over the objections of his family.

Three days later, Dowd awoke to more bad news—the case had finally made the newspapers. The New York *Daily News* published a brief story about the fact that John Wrynn was under investigation for leaking information, and a day later the *New York Times* ran a follow-up story. The reports were both short, skimpy on details. But Armanti was still elated; he expected a public outcry, an uproar demanding that Wrynn finally be held accountable.

Dowd wasn't as optimistic. Detectives often leaked information to newspapers in order to help turn up witnesses or lull potential suspects into a false sense of security. But publicity could also backfire: It shut people up, in particular, prospective witnesses and informants. At the Mollen hearings, IAB commanders had acknowledged that they'd short-circuited corruption cases by prematurely leaking information to the press. The bad guys were warned to stop doing anything to attract attention. Witnesses just faded. So brutal was the NYPD culture on cops who helped lock up cops that even honest people got cagey. In the weeks after the newspaper stories, the FBI began encountering problems from other previously cooperative officers. Two NYPD detectives who had warned Dowd that John Wrynn had been asking inappropriate questions about Tocco were now reluctant to provide the FBI with details.

Detective Wrynn also had an abrupt change of attitude. Finally, he seemed to realize that his predicament had grown far beyond the kind he could walk away from. At three A.M. on the morning after he was questioned, Wrynn called his father and left his pager number. But he had made some mistake with his phone and the Inspector couldn't figure out who the message was from. Four hours later, another message appeared on the Inspector's pager, and he called to find that it was John, paging him from his girlfriend's house. The Inspector knew that John was a whiz with his electronic gadgets; if he had messed up the earlier message, he must be in some shape.

"What's going on?" the Inspector demanded.

"Not good," John replied. "I was put on modified assignment."

The Inspector could tell that his son was in a panic. The kid was losing it. When they met to talk in person, the Inspector saw John's face quivering as he mentioned that the FBI was trying to link him to Mergenthal's death and the investigation into Lieutenant Williams's murder. John swore again and again that he rarely ever saw Tocco or the Ferrantis. He'd simply bumped into Tocco at a party in late 1992, exchanged a few words, and now someone within the department was trying to twist it into something sinister. He couldn't believe it.

Sensing the web that John was now enmeshed in, his father warned him to watch his step. Inspector Wrynn knew only too well that once the NYPD's inquisitors had someone in their crosshairs, they'd use any piddling infraction to ram him.

When John Wrynn arrived to testify before the grand jury, in April, Stamboulidis detected an air of smugness about him. But contradicting Wrynn's self-satisfied expression were signs that the pressure had gotten to him. His hair was shorter and thinner than the photos in his OCID identification badge, which had been taken two years earlier, and he looked as though he'd put on ten or fifteen pounds. He wore a sport jacket. Gone were the trademark cowboy boots; on this day he had selected business shoes, Sunday shoes. The kind his father used to badger him to keep shined.

Stamboulidis had spent days with Armanti, Dowd, and Peil, preparing a list of questions. He'd planned to ask Wrynn about his drug use, his conversations with Tocco, his admissions during his FBI interview. He'd demand to know precisely what he'd meant by telling Tocco to "watch who you talk to"—especially since Wrynn had already been told that Tocco was under investigation. He'd ask how it felt to know that his friend Eric Mergenthal's death was most likely due to Wrynn's own leaks.

Wrynn walked into the grand jury room and took a seat in the witness box. He raised his hand, took the oath to tell the truth. And he responded to every question with the same answer: He took the Fifth.

15

"WHAT ANY FATHER WOULD DO"

JUNE 7, 1994

INSPECTOR JAMES PATRICK WRYNN walked into the grand jury room of the federal courthouse in Brooklyn with a hardcover book in his hand and a determined look on his face. He had weathered twenty-nine rugged years in the NYPD—nearly three decades of thankless hours, headaches, blows to the ego and to the spirit. The next few hours would either make his career or break it into pieces that could never be reassembled. If he succeeded on the stand, the Inspector was in line to become a chief and finally wear the star that designated the high distinction of that office. If he failed on the stand, however—and it was hard for some, including his son, to consider the idea that Jimmy Wrynn could ever really fail—he could be forced to retire in disgrace and, quite possibly, face criminal prosecution for obstruction of justice or perjury. Jim Wrynn, the subject of criminal prosecution: It was almost unthinkable. After twenty-nine years.

It had been eleven months since an out-of-control Wrynn had been spotted in the Internal Affairs special projects office. Since then, the Inspector had been the subject of furious battles among police officials. Once IAB was thrown off the Wrynn matter in September, the investigation had become strictly a law enforcement issue. The NYPD and the U.S. Attorney's Office had been hammering it out. The battle had been treacherous.

In January, when his son was questioned by the FBI, the Inspector had begun raging about conspiracies and thundering over the lack of loyalty. But most of what he had to say centered on what he was owed by the department and its chiefs for all the years and sweat he had given. And John? John was innocent, the Inspector would insist. Then he would slam down a fist and swear to whomever was there that it was all a vicious plot designed to pressure him into retiring in order to spare his son further embarrassment.

The scheme gradually described by the Inspector was oddly convoluted, and it would become more labyrinthine as time passed, particularly given the rather obvious infractions of his many sympathizers. Inspector Wrynn conveniently failed to mention that he and John were both under scrutiny because of their own actions. He had nothing to say about his own hypocrisy or the standard he had demanded for so many years of so many other men. Instead he spoke of the never-ending back stabbing in the gladiators' ring of police headquarters. But, despite his nagging fears about being sabotaged by his unnamed, unseen rivals, Inspector Wrynn did receive signs of support from his higher-ups. A few weeks after John had been placed on modified assignment, the Inspector was called into the office of Chief Philbin, who had replaced Beatty as head of Internal Affairs. Philbin said he couldn't discuss the case, that IAB wasn't even handling it, but his words of reassurance seemed as comforting as those of "a father with a son," the Inspector later said. "Be patient," Philbin told him. "We're standing behind you."

In a real way, the change of administrations and the overhaul of IAB had made Inspector Wrynn an even more valuable commodity within the NYPD. Shortly after Mayor Giuliani was inaugurated and Commissioner Bratton took control of the police department, several other Internal Affairs commanders were urged to retire along with Chief Beatty. (Al James, the Inspector's friend, had been eased out shortly after his comments about "degenerates" made the papers.) Those departures created a leadership vacuum within Internal Affairs. Walter Mack, the civilian named to oversee the bureau, was an outsider. In a closed society like the IAB, he'd need at least one insider to guide him through the unwritten rules, hidden agendas, and minefields.

By June 1994, there were few people left in the bureau who could match the experience and savvy of Jim Wrynn. He *got* the place, every inch of it, and despite whatever had happened to his son, he knew how it worked and when it didn't. Who to manipulate and what to fix and what not to. And what would never, *ever* change. He was intimately familiar with the strengths and weaknesses of the chiefs at the top of the department; he could name the scars each carried and cite the dates when they'd been acquired and who had inflicted them. And, of course, he could remember, better than anyone, the exact circumstances of the offenses that had occurred. Wrynn also had a way of making his superiors comfortable; he knew never to embarrass them or fence them into uncomfortable or confining corners. He had been a pro in this place for about as long as anyone could recall.

On January 3, 1994, Giuliani's first week in office, IAB underwent yet another reorganization. In mid-April, just three months after his son had been questioned by the FBI, Wrynn was called back to IAB headquarters, to the same building in SoHo where he had burst into the office of those investigating his son. Walter Mack needed a pro. Or so the Inspector later explained.

"What was happening is, the chiefs were retiring from the Internal Affairs division and the commissioner, Mack, wanted a presence in the main headquarters who had some experience in Internal Affairs work," Wrynn said. "So I was asked to basically come down and run things while they were in the process of retiring."

But Wrynn's promotion to chief depended on the outcome of the investigation into his actions on behalf of his son, which were being examined by the same prosecutors and federal grand jury looking into the murder of Lieutenant Williams. Legally, the safe move for Inspector Wrynn on that June day when he stalked in to face the grand jury would have been to do what his son had done: take the Fifth, even if he had nothing to hide. By testifying, the Inspector would run the risk of inadvertently saying something incriminating, or making a misstatement that could lead to perjury charges. But if he took the Fifth, James Wrynn would essentially be giving in to the enemies he despised and announcing the end of his illustrious career. Police department employees can be suspended for taking the Fifth in court, and there was no way Wrynn could remain a commander at IAB if he wouldn't testify. Once word got out that he'd hidden behind the Fifth Amendment, it would be just a matter of time before he was shipped off into some disgraceful assignment or forced to retire.

So by the time the Inspector arrived at federal court on that crucial day, he was determined not to falter. As he waited outside the grand jury room, Wrynn kept his nose in his book, as usual, and if anyone doubted whether he would be his usual fearsome self on the witness stand, they needed only to glance at its title. He walked into the courtroom carrying *Boss of Bosses,* the story of the Gambino crime family's assassinated leader Paul Castellano, written by two FBI agents.

———

THE FACE-OFF BEGAN with the kind of silence that usually precedes a natural cataclysm or an unnatural disaster. Then, finally, it broke:

"Can you please state your full name, including any middle name or initial, and spell your last name for the stenographer in front of you," Stamboulidis asked the Inspector.

"James Patrick Wrynn, *W-R-Y-N-N.*"

"Mr. Wrynn, you are employed by the New York City Police Department, is that correct?"

"Yes."

"You are an inspector?"

"That's correct."

Inspector Wrynn had spent virtually all his life rising through the ranks of rigid, formal institutions—from Catholic school to the police academy to the upper level of the NYPD— and it quickly became clear that this background had also prepared him to present himself as a most diligent witness. He took great pains to appear meticulous, polite, and cooperative. As Stamboulidis began the questioning by dispensing with a few innocuous questions about the Inspector's past, he seemed pleased and proud to recite the names of the respectable institutions that had constituted his upbringing: St. Luke's grammar school, Fordham Prep, Fordham University. Later, as he finished charting his ascent through the NYPD—from patrolman to supervisor to the head of the police academy, then on to become the man sought to reform Internal Affairs—even Stamboulidis felt obliged to give him a tip of the hat.

"Thank you for helping us through that rather impressive career path," the prosecutor responded.

Yet moments later, when Stamboulidis first mentioned John, then asked the Inspector where he lived and whether his son owned his own house, the man in the witness chair shot back a fast, defensive remark that made it clear he would fiercely protect his son. "He has a mortgage on it," the Inspector cracked, "but he's paying it like everybody else."

When Stamboulidis moved on to Detective Wrynn's legal troubles, the Inspector remained strictly controlled, adopting the tone of an affectionate father—not worried, not anxious, just concerned. He listed the highlights of his son's career, recalling minor triumphs that only a proud dad would. In response to one question, he managed to share a long and anguished story about the anonymous caller who'd first informed him that

John was under investigation. He recounted the wrenching conversations and warnings to John that followed, then testified that his son had come to him with tears in his eyes—worried not about himself but about rumors that the Inspector's name had been picked up on a wiretap involving the Luchese family. Each time the Inspector mentioned the charges against John or himself, his face contorted into an expression that could only be termed a sneer.

Stamboulidis edged the testimony toward the main event, questions about whether Inspector Wrynn had ever interfered with the investigation or threatened the IAB detectives. Yet abruptly, the Inspector cut him off, slamming the subject closed with a defiant, outraged blanket denial. Still, Stamboulidis held his ground, narrowing his focus closer and closer to the incident that most compromised his adversary.

"When you went to IAB, did you have the ability to look into their files or their logs to see whether there was an investigation of your son?" Stamboulidis asked.

"I am not sure if I did have the ability," the Inspector shot back, politely but adamantly. "And I will say why: because I don't know what they did. The log on my son, whether they joined— Because I never looked, I never asked, looked, made a phone call, or inquired about anything to do with the investigation on my son.

"Never!" he snarled, for emphasis. "Not a thing!"

Stamboulidis had been prepared to grill the Inspector on every minor detail about his foray into the Special Projects Unit:

What on earth possessed you to barge into the office where the files were?

Did you, as Sergeant Matthiessen later told his colleagues, look through the file involving John?

Precisely what did you mean when you stormed out of the office, warning the detectives investigating your son that "there's gonna be trouble"?

Are you asking this grand jury to believe that you went to the trouble of charging into Internal Affairs, pawing through the file and threatening your subordinates, but never said a thing about it to John?

But Wrynn's preemptive denial was so unequivocal—*Never! Not a thing!*—that the prosecutor decided to move on.

"Now I have a series of names I would like to run by you. Do you know a man named Mario Ferranti?"

Shifting personas once more, Wrynn transformed himself from protective father to a solid, if slightly confused, pillar of the neighborhood. Mario? Mario the neighborhood degenerate wiseguy? The Inspector described him as that "boy" who had gone to Catholic school with his son but who had *long* since lost touch with the Wrynn family. Tocco? The Inspector spoke of Tocco—the gun-toting, drug-dealing, fire-setting Torch—as an affable neighborhood character whom the Wrynns had known, briefly and barely, in a past that seemed washed away by the years. Why, he drove his momma's Cadillac and was so goofy that his Doberman pinscher let you walk right up and pet it.

Myron Dobbs? The Inspector was friends with his father, a retired fireman. Wrynn recalled helping the family lug Myron's sister, a heavy child afflicted with spina bifida, from their driveway to the front door and up the staircase. The Inspector was jolted from these memories only when Stamboulidis brought up Myron's reciting phrases from Armanti's police report verbatim and saying that someone from the NYPD had tipped off his father.

The Inspector responded by emphasizing that he and Myron's father spoke only in generalities, one concerned dad to another, about Myron and his obvious substance-abuse problem. He even referred to Myron, who was known as Myron the Moron in Throgs Neck, by his full name, Michael, which few people in the neighborhood even knew.

"He should be a saint in heaven," the Inspector gushed about Michael's father. "A nice man, always has time, never has had a bad word to say. But in some brief conversations we had by ourselves, he indicated Michael's problem. I don't know if he was talking about alcohol or drugs, but you look at the kid, you figure he is a heavy drinker at least."

After a few minutes of this, Stamboulidis doubled back for more questions about John's IAB file. The Inspector had said he'd never *asked* about the file, but had never actually denied entering the office and tearing through it. So Stamboulidis tried to pin him down, make him state, under oath, exactly what report he'd seen from the case folder, just to be certain that the Inspector couldn't fall back on some semantic dodge later.

But the Inspector insisted he had never seen a single IAB document regarding John until January 12, 1994—the day after the FBI had questioned his son. Even then, the Inspector said, he'd seen nothing confidential, only a daily advisory distributed to every IAB office, which merely mentioned that John had been placed on modified duty. Inspector Wrynn testified that he'd even had a difficult time understanding just what that

message meant. (Apparently it was a computer printout written in a cryptic code that he couldn't quite decipher.) "This computer we have was
probably born before I was, and I never really could read these logs very
well," said Wrynn. "I would read the plaintiff's name, there is information in there but I can't decode it."

Stamboulidis decided to cut through all the Inspector's posturing and
ask him a question he couldn't hedge.

"If there is an IAB file investigating allegations of impropriety on the
part of your son, have you ever seen or handled any document in that
file?" Stamboulidis asked.

"Absolutely not," the Inspector replied.

Stamboulidis then asked Inspector Wrynn to step down from the stand
and leave the room so he could ask the jurors whether they had any questions they'd like him to ask. After his departure, it became clear almost
immediately that the jurors were troubled by the gaps and inconsistencies
in the Inspector's testimony. Part of the problem was that his memory
seemed to grow better or worse at the most convenient times. When Stamboulidis had asked about the cement job that Mario Ferranti was rumored
to have done for free, the Inspector had started talking about two different
occasions when he'd had concrete poured around his house. The first project was in 1970, nearly a quarter century earlier, yet he could remember the
most innocuous minutiae: the contractor's name, his day job as a security
guard at the United Nations, the lunch boxes the workers brought to the
Wrynns' home. Yet when pressed for details about the job in question, completed just five years previous, the Inspector's memory had gone fuzzy—
fast. He couldn't remember the names of the contractors or how he'd found
them. Come to think of it, the Inspector said, he'd had a court appearance
scheduled on the date they did the work, so the men had charged him an
extra fifty dollars for not being there to help. Whoever they were.

Most implausible was the notion that a man as well educated and liter-
ate as Inspector Wrynn, a commander in IAB, couldn't read a simple
computer log sheet and didn't bother to learn even when he found his
son's neck on the line.

"First, I would like to know," said one juror, "how could he get so high
in the police department and he cannot read these sheets? He says he
can't read nothing. In the next place, he is supposed to be a top man, he
is not supposed to discuss this stuff with his son and let him know he is
watching. Family you should not tell what is happening."

The juror was clearly angered—a good sign for the prosecutor—but Stamboulidis tried to calm him.

"I understand your sentiment, but what question do you want me to ask?" Stamboulidis said. "I am not allowed to give him speeches or discipline him in any way."

"Why did he feel he could tell his son there are people on him?" the juror replied.

A second juror had another concern: "After his son got the modified assignment, I'm sure there was a circumstance where he went to his father and said, This is not fair. . . . Could he tell us what that conversation was about and did he advise his son how he could appeal it?"

Yet another juror added, "It boggles my mind about the Luchese family. Where did the son hear it, see it? I mean he is in the Bronx and whatever. Where did that come in that he is connected with the Luchese family?"

Stamboulidis fielded a few more questions from the jurors, then promised that he'd try to get them answers. But when Inspector Wrynn returned, he seemed even more guarded than before. The more Stamboulidis questioned, the more adamant the Inspector became. Time and again he denied ever having lifted a finger to try to find out about John's case. He said John had never even asked him for help.

When Stamboulidis asked whether the Inspector and John had talked extensively about the investigation, or if they'd declared some aspects of the investigation off-limits, the Inspector exploded.

"My son is as innocent as I am, and I don't fear the truth!" he proclaimed. "It would be a lie to say I don't talk to my son about this. That would be ridiculous—"

"I'm not suggesting," Stamboulidis cut in. "All I'm asking is a question to find out—"

But the Inspector had begun his speech and he intended to finish it.

"I talk to my son as a father does," he declared, so enraged he began to stammer. "I am concerned for my son. I make him call me every day because I am . . . I have seen people commit suicide for less than this. My son is very sensitive with respect to this. There is no truth. He is very upset. He's kind of accepted it now as time has gone by. He knows justice has to take its path. He is waiting patiently."

After excusing Inspector Wrynn from the stand and dismissing the grand jurors, Stamboulidis walked to the end of the hall, where he waited for an elevator. Before a car arrived, however, Inspector Wrynn approached

Stamboulidis, a move that the prosecutor considered both highly inappropriate and supremely presumptuous. Yet the Inspector spoke as if they were comrades, explaining that he was about to be promoted to chief but couldn't get his star until the investigation had been settled. Stamboulidis got the distinct sense that Wrynn was trying to elicit a review of his performance on the witness stand. Although taken aback, Stamboulidis was certainly not flustered enough to tip his hand.

"When it's done, it's done," he said curtly. "I'll let the police department know."

"Anything you can do would be appreciated," Wrynn said.

By the time Stamboulidis arrived back in his office, where Armanti was waiting, he was livid. "He's lying," Stamboulidis declared.

AS ADDITIONAL WITNESSES were subpoenaed in the following weeks, their testimony blew gaping holes in Wrynn's account. Sixto Santiago, one of the detectives assigned to investigate John Wrynn, testified that he'd seen Inspector Wrynn march straight into the IAB office in SoHo where Sergeant Matthiessen sat with the file. Santiago repeated his assertion that the Inspector had stayed with Robert Matthiessen for several minutes before storming out, swearing, "There's gonna be trouble!"

But despite Santiago's vivid recollections, Matthiessen, during his hours on the stand, was afflicted with the same selective amnesia that had overcome the Inspector. The same day that Wrynn tore into IAB's special projects office, Dowd, Armanti, and the two fire marshals had all heard Matthiessen say that the Inspector had been rifling though his son's case file. But when he was called before the grand jury eleven months later, Matthiessen's memory seemed hazy. Did Wrynn say anything or make any threats to anyone in the office? Matthiessen just couldn't recall. Did he handle any paperwork or look through any files while he was there? Matthiessen just could not remember. When the Inspector barged into the special projects office, was Matthiessen in the same room with him or in the outer office? Sergeant Matthiessen simply couldn't say. As a matter of fact, Matthiessen testified, he couldn't remember whether his office had been on the third or fourth floor of IAB headquarters, even though he'd worked there for more than a year.

Despite his artless efforts to protect Wrynn—and himself—Matthiessen's testimony still contained damning evidence: He couldn't deny that the Inspector had had the nerve to burst into the office where his son's case was being investigated, as if it were his birthright. Matthiessen also managed to acknowledge that he was as stunned as everyone else to see the Inspector there and admitted to being too frightened to stand up to the guy. That made two witnesses, Matthiessen and Santiago, who placed Wrynn inside the special projects office where the case file on John was located. And it gave the prosecutors a solid foundation upon which to build a perjury case against the Inspector.

After the lunch break, Stamboulidis asked the members of the grand jury whether they had any questions they'd like him to pose to Matthiessen. Their reaction didn't bode well for Wrynn and his defenders.

"James Wrynn, he's the father of John Wrynn," said one juror. "Whether the father was involved or he wasn't, he's not supposed to be in that investigation because that's his son. So that's why I'm saying, Why should he be in the room? *Why?*"

Afterward, Matthiessen made a less-than-triumphant return to the stand. Every time Stamboulidis pushed him for details, he brandished an *I don't recall* or *I just don't remember,* using these dull shields to deflect the questions. Matthiessen's aversion to specifics grew so tedious and implausible that, ultimately, Stamboulidis did a one-eighty, throwing out the broadest possible question: Had Matthiessen ever seen anyone at IAB do anything to undermine the investigation into John Wrynn or withhold information from the other agencies involved?

"Counsel," Matthiessen replied, "we always made a bona fide attempt in our endeavors with the Detective Bureau, the marshal's office, and your office as well. I know of— I will tell you I don't know of any intention, it was done deliberately, intentionally, not to withhold information. It doesn't make sense."

BY THE TIME of the Inspector's performance before the grand jury, more than twenty-seven months had passed since Lieutenant Williams's death. It was obvious to most informed observers that Jack Ferranti, his brother, Mario, and Tocco had set the blaze. In fact, two months before the Inspector took the stand, Dowd had even located one of Tocco's neighborhood friends, someone willing to testify that the Torch had come to his house the night of Lieutenant Williams's death and admitted to setting the fire. But the witness, Vincent Marziano, was a heroin addict, and while his story about Tocco was plausible, his memory was chemically challenged—he remembered four different addresses where he'd been

living during the time in question, yet he couldn't verify where he was
when he'd spoken to Tocco.

The physical evidence from the fire was giving the investigators
heartaches, too. The FBI lab in Quantico had determined that a space
heater found in the rubble of the store could not have been the cause,
blowing a hole in the Ferrantis' contention that the blaze had been accidental. But when Dowd went to the police storage facility to retrieve other
crucial evidence—the floor tiles taken from near the fire's origin—they
were gone. Although the Williams case had been considered a homicide
from its earliest stages, a fire marshal had mistakenly listed the tiles as
evidence in a simple arson case—which meant the NYPD had to save
them for only a year. Conveniently, they'd been thrown into the garbage at
the evidence warehouse.

With the grand jury sputtering along, it was nearly impossible for
Armanti to convince the fire marshals—or himself—to wait patiently for
the criminal justice system to run its course. The fire marshals, in fact,
were threatening to deal with the dirty truth their own way, by taking their
files to the press and forcing the NYPD to stop protecting the Wrynns.

Armanti was tempted to help them drop their bomb. But after watching
the public flogging of the NYPD for months, he figured that the new
administration deserved at least a chance to correct the mistakes of its
predecessors. And Dowd warned them that if the whole case went public,
it would make it nearly impossible to lock up the Ferrantis. Before
Armanti went ballistic, he wanted to be able to say he'd at least tried all
the proper department channels. If the new regime turned its back on
him too, well, he would be sure to take names.

But from Armanti's point of view, IAB just kept outdoing itself. Filing an official corruption complaint against the Wrynns gave him a new
perspective on just how obtuse Internal Affairs could be. As Armanti
described how he'd used a surveillance van to make videotapes of people
outside Sebastian's, the lieutenant writing up the report interrupted. "Did
you have authorization to take that van?" he asked.

"You're fucking kidding me, right," Armanti said, flashing his serial-
killer look. "You think I stole the fucking van?"

"It's just a question," the lieutenant replied.

"Well, is it an appropriate question?" Armanti shot back.

By the end of June 1994, Armanti's friend Tommy used his contacts to
get word to Walter Mack, the civilian in charge of IAB, who called

Armanti into his office and promised to put his best men on the case. But Armanti trusted no one. He knew the IAB detectives would work a ten-to-six shift, so he called Mack's secretary at nine A.M., posing as someone with information to pass on. Armanti asked who was assigned to the team, and nearly lost what was left of his sanity when the secretary read back the names of three supervisors who had been involved in the Wrynn case—and had done their best to undermine Armanti.

"Tell your boss if he's gonna screw with me, he's gonna read about it in the papers!" Armanti yelled before he slammed the receiver down.

Later that day, at the NYPD shooting range, two IAB commanders sped up in a department car, sirens blaring and lights flashing. Commissioner Mack wanted to speak to Armanti. So the detective prepared himself for more bureaucratic back stabbing. Mack, however, promised he'd reassign the case to detectives with no conflict of interest. Again, Armanti tried his best to believe.

The longer the case dragged on, the more Armanti sensed that the Wrynns were no longer the target of IAB's investigation: *He* was the man Internal Affairs was gunning for. IAB continued leaving messages for Armanti in various police precincts, basically making in-house public announcements that Armanti was in trouble and being hunted down. Then Internal Affairs detectives called Detective Dowd, telling him, "You gotta talk to us. Your friend Armanti, who the fuck does he think he is?"

With Mack providing little help and the frontline IAB detectives intent on doing the opposite, Armanti hunted desperately for allies. To this end, his best friend, Tommy Dades, a detective specializing in organized crime, introduced him to Captain William Plackenmeyer, a highly respected commander who oversaw five detective squads in South Brooklyn. Plackenmeyer, a former undercover, realized the gravity of the situation. He asked Armanti to meet him and another senior officer in the back room of a bar in Bay Ridge, Brooklyn. The supervisors were astounded as Armanti told them how he'd been burnt on the set, how Internal Affairs had protected John Wrynn, and how Armanti had feared for his life.

Plackenmeyer's companion was especially alarmed. "Son," he said, "if I were you, I wouldn't leave the house without a bulletproof vest and a sawed-off shotgun."

Plackenmeyer then agreed to ask for help from a friend who was one of the NYPD's most powerful chiefs. (Plackenmeyer declined to identify his high-ranking ally, but Armanti later learned that it was First Deputy Commissioner John Timoney, number two in the department.) Plackenmeyer asked his friend to ensure that the Wrynns were dealt with immediately. During Plackenmeyer's meeting with his powerful friend, Commissioner Bratton's chief strategist and closest confidant, Jack Maple, stopped to listen in for ten minutes or so. Then Maple walked out, grousing that cases involving the feds can take forever.

This response left Plackenmeyer mystified, because it ignored the fact that the NYPD had left James Wrynn in a sensitive and powerful position and was allowing his allies to harass Armanti. Timoney promised Plackenmeyer he'd alert the police commissioner, but if the meeting ever led to any action against the Wrynns, Plackenmeyer never heard about it.

At the same time, Armanti was starting to worry about just how much he could trust his relationships with the federal investigators. In Throgs Neck, he and Peil had developed a close but stormy relationship, socializing with Dowd and the fire marshals and occasionally going out alone.

But Armanti began to worry that Peil might be concealing things about the case. Federal court rules require that prosecutors assemble witness lists—known as 6E lists—naming people who are privy to the confidential details of an investigation. But on the grounds that the undercover might be called as a witness, Stamboulidis removed Armanti from the 6E list. Armanti tried to fight the decision; the thought of exclusion was unbearable. Peil and Stamboulidis had always appeared sincere, determined, and on the level when Armanti was in the room. But how could he trust the feds? Why was it taking them so long to bring criminal charges against the Wrynns? he wondered. What could they possibly be discussing at all those meetings he was no longer invited to? Was it possible that the FBI and the U.S. Attorney's Office had cut some secret deal with the department and had joined IAB's twisted plan to treat him like a target?

At some point, when he stopped by the U.S. Attorney's Office to talk to Peil and Stamboulidis, Armanti's suspicions got the best of him. When Stamboulidis and Peil stepped out temporarily to meet with other prosecutors, Armanti could not resist peering into the canvas bag Peil used to tote her papers. He pulled out the case folder, strode down the hall to the nearest copying machine, and copied the entire file—more than 150 pages of documents and personal notes—before discreetly tucking it back into her bag.

Peil and Stamboulidis returned a while later and assured Armanti that, in time, things would work out.

"Just try to be patient," Peil told him.

"I'm trying," he replied.

By December 1995, Mack tried to placate Armanti's complaints by calling him to a meeting in police headquarters. On his way, Armanti stopped to chat with friends in the narcotics office on the eleventh floor, where he strapped on his hidden tape recorder and a microphone. A few minutes into their conversation, Armanti began to wonder whether Mack knew he was being taped.

Mack sure spoke cautiously enough, thanking Armanti for his courageous work on the case, then apologizing for the "missteps" his investigators had made for months. He was so smooth that Armanti couldn't take it.

"I have one more question," he blurted out. "Is Inspector Wrynn a subject of this investigation?"

"You'd have to ask George Stamboulidis about that," Mack said. "He'd know better than me. But I would think the answer to that is yes—"

"So why is he still in Internal Affairs?" Armanti interrupted. He had seen IAB suspend cops and ruin their careers for something as minor as taking care of a parking ticket. "When they're going to go after people, they get moved. I've seen it happen to detectives I've worked with. Just upon allegations they've been removed."

"He's an individual whose conduct is being investigated," Mack replied, adding that he did not believe the Inspector would be indicted. "My own feeling is, having dealt with the Inspector . . . I wanted to leave it to the grand jury."

Armanti walked out of the office and clicked off his tape recorder.

Several months later, in a conversation with Stamboulidis, Mack offered a slightly different explanation. "It didn't seem fair that one mistake should destroy a great, thirty-year career," he said. "He did what any father would do."

16

"GUYS WHO'LL TAKE CARE OF THIS"

MARCH 7, 1995

LIFTING WEIGHTS IN his basement, Armanti heard his phone ringing.
He ran upstairs to get it, but before he could manage a civil greeting, an
unfamiliar voice filled his ear.

"Vinnie! What's up?" the caller inquired, in a strangely animated tone
that instantly gave Armanti a chill. He had run upstairs sweaty and huff-
ing, but the shock of the voice completely knocked the wind out of him.

"Who is this?" Armanti demanded.

"Vinnie! Vinnie Blue Eyes, what's up?" the caller said.

Armanti's heart jumped. Vinnie had always been his nickname, and
he'd used it during a dozen undercover operations. But only one small
group of people had ever referred to him as Vinnie Blue Eyes—the
Ferrantis and their cronies in Throgs Neck.

They were calling to say they knew where he lived.

"This ain't Vinnie," Armanti said.

"Vin-nie, cut it out," the voice said, amused with its own power.
"How's it going?"

"There ain't no Vinnie here," Armanti insisted, trying to sound irritated rather than alarmed. And failing, he knew.

"Vinnie, I know it's you" the caller said, then the phone was slammed
down fast, as if to say "Joke's over!"

Armanti held on to the receiver, trying not to panic. But it was obvious:
They knew where he lived. The people who'd sliced up Bruce Bailey, the
twisted, demented sadists who used Dobermans and baseball bats to bat-
ter their tenants, and bullets to settle their debts. The men whose tainted
heroin had silenced Eric Mergenthal, who'd shot the mortgage broker in

the neck, and who'd killed Lieutenant Williams. They knew where he lived. They were coming. And Armanti had no doubt that someone from the police department had helped them obtain his home phone number and address.

Armanti hung up the phone, walked to the bottle of Zinfandel on the counter, and poured himself a glass. Then the phone rang again. This time it was a woman with an Hispanic accent.

"Hello, Vinnie," she said.

"Who's this?" he shot back.

"Hey, Vinnie Blue Eyes!" she said playfully.

"No," he said firmly. "There's no Vinnie that lives here."

"I know that's you," she said, then abruptly hung up.

Armanti ran to his closet, threw on a bulletproof vest, and grabbed a shotgun. Moving from window to window, peering out to see who might be waiting to send him to purgatory. Finally, he made his way to the phone and, finger trembling, dialed Cindy Peil's home number.

"They know where I fucking live!" he shouted.

Peil told Armanti to leave now, to get out of there fast and spend the night somewhere else. He stayed with friends for a few days. The NYPD ordered a car from Armanti's local precinct to swing by his home once an hour. When the FBI traced the calls, agents found that they'd been made from two pay phones, one in the Bronx, the other in Queens, just over the Throgs Neck Bridge.

In the months since Throgs Neck, he had been struggling, unsuccessfully, to restore some sense of equilibrium to the existence he only half-remembered as his own. Work had become a daily bout of agita, even beyond the ugly business with the higher-ups. The narcotics commanders, ostensibly concerned that Armanti's identity might be compromised, had clipped his wings and assigned him to a desk until further notice. But there was something else that nagged at him, too. The police department had announced two different sets of promotions since Armanti had returned from the set. And even though people in the chief's office had told him that he was at the top of the list sent to the police commissioner—number one on the list, to be precise—he had been passed over each time, without explanation.

There was no one who could share his disappointment. At home, Judy's absence was inescapable, but Armanti tried to fill the emptiness by force of will. He'd cook elaborate dinners, open a nice bottle of wine, put on dress slacks, as if the rituals themselves might mask the fact that Judith and the job had been all he had.

Every time Armanti began regaining his stride, another aftershock from Throgs Neck would roll in, leaving him emptier, just a little further away from caring about what might happen next. Internal Affairs detectives continued to taunt him any way they could. A neighbor had stopped Armanti on the street one day in late 1994 and told him that two guys who looked like cops had pulled up to his house a moment after he'd left that morning. They had spent about five minutes sneaking around his backyard.

During the eight years he'd worked as an undercover, Armanti had always tried to keep his routines from growing too predictable, to confuse anyone who might be watching. He habitually took alternate routes to and from work, and occasionally parked his car a few blocks from home so he could sneak up on someone who might be staking out his house. After Throgs Neck, he began placing a piece of clear tape across the gap between the door and its frame when he left, so he would know whether anyone had gotten inside. When friends visited, Armanti insisted on walking them out to their cars, even though it was a low-crime neighborhood and many of his guests were fellow cops. He wanted the chance to case the neighborhood, to see if someone was lurking, waiting to catch him when he was alone. Armanti hadn't been in the greatest condition. Too much had been happening.

Since two crucial witnesses in the arson case had received crude death threats, Armanti's anxiety had grown into something resembling full-blown paranoia. Two former clerks in Ferranti's burned-out store, Gina Esposito and her daughter Lisa Ziccardi, had both told investigators that in the months before the fatal fire, they'd heard Jack say that business was so bad he might burn the building down and cash in on the insurance money. Their testimonies could be devastating if ever uttered in court—but they couldn't hurt Jack if they were too frightened, or too dead, to testify. And that seemed to be the plan. On the morning Esposito was scheduled to appear before the grand jury she suffered the kind of gaudy, violent misfortune that always seemed to haunt those who troubled the Ferrantis. When Dowd and Bobby Thomson appeared at Esposito's home to escort her to court, they were greeted by a terrifying sight in the driveway. A charred, smoldering delivery truck that belonged to Esposito's boyfriend had been firebombed during the night. Dowd and Thomson raced to the stoop and pounded on the door. When no one answered, they forced their way inside, and found Esposito livid.

"I'm not going!" she screamed. "You can't protect me!"

"Calm down," Dowd said, attempting to soothe her but knowing he had little hope of succeeding. "We'll look out for you."

"I'm not going to do it!" she raged. "I told you they were going to find me! I told you! You can't protect me."

Within an hour, the captain at Dowd's detective squad in Queens had called Armanti. The powers that be had determined it expedient for him to move out of his house for a while, so once again he was forced to stay with friends.

The firebombing terrified the witnesses, but it also infuriated Dowd, Armanti, and the fire marshals. Bit by bit, month after month, they had been stitching together scraps of evidence about the fire. They weren't about to let the Ferrantis' pyrotechnics derail them. Then Esposito and her daughter disappeared, refusing to testify under any circumstance. It took weeks and the threat of an arrest for Dowd to finally convince them to appear before the grand jury. But when they finally came through, their testimony provided two of the last major pieces of evidence.

ON MARCH 2, 1994, after all the struggles, slipups, and delays, the grand jury had handed down an indictment against Jack, Mario, and Tocco, charging them with arson, homicide, conspiracy, and other crimes. After reviewing the case file and holding meeting after meeting, prosecutors, the police, and the fire marshals decided to time the arrests as close as possible to February 24, 1995, the third anniversary of Lieutenant Williams's death.

Ed Dowd was relieved to have the glorious opportunity to haul in Jack, who had recently relocated to Manhattan, more specifically to the decidedly un–Throgs Neck neighborhood of Chelsea. It had become a running joke among the investigators that a lowbrow like Jack Ferranti—a gangster slumlord with a well-established predilection for streetwalkers—had somehow connived a wealthy lawyer into marrying him. But in early 1994, he had moved into her apartment on West Twenty-fifth Street, where he'd wooed her by cooking risotto, collecting antiques, and renovating the apartment with a flair and attention to detail that would have stunned the tenants in the hovels he owned.

Jack's wife, Miriam Breyer, even saw a charming side of the ol' wiseguy with the bushy sideburns. Breyer had difficulty walking because she had suffered a devastating car accident a few years before she'd met Jack, but he encouraged her to work hard to rehabilitate herself. When they traveled to Turkey with Breyer's parents, Jack lugged her bags around the country for two weeks, and when Miriam was unable to walk up the steep steps of a coliseum on their tour, Jack threw her over his shoulder and carried her. Despite his own Italian Catholic upbringing, Jack was a mensch about Breyer's Jewish customs—he agreed to a kosher wedding and a Jewish ceremony, and he even insisted on fasting each Yom Kippur.

Dowd wasn't about to be lulled by the new, domesticated, downtown Jack Ferranti. When the day came for the arrest, the detective arranged to be accompanied by an Emergency Service Unit squad, one of the NYPD's highly trained, heavily armed SWAT teams, which are usually deployed only for hostage situations or barricaded gunmen. They scouted the neighborhood and decided that the rooftop of a nearby convent would be a convenient place to station the police sharpshooters. The plan was to take Jack by surprise, quickly and quietly, but the ESU unit also came prepared with overwhelming force in case Jack tried to shoot his way out or escape. But as Dowd drove toward Ferranti's home on the morning the arrest was to take place, a news report blaring out of the radio nearly caused him to career off the road. One of the city's all-news stations had picked up a story from *New York Newsday,* which had reported that morning that police were about to make arrests in the Lieutenant Williams case. Once again, confidential information had been leaked at an exceedingly delicate moment. This situation could easily veer disastrously out of control. If Ferranti happened to flick on the radio that morning, the newscaster might as well have been announcing *"Load up that forty-five, Jack, they're coming to get you."*

When Dowd arrived at the staging area, around the corner from Ferranti's apartment, he took his place behind a team of emergency-service cops equipped with riot helmets, shields, and bulletproof vests. It was a frigid morning, and as they stood, awaiting the go-ahead, their breath steamed out from under their plastic visors—an army of blue shrouded in a cloud of mist. With each long moment of delay, Dowd's anxiety shot up higher. He pictured Jack turning on his radio, then loading a shotgun. Finally, just before 6:00 A.M., they made a phone call to the apartment, ordering Jack downstairs. Miriam answered the phone and said she'd unlock the door and let the officers in. When a minute passed and she hadn't yet appeared, the commander gave the signal, and the ESU team bashed in the street door.

Jack's wife had been making her way down from their apartment on the top floor of the five-story brownstone. She was screaming for them to stop banging on the door when it flew off its hinges.

"What did you do to my door!" she screamed.

"Shut the fuck up!" Dowd replied as an ESU officer took her arm and continued charging upstairs. Jack, who apparently didn't listen to radio news in the morning, was still getting dressed when they burst into his bedroom. Wearing only boxer shorts and a white, wife-beater T-shirt, he had nowhere to hide a weapon. When he saw the shields, the helmets, and three rifles and Dowd's .38 all pointing at him, he threw his hands into the air.

"What the fuck!" he screamed, his face so ashen he looked like a ghost.

"Shut up!" Dowd screamed. "Don't say a fucking thing!"

"This is harassment," shouted Jack's wife, the consummate lawyer even under duress.

"He's under arrest for the murder of Fireman Tommy Williams," Dowd shot back. He and Thomson wrenched the cuffs on Ferranti's wrists and dragged him into the cold in his underwear.

Mario Ferranti and Tocco were also picked up at their homes. Oddly, both were walking menacing dogs when they were approached by the arrest teams.

The media were tickled by the timing of the arrests. The third-anniversary stories in all the papers were full of cheers from firefighters who remembered the day Lieutenant Williams had lost his life, but there was also praise for the tenacity of Dowd and the fire marshals. Patricia Williams, Lieutenant Williams's widow, appeared on TV and in the papers, thanking the police for getting the Ferrantis. She predicted that they would be convicted of killing her husband; her grieving family's ordeal was almost over. Such was the relief within the fire department that the media were content to present the case as a neat, gift-wrapped conviction just waiting to be presented to the Williams family by a jury.

But within the legal system, the morning after the arrests brought cold, unsparing skepticism. Viewed through the discerning eye of a lawyer or judge, the evidence against Tocco and the Ferrantis was more like a grab bag of odds and ends than a cohesive criminal prosecution. No one who had been involved in setting or planning the fire would testify. Although Tocco had been identified at the scene by Michelle and Shelly Anthony, eyewitness IDs are notoriously unreliable evidence, liable to self-destruct under cross-examination. Even if the jurors could be convinced that Tocco had lit the fire, his link to Jack was spun together with a tenuous thread: the testimony of Marziano, the career criminal and heroin addict who couldn't remember where he'd lived.

The prosecution couldn't even definitively prove that the fire had been arson. In most cases, fire investigators declare an arson only after a process of elimination that rules out any possible accidental causes. The fire at Ferranti's store had plenty of suspicious signs: Jack's statements about cashing in on the insurance; burn patterns near the origin of the fire that appeared to indicate the presence of gasoline or some other accelerant; the fact that the blaze had begun in the locked basement with no sign of forced entry. But the only ironclad proof of arson would have been traces of gasoline or kerosene spotted by the laboratory on the recovered floor tiles—and those tiles had been mistakenly thrown away by the clerks in the police storage facility before they could be tested.

In the hours after Lieutenant Williams died, the fire marshals had also neglected to perform tests to determine whether an electrical problem or other accident might have sparked the fire. This gaffe would certainly be exploited by the Ferrantis' lawyers. One of the fire marshals had even said early on that he thought a portable electric heater might have started the blaze, a statement that would come back to haunt the prosecution.

Wobbly though the case might be, Dowd and Armanti relished the thought of Jack and Mario finally housed in the sort of lodging suited to their depraved criminal hearts. But to Armanti's surprise, he felt more solemn than triumphant. He kept flashing back to that picture of Lieutenant Williams and his family, hoping that the trial might finally give them some peace. Dowd, on the other hand, was angry that IAB's meddling had prevented them from getting what they needed to nail the Ferrantis cold. He was beyond disgusted that neither of the Wrynns had yet been charged. "We got ours," Dowd said to one of the fire marshals the day of the arrests. "Now let's see if those fucks in IAB get theirs."

In any case, their moment of triumph lasted little more than a moment. Jack was held on $1 million bail. It was an amount he could conceivably raise, but when his lawyers appealed it, they won. Incredibly, a federal judge ruled that Jack should be released immediately, without posting any bond, saying that the evidence was too flimsy to prove that he was a danger to anyone. "Are you sure you have a prosecutable case here, Counselor?" the judge asked the U.S. attorney.

The prosecutors appealed the decision, so Jack and Mario remained behind bars, at least temporarily. But the judge's ruling was an ominous sign. With the case already teetering, Armanti and the others worried almost constantly about the Ferrantis attempting to pick off another witness. But as the legal battles intensified, Armanti's struggle within the NYPD grew more torturous. Just four days after Jack and Mario were arrested, Armanti's pager went off, displaying Walter Mack's private office telephone number, followed by a 911. Armanti raced home to get his recording equipment. But by the time he got back to Mack, it was too late: Mack's private line was answered by someone with a voice Armanti didn't recognize. When he asked to speak to the commissioner, there was an awkward pause, then a cryptic reply: "Commissioner Mack doesn't work here anymore, Detective."

Armanti watched the TV reports and scoured the newspapers the next day, trying to find out why Mack had been so abruptly fired. But the department offered only empty clichés and double-talk. The timing of the call to his pager left Armanti with the nagging suspicion that his case was a major factor. Mack's naïveté had at times made Armanti wonder how the hell the guy had ever made it through law school, but he had come to believe that the man was honest. With Mack out of the way, Armanti was once again at the mercy of Wrynn and his cronies in IAB.

ABOUT TWO WEEKS after the intimidating phone calls to Armanti's home he answered his cell phone and heard his sister-in-law crying hysterically. Armanti's ten-year-old nephew, Nicky, had been walking down the street with a friend when a strange car, a Pontiac, pulled up alongside him. A blonde in the passenger side leaned out the window, asking him to go for a ride. When Nicky refused, the car followed alongside him and the blonde held out a ten-dollar bill, saying, "Come on, we'll take you to get some ice cream."

Nicky looked at the ten-dollar bill, then stared at the face of the person holding it. It was a man, wearing a blond wig.

"Run!" he screamed, and his friend dashed off.

Nicky bolted in the opposite direction, and the car chased him. He clambered over a fence and sprinted home, with the car still in pursuit. He burst through the door of his house, crying for his mother, terrified.

Armanti ordered his sister-in-law to phone 911 immediately, then sped to her house. He lived less than a mile from his brother and his family, and he flew along the highway, feeling alternately infuriated and crushed. He had always been meticulous about insulating his family from the mayhem of undercover work: never discussing the details of his relatives' lives with other cops, never telling his family about his exploits. None of his relatives knew the first thing about his battle with the Wrynns, and Armanti felt overwhelmed with guilt at the thought that his brother's family—his own nephew—was somehow being dragged into the morass.

For two years, Armanti had endured all the shadow play, just waiting for the opportunity to beat IAB at its own game. But the sound of terror in his sister-in-law's voice and his nephew's bawling in the background were unbearable. He wanted it over. He had chosen the life of a police officer; he had taken the oath. If it cost him his life, he could accept it, as long as he went down swinging. But Armanti would not see his family brought down with him, and he would not stand by and do nothing.

Fuck the job! Armanti thought as he pulled into his brother's driveway. *Fuck being a cop! I've got to get these people!*

Armanti's sister-in law was still in tears when he arrived, and his brother, Gino, was upstairs trying to calm Nicky. The police had taken a report; they'd also found that Nicky's friend Jimmy had escaped.

"Are you listed in the phone book?" Armanti asked his sister-in-law.

"Yeah," she said. "Why?"

"This is about me," he said.

When Gino walked downstairs, Vinnie braced himself for a nuclear tirade. No one in the Armanti family had exactly celebrated when Vinnie had entered the NYPD (a few relatives had had their brushes with the cops in the past), but Gino had been particularly mystified. Six years older than Vinnie, he worked as a foreman on the docks in New Jersey. For years he had pressured Vinnie to come work with him. The job was rough, and the union he dealt with was mob-infested and notoriously violent, but if you worked hard and kept your mouth shut, at least it paid enough to support a family. As a police officer, you put your life at risk, and for what? Four hundred a week after taxes?

Now, with his son threatened, there was no telling what Gino might do. Vinnie threw himself at his brother's mercy, offering every apology he could think of, nearly bursting into tears. He told Gino about being burnt on the set, IAB's maneuvering, the Wrynns, and the wiseguys. He begged for forgiveness. He promised to do anything—anything—to protect Nicky in the future.

Vinnie was so desperate that his brother looked shocked.

"Worry about yourself," Gino said. "I'll take care of the kids."

Vinnie studied Gino's face to see whether he was angry. Instead, he saw concern there.

"You know, I can help you," Gino said. During twenty years of dealing with a union full of arm twisters and leg breakers, Gino had never had the first bit of trouble with the law; but he knew people. And for something this dire, he was willing to call in a few favors, use street justice to settle a score that the criminal justice system seemed unwilling to handle.

"I could make a few phone calls," Gino said. "I know guys who'll take care of this."

Armanti closed his eyes and shook his head. He could see it now: he and his brother locked up, while Wrynn and his father remained untouched.

"Please, just leave it," Armanti said. "I'm gonna handle this myself."

Then Armanti ran to his car and sped off, tires screeching.

17

"A TEST OF THE DEPARTMENT'S WILL"

MAY 1995

A CHANCE FOR redemption can appear at the most unexpected times and in the most unimaginable ways. For the Wrynns, such an opportunity presented itself on May 15, 1995, in the unlikely form of a pair of naked buttocks sliding down a beer-slicked banister.

On that storied day, more than ten thousand law enforcement officers from across the country had gathered in Washington, D.C., for a weekend memorial service in honor of the 125 cops slain that year in the line of duty. But a noxious combination of testosterone, alcohol, grief, and sophomoric bad judgment turned the solemn weekend into the frat party from hell. Drunken police officers marauded through hotels, spraying beer, trashing rooms, and verbally abusing those who just didn't understand that there was a party going on. The New York cops—being New Yorkers—were unabashed when it came to revelry. Reports circulated of female hotel guests being groped and fondled as they navigated through hallways. Hotel guests complained of inebriated officers firing off weapons during the mayhem. A fire alarm was pulled at the Hyatt Regency Hotel, and a fire extinguisher was sprayed into the ventilation system, forcing hundreds to flee the building through clouds of powdery chemicals. It was the kind of wreckage that might have been left behind by touring rock stars.

Reporters soon caught wind of the lollapalooza, and the papers ran stories about hotel guests terrified by the officers' pagan excess. There were pictures, too—photos, in fact, of the variety to set tabloid editors' hearts a-twitter: hordes of sweaty, glassy-eyed, drunken officers caught in an assortment of poses hardly befitting their stations. The uproar was amplified by the fact that four years earlier, the navy had been shaken by the

Tailhook scandal, an incident in which scores of women were assaulted by drunken cadets and which was followed by the resignation of the secretary of the navy. Now headlines shrieked from newsstands: ANIMAL HOUSE!, NYPD LEWD! The word *bacchanal* could not have appeared more often if the gathering had been hosted by Dionysus. Editorial writers reacted like schoolmarms, demanding decisive action.

Once the brouhaha had spiraled into a major public relations disaster, the mayor and Police Commissioner William Bratton swung into action, promising swift retribution. By May 19, Giuliani himself had scheduled a press conference at police headquarters to reassure the usually unshockable populace that the trespasses of the guilty would not be tolerated. Addressing the public, Giuliani described the officers' conduct as "a tragedy" for the vast majority of well-behaved cops and vowed that nothing like it would ever happen again.

Since taking office in the wake of the Mollen Commission scandals, Giuliani and Bratton had moved frantically to divert the city's attention from corruption in the headlines to crime-fighting in the streets. Nearly nineteen months earlier, the Mollen Commission had advised the city to establish an independent monitor's office to oversee Internal Affairs. But Giuliani, who previously embraced this concept, had since changed his mind. Rather than surrender control of IAB to some independent agency, the mayor hoped to create a review board run by his own handpicked appointees. But, to gain approval for this, Giuliani had to convince the world that under his watch, police misconduct would not be tolerated.

Police Commissioner Bratton, who normally sweet-talked the press, appeared tense and uncomfortable as he stood behind the mayor, awaiting his turn at the bank of microphones. To Bratton, the scandal was more than just a disgrace; it was an ill-timed distraction. The new commissioner had inherited a department so obsessed with procedures and protocol that fighting crime didn't seem like a top priority. Immediately, he had begun freeing up officers by dismantling many anticorruption safeguards, shaking up the management structure, instituting new and aggressive crime-prevention strategies, and devising computer-generated maps to carefully track crime patterns. Crime had begun to fall during the final year of the Dinkins administration, but the plummet was now accelerating, and Bratton was intent on letting the world know about the progress the NYPD had made on his watch. His reputation was skyrocketing. A fawning *New Yorker* profile had appeared, entitled "The CEO Commissioner," and like most CEOs, Bratton considered center stage to be his own personal playground. When the heat from the Washington imbroglio flared up, he reacted like a diva elbowed from the spotlight. When he sensed the depth of the outrage over the Washington incident, he became the megaphone for the public's indignation, blasting the marauding cops in Washington as "nitwits" and "morons," and ordering Internal Affairs to mount a massive investigation.

At the press conference, Bratton's new chief of Internal Affairs, Patty Kelleher, looked appropriately chastened as he watched the commissioner and the mayor rail on. Kelleher's rise through the ranks had been fueled by his amiability, his ferocious work ethic, and his ability to not only intuit his bosses' moods but also anticipate exactly what they hoped to hear. With Giuliani and Bratton seething for the cameras, Kelleher— who was himself a familiar face at off-duty parties—transformed himself into an intolerant prefect of temperance. The incident was more than just an embarrassment, Kelleher said with a face as straight as an altar boy; it threatened to undermine the moral authority of the police department. Kelleher issued an ultimatum to those cops responsible for the Washington antics: Turn yourselves in now or face worse punishment when we track you down later.

"This is a test of the department's will to take a strong stand on the whole respect issue," Kelleher said. "Not just the abuse of force, but how we treat people on or off duty."

A show of overwhelming force became such a high priority that Kelleher assigned fifty IAB detectives—the most ever put on for a single case—and ordered them to interrogate every single NYPD officer who was known to be in Washington that weekend. Hotel employees, guests, cops from other departments, and anyone else even tangentially involved would also be interviewed. As it happened, this massive show of NYPD muscle was to be marshaled by none other than the man Kelleher himself described as IAB's most capable, experienced, and trusted supervisor: Inspector James P. Wrynn.

NEARLY A YEAR had passed since the Wrynns had finished testifying before the grand jury, but the police department and the prosecutors were still struggling to figure out exactly what to do with them. In early 1994, John Wrynn had been stripped of his gun and placed on modified assignment in the gulag of the property clerk's division. The Inspector was still in Internal Affairs, waiting to see whether the U.S. Attorney's Office would drop the case against him and clear the way for his promotion. The delay had been torturous, but it contained at least a speck of hope: Every morning the Wrynns awoke to find themselves on duty and unindicted was another day they could search for some way out of their serious troubles.

Despite the alternately panicked and remorseful conversations that John had had with his father, he still maintained an unflappable front with his friends. Shortly after he was placed on modified assignment, he had again started dating Linda Nelson, the assistant district attorney whom he had asked for information about drug raids on his friends' apartments. Nelson was astonished to find that John still enjoyed playing the outlaw. Their dates often involved strange brushes with the kind of seedy-looking street characters that she thought Wrynn might, by now, have known to avoid. At a New Year's Eve party he introduced Nelson to someone he said had been indicted for murder. On another occasion, the couple had a chance meeting with a shabby character called Tommy Tocco, whom Wrynn described as a bookie and old friend.

Nelson tried to get John to talk about his troubles with the department, but he laughed the whole thing off. It was as if it was just a trivial annoyance that he'd put to rest with his clever decision to take the Fifth. Nelson wanted to get past John's bravado. She told him that she'd heard he was under investigation for the serious, possibly criminal offense of leaking information to criminals.

"You don't believe that, do you?" Wrynn said.

John assured her that his problems would soon be over, bragging that his father's testimony before the grand jury had gone so well that the old man expected to be promoted to chief. John even went as far as to tell Nelson that the Inspector felt partly to blame for the whole mess because he'd forced his son to grow up in a community as overrun with troubled characters as Throgs Neck. "He wishes he had gotten me out of that neighborhood a lot sooner," John said.

Although John may have been expecting news of his father's promotion, the Inspector's prized career had been languishing in a kind of limbo. After the Inspector's grand jury appearance, weeks had passed, then months, with no word on whether he'd finally get the coveted chief's star he was intent on adding to his list of career accomplishments. Every day, the Inspector faced the possibility that the press would learn of the allegations that he'd torn through the files of his son's investigation. Now, however, with the entire city watching, he'd unexpectedly been given the opportunity to ride to the rescue. And this time, instead of merely saving IAB, he had the chance to burnish and enhance the reputation of the man who could do the most to help him: Mayor Giuliani.

Unfortunately for the Inspector, his big opportunity began with a pratfall. The NYPD delayed a few days before responding to the D.C. incident, so by the time Jim Wrynn traveled to Washington to begin the investigation, the convention had ended, the hotel guests were long gone, and the rowdy police officers had slunk back out of town. The Inspector faced a tough task, as neither the mayor's howling nor the media's braying had done anything to stir the throbbing consciences of the four hundred New York officers who had painted Washington scarlet that weekend: Not a single officer had come forward to offer information about the worst offenders. Even the Washington police seemed eager to forget the entire affair. After the Hyatt Regency had been evacuated at three A.M. (with people stampeding out of the hotel in terror), some Washington officers had been seen chatting with a few of the inebriated cops who'd caused the uproar. The D.C. cops, in fact, had shrugged off the scenic display as hotel guests stood outside—some being tended by nurses—while police officers continued flashing their bare buttocks out the hotel's windows. In the days that followed, D.C. police union leaders ridiculed the NYPD for treating the ruckus like the biggest crime since the kidnapping of the Lindbergh baby. "All these allegations of mooning," the president of the Washington union scoffed. "Nurses should be familiar with anatomy. Nurses have witnessed a butt before."

So Wrynn found little support in the nation's capital, and when he returned to NYPD headquarters empty-handed five days after the memorial, his superiors were not the least bit amused. With Giuliani inconsolable and Bratton unable to appear anything but ineffectual, Wrynn was ordered to return to Washington with more IAB supervisors and a battalion of investigators. Every hour, it seemed, the media glare grew more blinding. Giuliani attempted to shame the truth out of officers, telling them they'd betrayed an oath they'd taken before God and man. Then, as his fury escalated, he tried threatening, swearing that they'd be caught anyway, so they'd make it easier on everyone if they just surrendered now. He also served notice to those cops who had witnessed the debauchery in Washington without actually taking part in it: If they were caught covering up for their colleagues, they'd be fired, too. Clearly, His Honor was not in a mood to be placated.

In the early days of the investigation, Bratton mirrored the mayor's bravado and assured the public that the rogue officers would be apprehended, fired, and perhaps prosecuted. But progress continued to be almost infinitesimal. As the days passed, it became more and more obvious that Inspector Wrynn and the IAB were struggling mightily to deliver enough evidence to back up even a portion of the fiery rhetoric. IAB approached hundreds of the NYPD officers who'd been in Washington, but the responses to their interrogations amounted to little more than blank looks, shrugged shoulders, and *I saw nothing*s. It took nearly three weeks for IAB, unlucky on all fronts, to compel the Hyatt to turn over its guest list so civilian witnesses could be interviewed. By then, the newspapers had already talked to scores of angry guests, who ridiculed the NYPD for failing to get their stories of trauma, mayhem, and mooning.

Sensing IAB's difficulties, Bratton started to prepare the public for the likelihood that few cops would be brought to justice. When reporters pressed him about his inability to break through the Blue Wall of Silence, he lashed out. "You guys keep harping on this," he snapped. "Why don't you get off it? You all have this fixation, reporting on it day after day after day. Nothing is going to change. Wake up and smell the roses." (Bratton couldn't resist adding a personal jab at the press: "I don't see too many [reporters] telling tales on each other," he said.)

But Giuliani wasn't about to let it fade. Nor would he forgo any opportunity to attempt to badger officers into coming forward. When the police academy graduated a new class on May 26, the mayor's commencement address sizzled with vitriol. In a voice that meant business, he chastised the drunken officers, and his words to the NYPD's newest recruits dripped with disdain for the cops who'd witnessed the Washington antics yet remained silent.

"You have to realize that anything that you do can reflect not just on you but on the thirty-eight thousand police officers in this city," Giuliani said. "Your loyalty is to the law; your loyalty is not to any police officers who act illegally or improperly."

AS POLICE OFFICERS and jaded city residents watched to see whether the Blue Wall could withstand the tornado of Rudy's continuing assaults, Ed Dowd and Armanti were staggered to learn of Inspector Wrynn's suddenly heightened importance. Armanti, still living in fear of reprisal from the Ferrantis or their associates, tried to keep the case against the Wrynns alive while preparing to fend off some ferocious attack on his home or one of his family members. But never was he tempted to relent in his efforts to push the U.S. Attorney's Office to finally charge the Inspector with perjury or obstruction of justice. For months, he waited, hoping to pick up a paper and see the Inspector being led away in handcuffs. Stamboulidis, Dowd, and Peil tried to put a damper on his spiraling fantasies, urging him, as they had so many times before, to calm down and be patient. No charges, they continually emphasized, would be filed against either of the Wrynns until after the Ferrantis and Tocco were tried. The authorities simply didn't have the manpower for a battle waged on two complicated fronts. In the meantime, prosecutors said, the Wrynns weren't going anywhere and the FBI could use the extra time to strengthen the cases against them.

But Armanti remained astounded by the hypocrisy of Inspector Wrynn's most recent ascension to the ranks of the powerful.

"Blue Wall of Silence!" Armanti shouted at the television one day during a news report about the mayor and his sanctimonious police commanders pursuing the cops who'd gone on a bender in Washington. "The wall is made of fucking brass!"

Armanti was convinced that someone with serious political juice had come to the aid of the Inspector. Each passing day he sweated the outcome, worrying that Wrynn would triumph by using the investigation to bail out Giuliani and Bratton, and reemerge as a major power in IAB. If that happened, then Armanti would be the only one involved who would have to worry about criminal charges. His anxiety was also exacerbated by the fact that in early 1995, after more than a year working inside, Armanti had finally been allowed to return to the street as an undercover. Leaving the office for the familiar hazards of the set was a huge relief, but everything somehow seemed more menacing now. Before signing on to an undercover case, Armanti vetted his fellow investigators with everything but a frisking, and agreed to work in situations only where he knew and trusted the backup team.

He also decided to change his cast of undercover characters. Armanti's street personas had always been slightly exaggerated versions of himself, so his alter egos—Vincent Penisi, Donald LaForte, Dino Mangelli—usually walked the streets unarmed. To protect themselves they used their mouth and their wit, rather than a gun. After Throgs Neck, Armanti rolled out a new persona, Charlie Scadero, who would go nowhere without his Glock, prominently displayed. Anyone who flashed a weapon that brazenly had to be hard-core, so Armanti had little choice but to raise the stakes. He gave Scadero more attitude than any of his previous characters. To a degree, this heightened the risk of provoking a gunfight with the subjects of his investigation, but after being burnt in Throgs Neck, Armanti thought it would be foolish to head undercover without taking along enough hardware to shoot his way to safety.

"Next time something happens out there," he told Dowd, "it's gonna be a messy one."

Between his undercover cases and his obsession with chasing the Wrynns, Armanti also tried to reconstruct some semblance of a social life. One Saturday in the summer of 1995, Ed Dowd, a saloon owner's son, dropped by to help install a bar in Armanti's living room. As he lay on the living room floor, Dowd noticed a woman's sneaker, which he immediately snatched and used as a prop to razz Armanti.

"Uh-oh," Dowd sang. "Who's the poor girl who left this behind?"

Armanti laughed but volunteered nothing.

"Come on, who is it?" Dowd said, twirling the sneaker like Gypsy Rose Lee.

"Fuck you."

"Who is it?"

"It's nothing."

Dowd was puzzled; he'd never known Vinnie Armanti to be bashful about his conquests.

"What's this about?" Dowd asked.

"It's nothing!" Armanti yelled, loud enough that Dowd understood he wanted the discussion ended.

They spent the rest of the afternoon working on the bar, and most of the evening drinking from it. As Dowd walked to his car that night, Armanti called out from the front porch.

"Hey, Eddie," he said. "You owe me Embers." He was referring to the restaurant where Dowd had promised to treat Armanti if he managed to woo FBI agent Cindy Peil.

"Get the fuck out of here," Dowd said, "It never happened."

Armanti shrugged.

"Get out!" Dowd said. "She wouldn't go out with you if you held a gun to her head."

"I'm not saying anything," Armanti said.

"No, no, no," Dowd said. "Not for some lousy sneaker. You want dinner, you've got to do better than that. Show me a bra. Show me panties. You've got to do more than a sneaker."

Armanti grinned.

"You owe me Embers," he said, and shut the door.

"I don't believe you," Dowd shouted back. "I'm not paying." And he never did.

AS THE WASHINGTON investigation spiraled into a full-scale NYPD inquisition, Armanti couldn't stomach the fact that neither the newspapers, nor the mayor, nor the police commissioner ever made reference to the irony that such a major investigation was led by an Inspector facing possible criminal prosecution. Or that Wrynn had done his best to deepsix the investigation of an officer, his very own son, who socialized with criminals and might well wind up involved in a murder-conspiracy case. If Armanti had fully understood the circumstances, he would also have been outraged by the history of the relationship between Patty Kelleher, Giuliani's new chief of IAB, and James Wrynn.

Less than five years earlier, in the wee hours of a Saturday morning, Kelleher was driving a department car near his home in Orange County, New York, when he swerved off the road and crashed into a tree. When a state trooper found Kelleher, he was so seriously injured that they feared he might die. The state police, realizing that Kelleher was a city cop, notified the NYPD's operations desk, which then called the head of the Organized Crime Control Bureau, Chief Anthony M. Voelker. Not only was a captain from the Bronx sent to investigate; Voelker also saw to it that Inspector James Wrynn, then assigned to the Bronx, took a role in the inquiry.

Deputy Chief Frank Biehler, Kelleher's commander as the head of narcotics, noted the accident's timing, in the early hours of a Saturday morning, and later acknowledged that it had led him and other police brass to worry that alcohol might be involved. But the state police did not request a blood-alcohol test. Although NYPD regulations require that cops be "fit for duty" at all times, Inspector Wrynn's investigation didn't ask for one either. Persistent murmurs had it that Kelleher had been at a police department party that night and that Patty—whose quick smile and twinkling blue eyes made pals point out his resemblance to a leprechaun—had been his usual jovial self. Yet police commanders concluded simply that Kelleher had been on his way home from work and careened off the road to avoid hitting a deer. Chief Biehler later said he was satisfied by that verdict. Chief Voelker, who considered Inspector Wrynn "sound as the dollar," also concurred; he felt that if Wrynn said that Kelleher was fit for duty, the case was closed.

The investigation was a model of discretion. Technicians from the NYPD motor pool retrieved the car, which was totaled. Everything was accomplished smoothly and quietly enough to avoid headlines, an angry police commissioner, or the rantings of an outraged mayor. Kelleher missed several weeks of work and returned with a limp, bandages on his face, and a sheepish grin. But his career was still viable.

Wrynn's delicate handling of the affair remained such a closely held secret that Armanti and Dowd never heard about it during their extensive research into the backgrounds of the Inspector and his son. Even after Kelleher appointed the Inspector his field general in the crusade to avenge the revels of Washington, their special relationship was never made an issue. But it was clear that Kelleher was determined not to let Wrynn's difficult task in Washington end in failure. Within ten days of Wrynn's appointment, IAB helped the Inspector turn up the heat by questioning cops and their supervisors under oath. First IAB detectives called in the bosses: seven captains, fifteen lieutenants, and thirty sergeants who were in Washington. Then they squeezed the probationary police officers who attended. Because the latter weren't full-fledged cops, they could be fired without department trials, so investigators considered them the weakest links. Kelleher warned that anyone who was evasive or untruthful would be dismissed.

"If our investigation reveals they were not forthcoming, did not tell the truth, or that they lied during the hearings, I will have absolutely no hesitation in recommending to the police commissioner that those individuals be terminated," Kelleher said.

But for all the pressure applied by Kelleher, Wrynn, police headquarters, and city hall, the real break in the case emanated from a barroom. In early May, Ramona Vicario, a police officer from the 103rd Precinct, was enjoying herself at a tavern in Ridgewood, Queens, when she decided to regale her drinking buddies with stories about her role in the D.C.

debauchery. Vicario laughed about seeing her naked fellow officers flashing civilians. She boasted about competing in a wet T-shirt contest and hugging one of the nude cops who had slid down the banister. After Vicario started snorting cocaine a little later in the evening, one of the people she'd enthralled with her story decided to call Internal Affairs.

With the mayor and police commissioner breathing down his neck, Inspector Wrynn wasn't about to let IAB blow this one. Internal Affairs put a tail on Vicario, using techniques far superior to those used to investigate John Wrynn. Vicario never spotted the tail. IAB also set up a sting operation and, within weeks, had nailed the officer for buying cocaine on two separate occasions. Vicario was defiant when first brought in for questioning. So IAB went after her husband, also a cop, by putting him on modified duty, even though he hadn't been in Washington the weekend of the memorial. Vicario was also ordered to take a drug test, which she failed, forcing her to either resign or be fired.

Rather than face criminal prosecution for possession or see her husband dragged through the flames with her, Vicario agreed to cooperate. She gave IAB the name of the officer whose nude frolicking had horrified the city: James Morrow was a twenty-five-year-old with such a serious drinking problem that he'd been given the name "Naked Man" months before the Washington debacle because of his tendency to strip down to nothing but cowboy boots at parties. Inspector Wrynn's investigation had finally gotten its man.

The NYPD could at last take the offensive. In early June, when the department announced that Naked Man had been identified, Bratton began the big job of bragging about the work of his crack team from IAB. Haughtily, he predicted that the matter would be quickly and efficiently sewn up. "We now have quite a bit of information to work with, based on statements by police officers involved in this matter, and my anticipation is that like dominoes they will all start falling into place," Bratton said.

Bratton wasn't about to deny himself the thrill of rubbing reporters' noses in his triumph. "A great deal has been made of this so-called Blue Wall of Silence," he said. "I would indicate to you . . . that there is no such thing."

A month later, when Inspector Wrynn completed his written report on the rampage, the mayor could barely contain his glee. After interviewing more than thirteen hundred people, IAB had determined that only seven officers had actually broken department guidelines. Thirty others would receive letters of reprimand for violating the NYPD's order not to take firearms to Washington. Wrynn's report blamed the media for exaggerating the scope of the misbehavior, pointing out that one widely publicized photo of drunken officers in NYPD garb actually depicted cops from Providence who had purchased NYPD souvenirs. Giuliani, whose day-to-day dealings with the press were usually as cordial as a pit bull's interactions with raw meat, praised IAB's investigation and denigrated the reporters who had erred. The mayor conceded that it was likely some guilty officers were escaping punishment, but he lashed out at reporters who suggested that IAB had captured only a small fraction of the wild officers involved in the fracas.

The Internal Affairs Bureau exists "within rules that you don't exist within," Mayor Giuliani replied, testily. "They have to prove what they are saying."

James Morrow and another cop who'd cavorted in the raw were given a formal administrative hearing in the NYPD trial room. The outcome was a foregone conclusion. Morrow utilized a "lost weekend defense," saying he'd downed so many beers he didn't know what he was doing. He claimed to not even remember his performance as the NYPD's Lady Godiva. Both he and his companion in the buff, Wayne Hagmaier, began alcohol rehab programs and vowed to stay away from the bottle.

By the time Bratton announced their dismissal, fourteen months after the Washington debacle, the public had already been mollified by the city's declining crime during the two years of Giuliani's term. From the city's street corners to its executive suites, New Yorkers were growing comfortable again, confident in their sense that the city was winning its battle against violent street crime. Bratton and Giuliani were not shy about taking credit; it didn't matter that crime was also falling in communities across the nation—including cities that used tactics far different from Bratton's. Like evangelical trigonometry professors, the commissioner and Giuliani bombarded the public with bar graphs and pie charts complicated enough to convince some New Yorkers that the pair had scared criminals as far off as Peoria and Baton Rouge.

In mid-January 1997, Bratton and Giuliani proudly announced that the number of homicides had dropped 38.7 percent during the first two years of their regime. Also noted was the fact that there had been 30.5 percent fewer robberies and 35.7 percent fewer auto thefts. The official end to Inspector Wrynn's investigation came the next month, when Bratton fired Morrow and Hagmaier, to the delight of the media that had once lambasted him for the NYPD's hesitant initial response to the ruckus. The *New York Times,* praising the department for its "impressive investigation," claimed that the case had come to a "successful conclusion." The *Daily News* also cheered: "Commissioner Bratton has upheld the department's good name," the paper wrote. "And he has offered a cautionary tale to pandering legislators who want to take the power to fire away from the commissioner."

With New York's crime wave finally receding, the Mollen Commission's focus on police corruption seemed a distant memory, and the brouhaha over Naked Man appeared a silly indulgence. "Perhaps," one columnist wrote, "we can all move on now."

Vincent Armanti, who had all but given up his hopes of seeing a photograph of the handcuffed Inspector Wrynn in the morning newspaper, often felt during these times that he was a man on his own, walking among those who had, as he put it, "sold their souls out." All around him, the pursuits that engaged his fellow citizens felt increasingly distant and unreal.

18

" I DO WANT JUSTICE DONE "

JULY 31, 1995

BURSTS OF BRILLIANT light flashed through Ed Dowd's field of vision as he sat in the hallway of Brooklyn federal court, watching a long line of firefighters file into the courtroom. It was the first day of Jack and Mario Ferranti's trial, and already on this sweltering morning, Dowd's eyes were signaling an approaching migraine. The firemen were buffed and polished in the same dignified, formal uniforms they'd worn to Lieutenant Williams's funeral almost three and a half years earlier. Back then, all the rich blue fabric and glittering gold trim had seemed mournful and solemn to Dowd. But today, as the two dozen muscular firefighters marched toward the courtroom en masse in their Class A's, the effect was so forceful and intimidating that even the Ferrantis' hard-edged cheering section vacated the hallway at this display of strength and unity.

In the years since he'd first seen Lieutenant Williams's colleagues hysterically trying to bring the unconscious firefighter back to life, Dowd had become increasingly impressed by the bravery and unwavering camaraderie of the firemen. While his bosses in the NYPD had been shielding their cronies and angling to advance their careers, nearly everyone he had encountered in the fire department was truly devoted to avenging Lieutenant Williams. Every time Dowd had thought about folding, walking away from the case, the firemen had kept him going. "The best part of my career in the police department," Dowd had begun to joke, "were the years I spent in the fire department." Now, as the trial was set to begin, those bonds only magnified the wrenching pressure he felt to deliver a guilty verdict, and the pressure set off the pounding in his head and the flashes of light that kept popping like strobes. He could not overcome the fear that his case was about to flop, crushing the firemen's hopes for justice and his own desire to finally do right by someone before calling this damn case quits.

From the very beginning, *United States of America v. Jack and Mario Ferranti* had teetered between turmoil and utter chaos. Now, as it arrived in the tense, steamy courtroom, it seemed especially vulnerable to any number of uncertainties. There wasn't a stitch of physical evidence linking Jack or Mario to the fire that had killed Lieutenant Thomas Williams. Nor was there testimony from coconspirators who could describe how the alleged arson plan had been conceived and carried out. Prosecutors were left to construct a circumstantial case with building blocks that were, at best, unstable: hostile witnesses, a flawed crime-scene investigation, and testimony from a checkered collection of so-called experts whose work ranged from superb to sloppy. The case against Mario Ferranti was particularly vulnerable. It dangled by a single, slippery strand: the testimony of Vincent Marziano, the heroin addict who had damaged his already shaky credibility by being arrested again several weeks *after* agreeing to become the prosecutors' star witness.

The strongest evidence against Jack, the swaggering older brother with the bushy sideburns, came from his own words. In the year before the blaze, as the Today's Styles store threatened to go belly-up, Jack fell behind on his rent payments and blustered about burning it down to collect on the insurance. He had also lied about his whereabouts after the fire. Furthermore—though financial records proved otherwise—he had told insurance adjusters that Today's Styles had been making money and was stocked with $55,000 in merchandise when it burned.

Most important, however, Jack Ferranti had asked an employee to lie about another crucial matter. Prosecutors believed that the old space heater found in the building's smoldering remains had been left by the arsonists as a way to trick the authorities into believing that the fire had begun accidentally. But it appeared that Jack had persuaded his employee, who later changed her story, to say that the heater had been in the store for months and had been in use near the spot where the blaze had ignited. Who knew whether the jurors would be able to follow the changing statements of the intimidated witnesses?

To further complicate matters, a variety of scheduling conflicts and personal issues had left the prosecution team in turmoil. Armanti had been ordered to stay away from the courthouse, to prevent the Ferrantis and their henchmen from getting a better look at him. Cindy Peil had barely spoken to Dowd since September 1993, when she'd confided in him and Armanti about a secret meeting that her supervisors and the NYPD had held about shutting down the undercover operation. (When word had gotten back to the FBI, Peil received a stern reprimand.) And Assistant U.S. Attorney George Stamboulidis, the lead prosecutor on the case, was missing in action. A month and a half earlier, Stamboulidis had told Armanti and Dowd that he wouldn't be able to argue the Lieutenant Williams case himself because he had a major organized-crime trial that the office considered a higher priority.

The new assistant U.S. attorney assigned to the case, Sean O'Shea, was a ferocious and impassioned trial attorney, but when he realized how precarious the evidence was, he began barking panicked orders at Dowd and the fire marshals, quickly aggravating the people he needed most. Lauren Resnick, the young prosecutor who had been assisting Stamboulidis, was eight and a half months pregnant, so it was unclear how much longer she'd even be on her feet. O'Shea's wife was also due to give birth just about the time the trial started, and, incredibly, Dowd's wife was expecting too. He was just waiting for someone's water to break, making his bastard case into a complete orphan.

The defense team, meanwhile, had won several important pretrial motions that would prevent jurors from hearing the full litany of the Ferrantis' long and bloody history. Tommy Tocco's lawyer had convinced the judge to grant the Torch a separate trial, so the prosecutors labored under the added burden of knowing that they'd almost certainly have to endure the entire ordeal again. Lawyers for Jack and Mario had also unveiled their own last-minute surprise for prosecutors, an expert witness—a fire investigator who would argue that the blaze had been an accident. This witness, Thomas Klem, had a dazzling résumé and the persuasive delivery of a star salesman. Concealing his name until the last minute, the defense had left O'Shea, Dowd, and the others little time to investigate his background or prepare to cross-examine their surprise guest.

But the wild card that worried Dowd the most involved the Wrynns. If evidence about the NYPD's corruption and the attendant cover-ups somehow made it into the case, the defense lawyers would be blessed with infinite ways to confuse jurors and undercut the prosecution's arguments. The irony was appalling: Dowd, who had devoted years of his life to trying to expose the Wrynns, now found himself praying that their secret stayed hidden from the jury—at least until after the trial.

Dowd paced the hallway, sweating, adding up the facts and berating himself about what else he might have done to strengthen the case. Without warning, Lieutenant Williams's widow walked up to say hello.

"Are we going to get a conviction?" she asked.

Dowd smiled, then reached out and gave her arm a reassuring pat.

"Yeah," he said, surprised he'd been able to muster such a confident, believable tone of voice. "We'll get 'em."

If only he could make himself believe it.

WHEN SEAN O'SHEA rose from the prosecutors' table to begin his opening argument, he could feel the sorrowful, unforgiving eyes of the firemen watching his every move. Before this, O'Shea had specialized in fraud prosecutions. He'd agreed to take the Lieutenant Williams case only because he admired firemen. As he faced the jury and started to speak, those sympathies only added to the anxiety and dread that weighed on him. How would he face them if he lost? And how could he manage to win a case in such sorry shape?

Of the few intangibles that might work to O'Shea's advantage, the most obvious were the mangy appearance and feral courtroom etiquette of the Ferrantis and their supporters. Jack sat at the defense table poker-faced, radiating rage, his eyes glowering straight ahead. Mario was almost cartoonish—his brow furrowed in defiant disapproval and his mouth hanging open. Also scattered among the spectators were several dozen of Throgs Neck's least presentable citizens. During a pretrial hearing, those friends and relatives of Tocco and the Ferrantis had behaved like people bounced from the bleachers of a professional wrestling match. They'd grunted and scowled at the police and the prosecutors, and when FBI Agent Peil had finished testifying, they'd shouted out a chorus of "Bitch!" and "Liar!" as she was escorted from the courtroom.

O'Shea prayed that they'd put on an equally menacing performance now. Given the evidence, his only hope was to inspire the jurors, motivate them to put the pieces of this thing together themselves. So he tried to rally his spirits and begin the task of reducing the entire convoluted story line to a simple morality tale about a moneygrubbing slumlord who'd hatched a crude plot with tragic consequences. O'Shea explained to the attentive jury that Jack's store had been losing so much money that he'd hired his brother, Mario, and Tommy Tocco to burn it to the ground. Once the fire claimed Lieutenant Williams's life, O'Shea said, Jack began to lie—to the police and the insurance company, among others—and had asked his employees to shun the truth as well. O'Shea told jurors that they owed it to the memory of Lieutenant Williams, and to all the men and women who risk their lives to fight fires, to ensure that the Ferrantis did not escape responsibility for what they'd done.

"This is a story about greed," he said.

Jack Ferranti's lawyer, Jeffrey Hoffman, used his opening argument as a sharp, direct rebuttal; he had an answer for everything. Jack had lied to the police because his lawyer had advised him not to volunteer information. He had never threatened to burn down the store or asked anyone to lie, Hoffman emphasized; those accusations were being fabricated by disgruntled former employees. But by far Hoffman's boldest gamble on the courtroom floor on that July morning was to blame Lieutenant Williams's death on the fire department. The FDNY commanders, Hoffman insisted, had underestimated the danger of the situation and had mistakenly ordered Williams into a building that they surely should have known was a death trap.

"Because there was a death to a fireman, and because that death may have occurred unnecessarily, somebody, it was determined, would be charged," Hoffman said. "Somebody other than the fire department, other than the people involved, had to become a scapegoat."

Mario's lawyer, Marion Seltzer, was even more audacious. She vilified Dowd, saying that his relentless pursuit of her client had failed to produce any solid evidence. Then, without pause or reluctance, she accused Dowd of trying to frame the Ferrantis.

"There are no tape recordings, no wiretaps, no fingerprints, no photographs, no hidden videos," she said. "Not one person will tell you that he ever had a conversation with Mario where Mario admitted his involvement in this fire. What you will hear is nothing. Nothing, nothing, nothing, nothing whatsoever links Mario Ferranti to the fire."

What's worse, Seltzer said, the big blaze hadn't been an arson in the first place. She urged jurors to pay careful attention to the flaws in the crime-scene investigation, because the defense planned to present its own expert, a fire analyst who had studied the evidence and concluded that it had ignited accidentally. "This," she declared, a touch of disgust in her voice, "is the case of the arson that never happened."

O'Shea knew that he desperately needed the jurors to engage emotionally, so he began his round of witnesses with his heroes. Since he couldn't present Lieutenant Williams to the jury, he did the next best thing: He called a handful of the firefighters who had risked their lives that night, trying to save the innocent people inside—people whom O'Shea did his best to portray as just like the twelve jurors. Fireman Anthony Sannella of Ladder Company 136 was the first to take the stand. Sannella had responded to the fire call at Today's Styles that evening, just as Lieutenant Williams had. By the time his shift had ended, Sannella had helped rescue three people from the blaze and had hopped a six-foot fence to look for more. Next, firefighter Michael Milner told how he and Lieutenant Williams had gone searching for people stranded inside and were overcome by the flames and thick smoke. Milner kept his composure as he told of their desperate effort to escape the inferno and the way Lieutenant Williams had flown out the window like an unrecognizable blur, but several jurors could be seen drying their eyes.

Defense lawyers couldn't attack the hero firemen, but during their cross-examinations they did use the firefighters to lay the groundwork for their own, alternate theories about what had happened that night in the building on Grand Avenue in Maspeth, Queens. When one fireman mentioned walking to the origin of the fire, defense lawyers jumped in to quiz him about the shape of the burn marks on the walls, a detail that would be crucial to the Ferrantis' claim that the fire had been accidental. Jack's lawyer repeatedly asked Milner whether anyone had responded to the mayday call that he and Lieutenant Williams had issued—attempting to imply, none too subtly, that the fire department had abandoned the men in the blaze. Hoffman's questions to Battalion Chief Robert Stamphel, the ranking commander at the scene, suggested that he had failed to warn Lieutenant Williams that the fire was raging out of control. The firemen in the spectators' benches glared at Hoffman, and several grunted, but Chief Stamphel just brushed his questions firmly aside.

All the defense lawyers had to do was raise reasonable doubts, and it was clear that they would look for them anywhere and everywhere.

By day two, however, it appeared as though the defense attorneys would have to expend little of their expensive efforts: The case started falling apart all by itself. Lisa Ziccardi, who had worked at Ferranti's clothing store along with her mother, was called to the stand and asked to describe the comments she'd heard Jack make in 1991 about torching the business to cash in on the insurance.

"I don't remember him saying anything like that," she testified.

The prosecutors had feared this moment ever since the firebomb that had burst into flames outside Ziccardi's mother's house. Ziccardi had first refused to testify, then reluctantly agreed to come to court. In early July, when prosecutors had arrived to prepare her for the trial, she'd refused to open the door. Instead, she'd sat on the sill of a second-story window painting her nails, like some character out of *West Side Story*, while the very pregnant assistant U.S. attorney Lauren Resnick had stood in the ninety-seven-degree heat, shouting up questions and fighting the urge to vomit.

Ziccardi's memory loss during the trial itself forced Resnick to switch gears and treat her like a hostile witness. Resnick confronted Ziccardi with a copy of a written statement she'd given investigators several months back, stating that she'd heard Jack threaten to do "an insurance job" on the store. Growing increasingly defiant, Ziccardi denied that the name on the document was hers, even though she'd written it herself.

Judge Jack B. Weinstein had the jurors led out of the room. Then he assigned Ziccardi a lawyer, to warn her about the penalties for perjury, and ordered her to return the next day.

"What if I can't come tomorrow," she shot back.

"If you can't come tomorrow at nine A.M., I'll send a marshal out to arrest you, make sure you come!" Judge Weinstein replied.

"For what?"

"For not coming," the judge said, "because I'm ordering you to come."

"This is fair?" Ziccardi shouted. "I'm involved in this for no reason! This is good, thanks a lot! Real nice. I don't know nothing about the case. You're asking me everything—I don't know, I don't remember! I've been to a psychiatrist. I'm a sick person. I'm a sick person! I have family problems and you expect me to do this? Oh my goodness gracious! I'm an emotionally sick person! I'm going to have a heart attack here. My heart beats fast, I get nervous!"

The judge commanded her to leave the courtroom.

In the hallway, Ziccardi ran into Cindy Peil and said she simply couldn't tell her story with Jack Ferranti staring at her. She was literally too scared to speak.

"I'm nervous," she said. "I'm scared! He's sitting right there!"

Ziccardi returned the next day with her lawyer, but her attitude seemed far fresher than her memory. After retaking the oath, she said that, come to think of it, she *had* overheard Jack tell her mother that he would take care of the unprofitable business. But Ziccardi insisted that Jack had never suggested burning the store. In fact, Ziccardi said, she'd never even heard the phrase "insurance job" until the day fire marshals came to her house asking for a statement about Jack.

"When they came to my house and questioned me, they told me about the insurance job, stuff like that—'You think Jack Ferranti did this for money?,' stuff like that," she testified. "I said, 'I don't know.'"

Ziccardi's mother, Gina Esposito, was next on the stand, and she muddled things even further. Esposito said she'd never heard Jack talk about burning down the business, but she remembered Lisa telling her that Jack had threatened to torch the store.

Their back-to-back testimony was as dizzying as the old Abbott and Costello "Who's on First" routine. It was clear that Jack had said *something* to *someone*, but the details had become lost in a tangle of evasion, misunderstanding, and confusion. Because the judge had forbidden the prosecutors from presenting evidence about the firebombing that had clearly intimidated both witnesses, there was no telling what the jurors would make of it all.

When O'Shea walked into the hall after Esposito's antics on that grim third day, he looked so alarmed that Dowd wondered whether the prosecutor's wife might have gone into labor. Something else was weighing on O'Shea, however, something he didn't dare say aloud: If things continued to go this badly, the judge might dismiss the charges before the case ever made it to the jury. But for the time being, the fun continued.

Getting Jack's other employee to take the stand had been a harrowing adventure for Dowd, O'Shea, and the fire marshals. Theresa Rodriguez had closed the store at 5:00 P.M. on the day of the fire. The next day, when investigators asked Jack for her address, Jack said he didn't know it—even though she was his tenant. A few days later, Jack drove Rodriguez to the precinct and—what do you know?—she repeated Jack's specious claim that she'd purchased a space heater several years earlier and it had been operating in the store on the night of the fire. Months later, before the grand jury, Rodriguez had a change of heart that was especially surprising given that she was represented by an attorney paid for by Jack Ferranti. She admitted that she hadn't purchased a space heater and had never seen one in the store. Jack had told her to lie earlier, Rodriguez claimed, explaining that she was afraid he'd kill her if she refused.

The Ferrantis hadn't made her return to court an easy ride. Three weeks before the current trial was scheduled to begin, Rodriguez had mysteriously disappeared. She had made an unexpected trip to Florida with her husband and sister-in-law, Charito, who worked as a secretary for Jack Ferranti. Dowd, Peil, and the fire marshals tracked down friends and coworkers of Charito and her husband, who said that the two were heading back to their hometown in the Dominican Republic because "they had a problem." Prosecutors issued a material-witness warrant for Rodriguez, alerting police at airports in Miami and Orlando not to let her leave the country. When Rodriguez resurfaced, Dowd had her cuffed and taken into custody, warning her that, if she didn't cooperate, he'd keep her locked up until the trial and then have her deported once it was over. In the weeks before she was scheduled to testify, Dowd would swing by her house each night, just to be certain she hadn't been whisked off on an all-expenses-paid trip to Anywhere the Cops Can't Find Me.

Rodriguez was escorted to court and took the stand so warily it appeared as if she suspected it might be booby-trapped. After swearing her oath, she proceeded to testify that there had been no heater in the store on the day of the fire. She also verified that Jack had asked her to lie and claim that there had been. But Rodriguez also gave the defense attorneys a lot to work with. She said that Dowd had threatened to deport her (and separate her from her daughter) if she didn't change her story about the space heater. She went on to say that she had indeed used a space heater in the front of the store in the months before the blaze. She also told the jury that about two weeks prior to the fire that killed Lieutenant Williams, a lighting fixture in the front of the store had begun smoking and shooting out sparks so violently that it had burned her hair. As far as she knew, the electrical problem had never been repaired.

By the end of the trial's messy third day, jurors had been shown a variety of evidence that suggested that Jack Ferranti had something to hide. Proving that Jack had actually ordered the fire would be a far more complicated task and the difficulty was written all over Sean O'Shea's exhausted face.

MICHELLE AND SHELLY ANTHONY had moved to Long Island two years after the fire destroyed their home, but the terror of that night still haunted them at odd and unpredictable moments. Immediately after they'd fled from the burning building into the street, Shelly had waited patiently, even though he was barefoot. He'd figured the firemen would douse the flames and they'd be able to return to bed in fifteen minutes or so. But the blaze consumed the entire building, and the Anthonys were left with nothing more than the pajamas they were wearing. They had no insurance, either. Most insurance companies refuse to write fire policies for renters who live above commercial storefronts, so their finances were in ruins.

They had spent that first night sleeping on a couch at her brother's apartment, and when they awoke—wearing socks and coats that had been given to them by some Good Samaritan they could no longer recall—Michelle thought to herself, *So this is how it feels to be homeless.* In the weeks that followed, they had slept at the homes of friends, relatives, coworkers—anywhere they could find a bed and a hot meal. It took a month or so to find a new apartment, and Michelle couldn't get over how tiny it was. Soon, however, she learned she was pregnant, and she realized just how lucky she and Shelly had been that night of the fire. How sad to think that once the baby was born, she and Shelly would bring it home to a cramped, unfamiliar apartment full of other people's things. They were starting a family, but it felt like their own history had been completely erased.

For months, Michelle would find herself searching for some household item—a necklace, a T-shirt, a favorite brush—before realizing that it had been lost in the blaze. She talked about the fire constantly; if anyone so much as asked her the time of day, she'd find a way to tell them about the fire that had changed her life. Shelly rarely talked about how disorienting it all was. He went to a few counseling sessions, but mostly he suffered in silence, which made Michelle worry that the stress would one day sneak up on him.

A month or so before the trial, Michelle had answered a knock at the door and found two muscle-bound private investigators who said they worked for the Ferrantis.

"Are you Michelle Anthony?" one of the men asked. "We just wanted to see if there was anything you remembered."

Michelle and Shelly were enraged and terrified that the Ferrantis had found them. As their day in court approached, Michelle was so worried, she stopped talking about the fire to anyone.

Shelly, who had trained as a transit police officer before the couple's marriage, was called to testify first. His background had taught him to stick close to the facts, and he did not hesitate when asked to describe how he had picked Tommy Tocco's picture out of a photo array and identified him as the man who had been lurking outside the building the night of the fire. Yet as he told his story—waking to the sound of the smoke detector, leading his wife, who turned out to be pregnant, through the darkness by her hand—Shelly started to look shaken. During the cross-examination, spectators in the courtroom noticed that he was caught off guard by questions about the counseling he'd undergone since the fire. When a defense lawyer made a disparaging reference to the lawsuit the Anthonys had filed, seeking $75,000 to replace their lost belongings, Shelly began to break down completely.

Michelle had been ordered to wait outside the courtroom while he testified, and she was surprised to see her husband walk through the doors teary-eyed and obviously overwrought. After all the suffering the Ferrantis had put them through, all the pain and harassment, it enraged her. Shelly was her rock—how dare they do this to her rock! She hugged Shelly and they spoke for a moment or two; then she was hustled inside the courtroom to testify. *He was so strong for me that night,* she thought, as she marched toward the stand, *so I'm going to be strong for him today.*

Michelle wedged herself into the witness box, and the fact that she was quite obviously with the Anthonys' second child made her determination even more endearing. She then described her narrow escape from the building with her husband, and their brief encounter with Tocco. When the defense lawyers took aim at Michelle, she swatted them away like lazy flies. Marion Seltzer tried to rattle Michelle, using her high-pitched, high-speed Queens accent to ask a follow-up question before Michelle had finished answering the first. Seltzer raised an eyebrow when Michelle referred to Dowd by his first name, and asked precisely when the two had become so *familiar.*

"He's not Police Officer Dowd?" Seltzer asked suggestively. "You never referred to him as Police Officer Dowd?"

"Do you have a particular way that you would like me to address him?"

"I'm just wondering how it came to be that you referred to this police officer that you didn't know as Eddie Dowd."

"If he introduces himself as Eddie Dowd," Michelle said, "then how else would I address the gentleman?"

Seltzer then tried to cast doubts on Michelle's ID of Tocco. Had Michelle been wearing her glasses that night? Had the smoke made her eyes tear up? She had seen him only briefly, during a tragic, chaotic blur of a night, so how was it that five months later, she had still remembered him well enough to recognize his face in the photo lineup that her good friend Eddie the detective had presented? Michelle said it was simple: Tocco seemed concerned that night, worried that people might be stranded in the burning building.

"So you were moved by the fact of his personality," Seltzer asked, "by his warmth?"

"He didn't give me roses," she said. "He wasn't particularly warm, but I thought that there was concern. He asked if there was anyone left in the building."

She left it for the prosecutors to remind the jury that once Tocco had learned there were people still inside, he'd just walked away.

Shelly had watched her testify, and when they walked outside, he hugged her. This time they both broke into tears.

Placing Tocco at the scene of the blaze was one important element of the prosecutor's case. But the only link between Tocco and the Ferrantis was Vincent Marziano, whose testimony was just what you might expect from a career criminal whose heroin habit made him unable to recall where he used to live.

Under questioning from O'Shea, Marziano told jurors that Tocco had been looking for a score in the weeks before the fire. At one point the Torch proposed holding up a city bus and robbing the driver and all the passengers. Then Marziano moved on to discuss the actual night of the fire. He said that Tocco had visited his house, wherever it was, and announced that the police were looking for him because he and Mario had just burned down a building.

A few days later, Marziano testified, he saw Mario at a bar and asked whether he had helped Tocco set the blaze. Mario responded with a nod, Marziano said. Not a word, not even a grunt. A nod.

On cross-examination, the defense lawyers opened fire, poring over Marziano's lengthy criminal record and giving extra attention to the jail time he'd served for kidnapping. They quizzed Marziano about the three children he'd fathered, by two different women, and his refusal to support one of them. When they asked how he'd spent the $16,000 in taxpayer funds prosecutors had given him for living expenses since he'd begun cooperating, the defense counselors were delighted to hear that Marziano had used $1,000 to pay off a loan shark who was threatening to kill his pregnant girlfriend by cutting the baby out of her belly.

Then Marziano did the seemingly impossible: He made matters worse. When the defense lawyers asked about his arrest for stealing a camera after he began cooperating, Marziano insisted that he was innocent. But he went on to explain that the prosecutors had told him they'd get his sentence reduced to community service if he pleaded guilty. The jail was so hot and crowded, Marziano said, that he'd agreed to lie under oath just to get the hell out. For the Ferrantis' lawyers, this statement was a smorgasbord. Not only had Marziano lied in court, but the prosecutors had asked him to.

"Did the U.S. Attorney's Office say to you, 'We won't allow that, that's not the way the system works, to have innocent people convicted of crimes'?" Hoffman asked.

"No," Marziano replied.

"The government— Even though you're innocent and you walked into court and lied and pleaded guilty, which you weren't, right? You weren't guilty, right?"

"No," Marziano insisted.

"They never told you that that has to be rectified or changed, correct?"

"No."

"So it's not, as it wasn't here, inconceivable to you to lie, even to a judge, if it will get you out of jail," Hoffman said.

"Sometimes it's easier," Marziano said.

"Sometimes it's easier," Hoffman said, pausing between words to give them maximum impact. "I agree."

Some of the firemen watching the trial worried that Marziano had demolished his own credibility and, with it, the chances of convicting Mario. But later that afternoon, they got the first bit of indisputably good news since the trial had begun. Bobby Thomson, the fire marshal investigating the defense team's surprise witness, ran into the courtroom with a sparkle in his eye.

"This guy Klem," Thomson said, referring to the defense team's lauded, last-minute expert witness. "He's not what he says he is."

THE MOST PRECARIOUS aspect of the case, proving whether or not the fire had been set intentionally, ultimately boiled down to a courtroom duel between scientific experts. The prosecutors had to rule out any possible accidental causes, so they first brought in an engineer from the General Electric company who examined the charred space heater found in the debris. The witness determined that it had not short-circuited or malfunctioned in any way. Next, an FBI metallurgist testified that he had used a precision stereomicroscope to inspect the heater and its electrical cord and had concluded that the appliance had not been receiving an electrical current when it was burned. In other words, it could not have caused the fire.

The prosecutors also called James Kelty, the original fire marshal on the scene, to the stand to explain the physical evidence that had led the fire department to rule the blaze an arson. The distinctive burn patterns on the floor were a sign that flammable liquid had been poured and ignited, Kelty said. (The fire marshals had concluded that the heater had been left at the scene as a decoy.) The defense attorneys, however, riddled Kelty with questions about the lack of hard empirical evidence. They pointed out that the floorboards from the store had mistakenly been trashed at the NYPD warehouse and that no traces of any flammable liquid had been found near the origin of the flames. Kelty had not been involved in most of the day-to-day decisions in the case, and his lack of familiarity with specific details allowed the defense lawyers to pretty much have their way with him. Kelty also lost ground when he mistakenly said that the electrical circuits in the wall had never been tested. Furthermore, he was unaware that a short circuit in the store had singed Theresa Rodriguez's hair two weeks before the fire; he said that if he had known, he would have ordered electrical testing. Kelty, perhaps a little worn down, let the defense lawyers insinuate that the fire might have been started by a can of oil stored near the air-conditioning unit in the basement. Kelty even conceded that the burn patterns on the floor tiles might have been caused by a rapid "flashover" of fire.

Afterward, when O'Shea emerged from the courtroom, his manner was grave.

"He's getting hammered," O'Shea remarked to a fire marshal.

O'Shea had prepared for exactly this possibility by having one more expert witness waiting on deck before resting his case: Fire Marshal John Stickevers. If Kelty had frozen like a deer caught in the headlights, Stickevers was an ox—methodical, unshakable, and unstoppable. He testified that there had indeed been a test of the electrical system, and that no signs of any malfunction had been found. Next, he explained that an examination of the air-conditioning unit had indicated that the fire had actually started a considerable distance away, ruling out the oil as a possible cause. Stickevers calmly disputed Kelty's statements about the burn patterns, insisting that a flammable liquid had obviously been poured near the origin of the fire because it had seeped up under the moldings and caused burn damage there.

O'Shea rested his case and let out a sigh of relief. *Okay,* he thought, *at least we got in enough evidence that the judge will have to send it to the jury.*

Taking over, the defense quickly brought in its hired gun, and it wasn't long before his smooth delivery and confident bearing had captivated everyone in the courtroom. Thomas Klem touted his master's degree in fire-protection engineering, noted his work with the National Fire Protection Association, and drew attention to his time as an investigative officer for an ominous-sounding federal agency called the United States Fire Administration. Klem described his extensive experience training fire marshals, developing protocols for investigations, and writing fire-investigation instruction manuals, then nonchalantly mentioned his work investigating some of the most devastating fires in recent history: the Dupont Plaza fire in Puerto Rico, where ninety-seven people died; blazes at the MGM Grand Hotel in Las Vegas and the World Trade Center; the 1989 Happy Land fire in New York, where eighty-seven people lost their lives when a social club burned. He'd even investigated a fire at Windsor Castle—a royal blaze, one might say.

Having claimed credit for subduing every major fire since Mrs. O'Leary's cow burned down Chicago, Klem proceeded to blast the investigation of the fire at Jack Ferranti's store and offer a drastically different explanation. He said that New York fire marshals had fallen victim to one of the "myths" of fire investigating by leaping to the conclusion that the burn patterns they found automatically indicated arson. He went on to hint that a more sophisticated analysis by more seasoned investigators might have revealed that the burn patterns could have been caused by other sources, including melted plastic, synthetic fabric, or floor tiles that had been heated and had liquefied.

Klem blamed the fire on an electrical problem. To explain his intricate theory, he stepped down from the stand and walked to his charts, where he argued that burn patterns behind the wall paneling had led him to this conclusion. But the prosecutors weren't just worried about his reasoning. Klem had such an eye-popping collection of cross-sectional diagrams and whiz-bang graphics that he seemed like the man who'd invented fire. *Oh my God,* Resnick thought. *Look at those charts!*

Klem's most provocative claims concerned the space heater. Contradicting the other experts, he said that there were clear signs of short-circuiting on the cord of the appliance, and he began to advance his case that the heater had sparked the fire. He even hinted at foul play, saying that an early photo of the heater's cord showed that a "metal glob" had been formed near the plug—presumably when the heater had malfunctioned. But, he continued, after the heater was returned from the FBI lab, it had been "altered" and the glob was gone.

During a break, O'Shea was confronted by a fireman, who looked alarmed.

"This guy's doing some damage. Why aren't you objecting?"

O'Shea told him not to worry. There was little doubt that the outcome of the case might be determined by the outcome of his cross-examination, but O'Shea had a few surprises in store for the surprise witness.

He began by softening up Klem with questions about his methods. He pointed out that Klem hadn't been hired until after the building had already been renovated, so his assessment was based solely on reports and photographs from the scene. A few minutes later, however, O'Shea commenced with the carpet bombing. Fire Marshal Bobby Thomson's frenzied background check had found gaping holes in Klem's résumé. Although Klem presented himself as a top-notch investigator, much of his experience was doing administrative work, and in many of these cases Klem boasted about, he'd simply written reports summarizing the work of other investigators. Worst of all, Klem had left his job at the National Fire Protection Association after being accused of abusing his expense account by billing his employers for more than $5,000 in personal expenses. Klem, obviously uncomfortable and visibly deflated, attempted to explain the expenditures as minor bookkeeping errors. But O'Shea spent the better part of an hour dragging him through each uncomfortable fact—while the defense lawyers tried in vain to object and the Ferrantis fought back smirks.

"Now, was it a mistake when you paid for airline tickets for your children and charged the NFPA?" O'Shea asked.

"It was, indeed," Klem replied.

"And you did that, sir, didn't you?"

"It was a mistake."

"You misrepresented facts to get money, correct?"

"That is absolutely incorrect."

"That's not what happened?"

"That is not what happened."

"And certainly that's not what you are doing with this jury," O'Shea said sarcastically, "misrepresenting facts to get money from Jack Ferranti, correct?"

"I'm not misrepresenting anything here," Klem said, growing more defensive with each passing moment.

O'Shea pummeled Klem mercilessly about paying for his family's personal vacation at a Vermont ski resort and buying luggage with NFPA funds. Then O'Shea moved on to the visiting expert's glittering credentials. The ebullient O'Shea cited critical performance reviews from former employers, noting sloppy paperwork and reports handed in late. O'Shea quoted one of Klem's former supervisors as saying that he "had no conscience." In a blatant appeal to the big-city chauvinism of a New York jury, he pointed out that Klem had earned his credentials as a fire investigator in Prince George's County, Maryland, where the largest town was Bowie, population 33,695.

By the time O'Shea got around to grilling Klem about the specifics of the fire that had killed Lieutenant Williams, no one would have blamed the witness if he'd crawled behind one of his snazzy charts and raised a white flag.

The defense lawyers jumped from their chairs and scrambled to resuscitate Klem's moribund credibility, but the damage had been done. After devoting most of the trial to trying to explain away Jack Ferranti's lies, the defense had presented an expert witness who looked like a forensic fraud. Judge Weinstein had the jurors escorted from the room, but he told Klem to remain. He questioned Klem, looked at photos of the heater, and said he didn't see any "metal glob."

"I won't come to an official conclusion that you're lying or that you've misstated what you've observed, but I think that is the case," the judge said. "However, we'll let the jury decide."

The jurors deliberated two days before announcing that they'd reached a verdict. Dowd was racing down the Long Island Expressway toward home when the foreman announced that the jury had found Jack Ferranti guilty of all nineteen counts of arson conspiracy, witness tampering, and mail fraud. Mario Ferranti was convicted of a single charge of arson conspiracy but cleared of everything else. Cheers broke out in the courtroom as the firemen took turns hugging each other and Mrs. Williams. Mario sneered, snorted, and wagged his head in disgust, but Jack merely let out a long sigh.

When he learned of all this, Dowd called Armanti with the good news. "We fucking did it!" Armanti howled with joy.

That night, prosecutors, fire marshals, and police officers celebrated at a bar near the courthouse. Dowd felt like he could relax for the first time in years. His headache was even gone. O'Shea had a half dozen beers lined up in front of him when his wife wobbled in, so visibly pregnant that Dowd wouldn't have been surprised to see a stork circling above.

"Sean," she said. "It's time!"

The next day, she gave birth to a nine-pound, three-ounce boy.

BEFORE JUDGE WEINSTEIN imposed a prison term, he first saw to it that the Ferrantis repaid their many victims. As the Ferrantis remained behind bars awaiting sentencing, it took more than a year for the authorities to assess the market value of Jack's tenements and to figure out how much would be left to divvy up once the back taxes were paid. It was an enjoyable chore, because its outcome would ensure that Jack would lose both his freedom and his fortune. The judge ordered Ferranti to repay the insurance company $275,453 and the building owner $136,131. The Anthonys received $59,569 for their possessions; other tenants got smaller settlements. The Federal Bureau of Prisons received an advance payment of $318,037 to cover the cost of Jack's incarceration. Jack was also forced to give the fire department $949,000—to pay for its contribution to the $1 million pension Mrs. Williams would receive, the cost of fighting the blaze, and the $8,000 for Lieutenant Williams's funeral. Judge Weinstein then levied a fine of $2,911,599, to drain the rest of Jack's portfolio. If Jack ever made it out of prison he'd be both old and broke.

When the morning of Jack Ferranti's sentencing finally arrived, Lieutenant Williams's daughter Kathleen approached prosecutors with an unexpected request.

"I'd like to speak," she announced, just moments before the proceeding started.

During the trial, she had sat with her mother, watching intently but saying little. Now she wanted to bid the Ferrantis, and her father, one final farewell.

"I am a little nervous," she began. "I was not expected to speak today. Let me start by saying my father was the most important thing in the world to me and to my sister. He had the most influence [of] anyone in my life. It is not to say that I love my mother or sister any less, but the person I am today is because of this man."

She told of the horror of having her last memory of her father be the sight of his crushed face in the casket. How her sister, who was never the touchy-feely type, grabbed her at the cemetery and held on for dear life. After the funeral, people kept talking about how stoical Lieutenant Williams's widow and daughters had been—like Jackie Onassis and her children at JFK's burial. But in the years that had passed, she'd seen her mother, who had been so strong, disintegrate into tears countless times. Kathleen herself felt so enraged that she'd once thrown a glass across the room, just to hear it shatter.

"I don't feel angry anymore," she said. "I don't feel. I don't hate these men. I do want justice done, and I hope that there really is a heaven and hell and that they will get what they deserve in the afterlife."

Kathleen walked back to the spectators' bench and took a seat. Her mother, Patricia, then rose and stepped toward the judge's bench. Lieutenant Williams's widow told the judge that the Ferrantis had destroyed the life she had once cherished, and she then shared her last memory of her husband. Before she'd left for work that morning, Tommy Williams had woken early to make her lunch, and as he'd handed it to her, he'd said, "Pat, I will miss you."

Their eyes met, Mrs. Williams said, "and I felt my heart drop. I told him I would miss him too, and quickly looked away, knowing I would never leave for work if I let this feeling take over. Little did I know that this would be the last time I would see him.

"My heart has been broken. I am deprived of a very special person who has shared my life. He was my confidant, my best friend, my soul mate. To know that I will never be able to see, touch, or feel him again has been impossible to bear. My only comfort has been in knowing these criminals would someday be held accountable."

The federal court system has strict sentencing guidelines, which limited the amount of prison time Judge Weinstein could impose. Mario, who was convicted only of arson conspiracy, received five years. Tocco pleaded guilty to reduced charges three days after the Ferrantis were convicted and got a five-year federal sentence—but he still faced the prospect of an additional and lengthy prison term for selling cocaine to Armanti. Jack faced the heaviest time because he had been convicted of masterminding the arson plot—but the federal guidelines mandated that his sentence be less than life. Judge Weinstein took that as a personal challenge, using actuarial tables to determine Jack's life expectancy, then calculating how much time Ferranti would get shaved off his sentence for good behavior. Calling the fire "a particularly heinous crime," he imposed a sentence of 435 months in prison—thirty-six years and three months. Jack was forty-three, so if his health held up and he stayed out of trouble behind bars, he'd get out at age seventy-three—precisely fifteen months before he was likely to die.

Walking out of court the day of the sentencing, Patricia Williams caught up with Dowd and gave him a hug.

"Thank you," she said. "You don't know how much this means to me."

Dowd left the building alone, then sat on a bench outside the courthouse. When Mrs. Williams had made her statement to the judge, he'd become so choked up that he'd nearly had to leave the courtroom. Dowd had a wife and three children, so he was particularly moved by the way she and Kathleen had described the gaping void left by Tommy Williams's death. How Kathleen's college graduation had felt meaningless without her father there. How her sister's wedding had seemed hollow without Lieutenant Williams to walk her up the aisle.

Some victory, Dowd thought. *We win, and Tommy Williams is still dead.*

19

"HEAD ON A SILVER PLATTER"

DECEMBER 18, 1996

TOMMY TOCCO, SWEATING profusely, writhed in his chair at the Bronx district attorney's office. Squinting and stalling, he searched the recesses of his colorful vocabulary for the magic words that would set him free. He needed to say something, to play the perfect chord in order to spare himself a forty-year stint in prison for selling cocaine to Vincent Armanti. But if he said too much, his existence would be worthless. If he said too much, he'd be a gravelly voice nobody remembered.

Tocco was trying to convince his prosecutors to reduce the coke charges against him in exchange for facts about John Wynn and the brutal 1989 dismemberment of rent activist Bruce Bailey. (Mario Feranti had bragged about chopping up the body but the police didn't have enough evidence to charge him.) But Tocco knew that once he started, the DA would want him to rat out every other criminal he knew. That carried risks that would make prison seem like just another upstate health spa.

During the previous months, Tocco's lawyer, Ron Kuby, had rallied his considerable portfolio of skills in a last-ditch attempt to prevent events from reaching this particular juncture. He had cut his teeth with the renowned civil-rights lawyer William Kunstler, who had been hired by Tocco's family in 1994, then died a year later. So now Kuby had inherited the entire mess. Practicing law with Kunstler—who had defended the Chicago Seven, the terrorists behind the 1993 World Trade Center bombing, and inmates in the Attica prison uprising—had helped Kuby develop a name as a movement lawyer and an expert in high-publicity political trials. But he also knew the cold realities of drug cases involving suspects whom the media deemed unworthy of obituaries; when the DA has the evidence, you push for a plea deal.

Tommy Tocco had been caught selling a little more than two ounces of cocaine—just enough weight to trigger the severe penalties of an A-1 felony under New York's stiff, Rockefeller-era drug laws. At a time when cartels were moving a torrent of cocaine through the sprawl of metropolitan New York (often in shipments of hundreds of kilos at a time), it was a trivial amount. Then there was the fact that the sale to Armanti was, unbelievably, Tocco's first drug arrest. In any vaguely comparable case, Kuby argued, the DA would routinely cough up a plea agreement with a sentence of five to fifteen years. No cooperation necessary. No strings attached.

But other cases didn't involve a suspect responsible for killing a heroic fireman, and on top of that the DA had tapes of Tocco making the sale. Armanti was eager to testify. Why should the DA cut a break for someone as odious as Tocco when he held cards so strong? Although Kuby complained expertly, incessantly, and quite accurately that Tocco was being shafted, the prosecutors just shrugged their shoulders. During one exchange, a Bronx DA simply grinned and advised Kuby, reassuringly, "Bad things happen to bad people."

Tocco had rather pressing personal reasons to cut a deal. He had recently married his girlfriend, Angelique Montemurro, and before he began his prison sentence for the arson in the summer of 1996, the couple had conceived a child. If Tocco were convicted, the kid would be a middle-aged man before he saw his father any place other than a prison visiting room. Following the convictions of the Ferrantis, Tocco had pleaded guilty in the arson case and had started sending mixed signals about cooperating in the Bailey and Wrynn matters. But he kept backing out before anybody got near the negotiating table. Finally, in December 1996, with his trial for dealing cocaine approaching, Tocco agreed to sit down with Dowd and the DAs in the Bronx to discuss a possible deal.

As Tocco was led into the room and his handcuffs were unlocked, Dowd was stunned by how defeated the guy appeared. Tocco had put on some muscle since he'd been locked up, but he hung his head like a scolded dog. When the discussions kicked in, Tocco played it very coy about Bruce Bailey's hideous murder, which had ended with the victim's body parceled into four garbage bags. He said he'd heard Mario once make a snide reference to it, but had no idea who had actually killed Bailey.

Yet Tocco, surprisingly, didn't hesitate about giving up John Wrynn. His coarse voice as grating as ever, Tocco started by conceding that in October 1992, Wrynn had warned him to watch out. He was the target of an investigation. Then in mid-November, Eric Mergenthal, whom Tocco had known practically all his life, introduced him to an undercover he described as a "cousin" looking to purchase a gun. On November 21, the undercover gave Tocco $750 for a semiautomatic. A day or two later, Tocco said, John Wrynn told him to back out of the deal: Mergenthal had introduced him to a detective.

"He told me not to do the deal," Tocco said.

At the sound of those words, Dowd grew disgusted: Eric Mergenthal had been a messed-up kid, but he had also been somebody's son. He had been Dowd's responsibility, his informant, and he'd ended up dead. Tocco had put his finger on a sore spot that, for Dowd, just wouldn't go away.

"Tommy, we have you taped, talking about who killed Eric," Dowd said. "Who killed Eric?"

Tocco said nothing.

"Come on, Tommy, don't bullshit us now," Dowd demanded. "Who killed Eric?"

Tocco turned to Kuby, and they began a whispered consultation that ran all of a few moments. When they separated, Tocco said he needed a break and promised to continue the conversation the next day. Dowd raced to the phone to call Armanti, who was at home, waiting restlessly.

"We've got it!" Dowd said. "He gave up Wrynn. We're going to meet again tomorrow and he's gonna give up the Mergenthal murder and give up Bruce Bailey."

"I was right!" Armanti announced into the phone, his vision blurring with tears.

"Tomorrow!" Dowd said. "Tomorrow he gives it all up."

AT A DIFFERENT point in their careers, Dowd and Armanti might have been repulsed by the ugly truth that their case against the Wrynns was now at the mercy of ugly, untruthful Tommy Tocco. But the two worn-out detectives were in no position to be choosy. After the Ferrantis were convicted, Dowd and Armanti had mistakenly assumed that the U.S. Attorney's Office would finally turn its attention to the Wrynns. But George Stamboulidis said there still wasn't enough evidence to press charges. Prosecutors had hoped to stick John Wrynn with an obstruction-of-justice charge, Stamboulidis said, but the federal statute would apply only if he had interfered in a federal case. The gun investigation involving Tocco and Mergenthal had been a state case. So, Stamboulidis said, he still needed to research the statute to figure out the best way to proceed legally.

As for Inspector Wrynn, Stamboulidis wanted more evidence before trying to press perjury charges. It was clear that the Inspector's grand jury testimony was directly contradicted by IAB investigators Matthiessen and Santiago, who had testified that they'd seen him rampaging through the office where his son's secret file was kept. But perjury cases were dicey, Stamboulidis said, and this one involved a major cast of characters. The Inspector and his allies could try to come up with some nuanced explanation for what he'd done or the way he'd described it on the stand. Matthiessen and Santiago could be put under intense pressure to change, or at least slightly shade their stories. Stamboulidis said he wanted to see if he could find another eyewitness before moving forward.

"You're telling me that the United States attorney is going to let them go because you're afraid of the witnesses lying?" Armanti yelled. "So lock up Matthiessen and the rest of those IAB scumbags, too! They've already testified before the grand jury. If they change their story and lie, lock them up, too!"

Armanti didn't even hear Stamboulidis telling him for the umpteenth time to have a little more patience. Now he could feel his temper roaring out of control. He was tired of excuses. "What's the matter? Usually you feds love going after cops. Why aren't you doing it this time? Because it's IAB and it's *political*," he thundered, spitting out the final word as if it were poison.

For some time, Dowd had attempted a more conciliatory and diplomatic approach with the U.S. attorney. He had brought Stamboulidis bits of new evidence, hoping to nudge him into something vaguely resembling action. A few months before the Ferrantis' trial, Dowd had been driving in Queens when Sixto Santiago, one of the IAB detectives assigned to the John Wrynn case from its earliest days, had come up behind him and begun flashing his headlights. When Dowd pulled over and got into his colleague's car, Santiago showered him with unexpected apologies. He said, with apparent sincerity, that he felt terrible about the way Internal Affairs had undermined the Lieutenant Williams investigation. Then he went on to tell Dowd that the interference went even beyond what Dowd knew.

Every week, the case was discussed at IAB screening-committee meetings, Santiago said, where one of Inspector Wrynn's best friends was present. "We might as well have been talking directly to Inspector Wrynn," Santiago said, shame spreading across his face. "But there was nothing we could do about it."

Dowd urged Stamboulidis to drag Santiago back in front of the grand jury and press him for details under oath. But the detective was never recalled to the stand, for reasons that were never fully explained. Dowd, who was now beginning to question whether Stamboulidis had the grit for a take-no-prisoners brawl with the Wrynns and IAB, tried to personally strengthen the case against the Inspector by doing some freelance video surveillance outside the Wrynn family's major social gatherings. When Inspector Wrynn married Lieutenant Nancy McLaughlin, his girlfriend from the Bronx borough headquarters, Dowd used an unmarked van to make videotapes of everyone who attended. He also taped the mourners who came to attend the funeral of Inspector Wrynn's mother. Sitting in that van all by himself, just waiting and waiting for the familiar NYPD bosses to parade by in their civilian finery, Dowd was beyond caring about what would happen if the police department learned of his unauthorized mission. He could have been home with his kids, but there was something thrilling about treating Wrynn to the kind of tactics usually reserved for a Gambino capo. Unfortunately, neither outing yielded anything.

Without new evidence to force the prosecutor's hand, the case languished, and the foot-dragging by the U.S. Attorney's Office provided the NYPD with a convenient dodge: Police commanders said they couldn't do anything until the federal case against the Wrynns was completed because the feds had asked them not to interfere. In March, however, Commissioner Bratton was fired and his successor made Armanti hopeful that his problems would soon be solved.

Bratton was replaced by Howard Safir, a former Drug Enforcement Administration undercover who had once managed the federal government's witness protection program. Surely, Armanti told Dowd, this was a man who would recognize the heinousness of what the Wrynns had done. Then there was the fact that Safir had also been the fire commissioner between 1994 and 1996; he almost certainly had to be aware of how blatantly Inspector Wrynn and Internal Affairs had disrupted the investigation into Lieutenant Williams's death. In late 1995, in fact, Armanti and Dowd had been invited to a Fire Foundation awards banquet aboard the U.S.S. *Intrepid* museum, to thank them for helping convict the Ferrantis. During the dinner, Armanti had been introduced to Safir as the undercover in the Williams case. A look of concern had flashed across Safir's face.

"It's a shame what they've done to you, son," Safir said.

By the time Safir became police commissioner, John Wrynn was still on modified duty in the property clerk's office, where he had cooled his heels since being questioned by the FBI nearly three years earlier. It was hardly a demanding job, and he often spent the day studying for the computer classes he was taking at night school. Maybe he really wasn't sweating it. Maybe he believed that he and his father would never be abandoned by those who had seen them this far. Dowd and Armanti knew that the father and son had friends in high places that neither of them had yet even begun to discover—including, they suspected, the powerful detectives union. One day when Dowd was leafing through the Detectives Endowment Association magazine, he was mortified to see a photo of Wrynn and Linda Nelson, the ADA who had supposedly stopped seeing him back in 1994. They were in bathing suits, photographed on a diving trip to the Cayman Islands. *Where the hell,* Dowd thought to himself, *are the Cayman Islands?*

Inspector Wrynn had not yet received his promotion, but the Naked Man case had definitely elevated his standing within IAB, and he made no secret of his impatience to have the chief's star pinned to his lapel. IAB's other Throgs Neck operatives had already been given better assignments after their faithful duty in the Wrynn case: Lieutenant Shields had received a special-assignment bonus and command of a detective squad. The memory-impaired Sergeant Matthiessen was on his way to the NYPD dignitary protection unit, assigned to safeguard such visiting VIPs as the president or foreign heads of state.

Chief Kelleher also continued his ascent. Since the resolution of the Washington scandal, the mayor and the police brass had all been quick to pronounce Kelleher's efforts to reorganize IAB as the kind of rousing success that proved the NYPD fully capable of policing itself. Kelleher had tripled the number of Internal Affairs sting operations—known as "integrity tests"—used to catch cops prone to accepting payoffs, stealing drugs, or shaking down streetwalkers. Corruption allegations dropped by

14 percent during the first six months Kelleher was in command, and while his critics said the decline was due to the fact that rogue cops now saw IAB coming a mile away, the NYPD held the statistic as an empirical measure of his success.

Kelleher had had a few harrowing moments during his first year at IAB, however. In the fall of 1995, he was being driven up the FDR Drive by an aide while engaging in one of his most dependable routines: unwinding with a cold beer on the way home from work. Just north of the Queensboro Bridge exit at Sixty-third Street Kelleher took a sip from his can of Budweiser, placed it in the cup holder between the two front seats, and noticed an unmarked police SUV pulling alongside them. In the passenger seat was Louis Anemone, the chief of patrol and one of Kelleher's fiercest rivals—a man who would have loved nothing more than to talk about seeing Patty violating the state's open-container law by sipping a beer in a moving vehicle while still technically on the job.

"Hide the beer!" Kelleher shouted.

His driver, Captain William Gorta, keeping one hand on the wheel, grabbed a folder from the backseat, and concealed the can. Career disaster averted. Another stroke of luck for Patty, for whom the victories just seemed to mount in succession: In July 1996, Kelleher was promoted to chief of detectives, and in police headquarters, people began whispering that he was being groomed to become the next commissioner.

Dowd, meanwhile, was watching his career veer toward the scrap heap. The Ferranti case was the kind of high-profile victory that the NYPD customarily rewarded with a pay increase and a promotion. But months passed without Dowd receiving any thanks whatsoever. He and Piel had patched up their friendship, and they kept pulling at the loose ends of the case. But Dowd's supervisors didn't want his time spent on investigations that wouldn't reduce the homicide closure statistics in their squads. Already, a supervisor cursed Dowd out for driving to Fort Totten to pick up files in the Bruce Bailey murder. The next day, Dowd learned that he'd been unceremoniously dumped into another precinct.

Armanti was returned to undercover duty in early 1995, but the danger of the set paled in comparison to assorted threats on his life and his career. In early July 1995, he walked into his backyard to clean his pool for a Fourth of July barbecue. When he saw that the water level was eight inches below where it should have been, he inspected the pool and found that a small hole had pierced both the liner and the aluminum sidewall. Resting at the pool's bottom was a shell from a .380 automatic. Armanti could only wonder whether he had been swimming when the shot had been fired.

IN LATE 1995, Armanti bumped into an old friend from Brooklyn, Jerry Walker, who had recently been assigned to answer phones in Internal Affairs. Walker looked alarmed, and slightly guilty.

"Are you all right?" Walker asked, concerned. "I've been meaning to call you."

"Why, what's going on?"

"They're gunning for you," Walker said. "The bosses are gunning for you."

"No shit," Armanti replied.

"No, this is serious," Walker said. "I was in Kelleher's office the other day. He was having a meeting with his upper echelon of bosses, and something just happened with your case. He slammed his hand on the desk and screamed out that he wants your head on a silver platter."

Armanti reported the conversation to Stamboulidis, and Kelleher had been summoned to the U.S. Attorney's Office the following day. When asked about the statement, Kelleher had turned red, glared at Stamboulidis, but said nothing. Then Kelleher had charged out of the room, leaving Stamboulidis and the others convinced they'd hit a nerve.

One Friday night not long after, Armanti was out with friends when his pager went off, displaying a callback number he'd never seen before. Armanti called the number and heard an unfamiliar voice.

"Don't go home!"

"Who is this?" Armanti asked.

"Never mind," the caller said. "Just *don't go home.* They're gonna try and lock you up tonight."

"Who the hell is this?" Armanti shouted.

"Have you been drinking?"

"I'm sure as hell not gonna tell you!" Armanti replied.

"They're going to try and DWI you, so don't go home," the caller said before hanging up. Armanti then phoned a neighbor, who told him that there were unfamiliar vehicles driving up and down his dead-end street. The neighbor thought they appeared to be unmarked police cars.

Armanti spent the night at a friend's house. Later he tracked down the place where the warning call had been made: a pay phone on Hudson Street, a block from Internal Affairs headquarters.

By November 1996, Armanti had had just about enough of patience and protocol. It was time to demand that *someone* do *something* about the Wrynns, and he knew that he wanted to demand it, personally, from the man at the very top. Sitting at a computer terminal in the Brooklyn DA's office, Armanti decided to personally inform the police commissioner about the situation, in writing.

Police Commissioner Howard Safir
One Police Plaza
New York, NY

November 18, 1996

Dear Commissioner Safir,
I would like to introduce myself to you. My name is Detective Vincent Armanti, Shield #4126. I am assigned to the Special Projects Unit, Narcotics Division.

He told Safir his background, how he'd risked his life on dozens of undercover assignments. He laid out the details of his role in the Williams case, just in case Safir might have somehow lost track of who he was. He described how Internal Affairs had sabotaged, misled, maligned, and endangered him. Then he ended with a personal appeal, hoping that Safir might identify with his predicament and do something out of sheer guilt.

During the past three years, my life has been far from one of normality. I come to work with the knowledge that the Department I risked my life for has turned their back on me instead of rewarding my achievements and integrity. I go home with the knowledge that murderers know who I am and possibly where I live, due to a leak in the Police Department. And, to add insult to injury, these members with the integrity problems are the same members who were rewarded with the transfers to elite divisions. These are the same members who forgot their oath to the New York City Police Department while testifying in a Federal Grand Jury.

I take a deep breath and still believe that justice will be served.

I know the integrity problems with other members of the Department have had a negative impact on my chances for advancement and my career. I could never imagine that believing in the truth could have put me in this position. I believe that the information and intelligence that I have gained and maintained through this investigation on members of the Police Department and alleged corruption involving prominent City officials has placed me in a no-win situation. The only people interested in this information are people who have something to gain by tarnishing the reputation of our great department.

Thank you for your attention to this matter.

Very truly yours,

Vincent E. Armanti
Detective

Armanti hand-delivered the letter to Safir's secretary, then sat in the waiting area until the commissioner arrived. He watched as she handed him the envelope. As Safir walked into his private office, Armanti's eyes followed him, wondering which side of the man would prevail. Would he respond like a retired DEA undercover, a former fire commissioner, the man who had apologized to him at the Fire Foundation ceremony? Or would Safir's cautious, political side make him ignore the matter—or, worse yet, allow IAB to ratchet up the pressure? If Safir refused to move against the Wrynns and tried to buy his silence with a promotion, Armanti already had a script prepared. NYPD promotion ceremonies were usually held in the police auditorium, attended by hundreds of spectators, including police commanders, city officials, and journalists. If Armanti was somehow allowed up on the stage with Safir, and the Wrynns were still unpunished, he'd put on a performance that no one would ever forget.

But the Wrynn case had been such career poison to anyone who had seriously pursued it that Armanti had a better chance of being crowned Miss Staten Island than getting the promotion that was now three years overdue. Armanti waited for the police commissioner to respond. He left phone messages and asked fire marshals to have their friends in the department reach out to Safir. But he never received a reply.

By the time Tocco sat down to talk about cooperating, a month had passed since Armanti had delivered his letter, and he had few options left. Despite the promising start Tocco had made during the first day of plea discussions, he would have to do a lot more if he wanted a deal. Being a cooperator is like being pregnant—either you are or you aren't. Prosecutors can build a case around a snitch only if he tells everything. Otherwise, defense attorneys might bring out crimes during cross-examination, destroy his credibility, and make the DA's office look foolish in front of the jury. The DA's office would want Tocco to give up everything—about the Ferrantis, Wrynn, and even his cousin the Bonanno capo Vinny Bosciano.

When Tocco arrived for the second day of the talks, Dowd noticed that he seemed more energetic. His forlorn shuffle had become a strut. He held his head up.

"Okay," Dowd said, "let's keep going. Tell us more about Eric Mergenthal."

Tocco looked around the room, snorted to himself, but said nothing.

"Tommy," Dowd said, wishing that the lawyers would leave the room for a moment so he could lay his hands on Tocco, "you've got to tell us who killed Eric."

Tocco cleared his throat, but he still didn't speak.

"Tommy, give it up!" Dowd demanded. "Who killed Eric!"

Tocco smiled, glared at Dowd, and pointed a finger straight at him.

"You killed him," Tocco said with a sneer.

20

" I TOOK AN OATH "

APRIL 7, 1997

"RAISE YOUR RIGHT HAND."

Vincent Armanti, NYPD Undercover Detective #4126, leaned forward in the witness box, so eager to shout out the truth that every nerve in his body was crackling. In his pocket were his grandmother's rosary and his stone marked *Courage,* and he had chosen his clothing as carefully as if this were his wedding day. Taking a deep breath, he reminded himself that it was essential to appear calm. Only cool, professional detachment would win over the jury. There was a lot he had to get right, many complicated details to convey in order to explain what had happened. Armanti took a last deep breath as he placed his left hand on the Bible, then lifted his right with a motion as slow and steady as a farewell salute.

"Do you, Detective Number 4126, swear that the testimony you are about to give is the truth?"

Armanti checked out the jurors. Gradually, carefully, he surveyed what he could see of the courtroom, which had been divided in two by an opaque plastic screen that ran from ceiling to floor for the entire width of the place. It was designed for the purpose of protecting his identity. Inside the screen, besides himself, were the judge, the jury, the lawyers, Tocco (the law gives defendants the right to look face-to-face at witnesses), and a few members of the press. Outside was the rest of the world, including Tocco's relatives and a half dozen thugs who habitually roamed the streets of Throgs Neck with Tommy and the Ferrantis.

The screen gave the entire scene the surreal, excited energy of a revival tent or a movie set. Armanti glanced at Tocco, who had snorted as the detective entered the courtroom and was now scowling at him from behind the defendant's table. Then Armanti peered coolly into the eyes of the court clerk administering the oath.

"Yes, I do," Armanti replied at the end of the oath, hearing his own words as if they had been uttered by someone else.

The truth. Finally, the truth. Armanti was about to give the police department far more of that particular commodity than it wanted to hear. After years of evasions, deceit, and humiliations, his moment had finally arrived. The DA's office was at last prosecuting Tommy Tocco for selling cocaine to Vinnie Blue Eyes, but to Armanti that was only part of the story, for on this day he was determined to put IAB and the NYPD on trial for flouting the law and disregarding his life.

William Zalenka, an assistant Bronx district attorney with the studious demeanor of a tax auditor, approached Armanti, offering him a warm but slightly wary smile. Zalenka had a simple mission: Convict Tocco of the drug sale. The road to this goal was so straightforward that the only prosecution witness besides Armanti was the police chemist who'd tested the drugs. Zalenka's expression suggested a certain trepidation. As appalled as he was by the travesty IAB had dragged Armanti through, his supervisors had ordered him to avoid the subject of police corruption during the trial. Bronx juries were notoriously distrustful of the police in the best of times. So the smartest, safest play was to keep things tightly focused on Tocco's crimes.

But Armanti would not go unheard. Whatever else the prosecutors had planned, they could not avoid giving him the stage, and he had no intention of stepping off it until he was finished. For too long, silence had been the shield of the tainted cops and shameless bosses.

There was also a practical reason Armanti needed to get the facts on record: He had to prepare himself for the next onslaught from within the NYPD. It seemed inevitable that if the friends of the Ferrantis didn't manage to kill him, he would soon face some kind of trumped-up departmental charges. If that happened, his sworn testimony could provide some necessary protection. So Armanti was happy to answer the DA's questions about Tocco, but he would not hesitate, when he saw an opening, to testify about everyone who had aided the Torch—Wrynn, IAB, all the gutless chiefs. In his mind they were all equals, different gears in the same corrupt machine. The DA's office could dictate the questions Zalenka asked, but no one would control what answers Armanti would give. Not any longer.

"Good afternoon, Detective," Zalenka said.

"Good afternoon, sir," Armanti replied.

He had spent months studying his notes, preparing his script. But then, in the week before the trial, two last-minute glitches had threatened to scuttle the whole case. When Armanti had called the NYPD property clerk's office to retrieve the cocaine Tocco had sold him, it was missing. It had been sent into storage nearly three years earlier, marked as evidence with a bright red DO NOT DESTROY sticker. But somehow, the property clerk's office—the unit where John Wrynn had been working—had lost track of the drugs. Armanti called back and begged the officer to search again, try another place. Finally, after three hours of rummaging through the byzantine depths of the NYPD storage warehouse, the cocaine had turned up. It had mysteriously been placed with a batch of other evidence that was to be destroyed that very day.

"Please, please, hold on to it!" Armanti pleaded. "I'm heading down there this minute. Do not let that bag out of your hands until I get there!"

Then, two days before trial was scheduled to begin, the DA's office had balked at Armanti's request to close the courtroom. Armanti had never testified in open court, and he wasn't about to make an exception for the people who had sliced up Bruce Bailey and disposed of Eric Mergenthal. In a panic, Armanti called the NYPD's Legal Bureau to ask for some kind of help. Many of the lawyers there were cops with night-school law degrees and no real experience, but Armanti got lucky. His call was answered by Marlene Besterman, a former Manhattan DA with enormous determination. Immediately grasping the situation, she raced to the Bronx to demand a closed courtroom to protect the obviously imperiled undercover. Meanwhile, Armanti turned up the pressure on the DA's office, with a performance more difficult than anything he'd ever tried to pull off on a set.

"You tell your bosses: no screen, no undercover," he told Zalenka, improvising.

A radioactive minefield and a pack of frothing pit bulls couldn't have prevented Armanti from climbing onto that witness stand, but his bluff worked. Zalenka was permitted to join with Besterman as she argued for the screen, and the judge agreed. Still, the police department wasn't about to do Armanti any favors. During Armanti's previous major cases, the NYPD had provided an armed escort to and from court. This time he was told to take a handheld police radio and call in if there was trouble. But his supervisor, Sergeant James Henry, ignored that order and two narcotics detectives, John Cieriello and Paulie DiGiacomo, volunteered their own time to whisk their friend in and out of the back door of the courthouse. Armanti was given a bulletproof vest for the ride up the FDR Drive from police headquarters to the Bronx courthouse on the Grand Concourse. But he had carefully removed it the moment he entered the courthouse. He didn't want to wrinkle the carefully starched, French-cuffed shirt he had chosen to mark this occasion. He was taken up the service elevator, to minimize the chance that he might be seen by any cronies of Tocco or the Ferrantis.

When Armanti strode into the courtroom that first day, the walk to the stand seemed endless. Hours seemed to pass between the time he entered and the moment when he seated himself on the witness stand, behind the screen. As he prepared to pull back the curtain that had concealed the machinations of Internal Affairs and the NYPD, he wondered if the mayor himself might somehow be listening.

Then suddenly it was actually beginning and, luckily, Zalenka's early questions were simple and direct. Armanti described his background, the origin of the Lieutenant Williams investigation, and the way Dowd had lured him into taking on the case. His attitude on the stand was all business. He would present himself as a pro, unlike all those cops who wore crumpled corduroy jackets and mumbled answers while nervously watching the clock. Armanti knew the jurors would hear tapes of his performance as Vinnie Blue Eyes—all those furious *fucks*, dick jokes, and the bullshit swagger. So he would counterbalance the crudeness by transforming himself, on the stand, into the kind of dependable officer who would leave an unassailable impression. He carried a duffel bag bursting with hundreds of pages of documents, neatly organized by date. He decked himself out like a CEO or, some might have said, a mob capo: Hugo Boss double-breasted suit, hand-painted silk tie, Italian loafers. Every hair on his head had been slicked meticulously into submission. Each day of his testimony, he engineered a new dashing outfit, giving jurors a few moments to check out the threads as he entered the court-room. People in the Bronx might not like cops, but Armanti would be damned if he couldn't make them like him, remember him, listen, and believe. It was a performance, and he knew how to deliver.

Despite his resolve to maintain his calm exterior, however, Armanti found himself rattled by surges of emotion as the hours and days passed and he delved back into the details of his story. Once more, he experienced the terror of learning, on the set, that his cover had been blown. Again he felt the fury of realizing he'd been betrayed by a fellow cop. The rage of watching Internal Affairs scheme and lie came back to him in waves. The nauseating feeling of Carlo Cuzzi's fingers frisking him, the humiliation of having to drop his pants to convince Tocco that he wasn't wearing a wire. As he recounted all of it, Armanti remembered to make eye contact with the jury, keep his speaking voice measured, say "sir" and "thank you." Inside, though, he was screaming, *Can you believe this!*"

Halfway through that first day of testimony, Armanti finally got to utter the two words he'd been longing to say. He knew the moment was coming when Zalenka began to ask about the day Myron Dobbs offered to take Vinnie Blue Eyes to City Island, the day they were supposed to meet his friend on the force. Determined that the truth would, at last, get a little attention, Armanti spoke the name John Wrynn.

Armanti stared straight at the jury. He would speak only three sentences about the Wrynns that day. But at some point, as he tried to get across what had happened and, more important, what had been ignored, he saw a female juror uncross her arms. Then a male juror leaned forward to look at Armanti with a concerned furrow of his brow. Armanti also noticed a commotion among the spectators. He had heard whispers that the first deputy commissioner's office would be observing his testimony, and once he said the name Wrynn, two men who looked an awful lot like cops began scribbling in their notebooks.

Armanti also glanced at another spectator taking notes, a newspaper reporter whom he had invited to write about the proceedings. He had resisted running to the media for years, had waited for the department to do the right thing, and worried that if he went public at the wrong time, or with the wrong reporter, he'd come off like every other disgruntled cop. But when the DA's office had balked at closing the courtroom, a friend had referred him to a reporter from, of all unlikely places, the *New York Times*. Most cops read gritty tabloids like the *Post* or the *Daily News*; the *Times* was too highbrow. But the more Armanti thought about it, the more sense it made. The *New York Times* had broken the Knapp Commission scandal twenty years earlier, and while every New York paper would be read at City Hall, the *Times* would also be read in FBI headquarters, the corridors of the Department of Justice in Washington, and in the offices of the White House. Surely if all those powerful people found out, someone would have to do something, wouldn't they? Armanti had met with the reporter three different times in the week before the trial to describe the case and show him the documents. One of the meetings took place in the apartment of Armanti's babe of the moment, a model for Guess jeans. Armanti viewed their liaisons as more of a diversion than a true relationship, but she cared enough to become concerned when she heard the reporter asking him the same questions over and over.

"Are you sure you should trust this guy?" she asked later.

Armanti shrugged. "What the hell else have I got?"

Armanti had no better answer to that question on the day he began to testify, watching the reporter turning the pages of his notepad. Would this guy screw him too? He didn't know. But he did know that the subject of Internal Affairs would come up again very soon in this very room, and when it did, the jury—and the world—would be watching.

NO ONE WHO had ever seen Ron Kuby cross-examine a police officer was surprised when Tommy Tocco's lawyer later emerged as one of New York's most bombastic, provocative talk-radio hosts. Quick with a joke and quicker with a cutting comeback, Kuby can segue seamlessly between overheated left-wing dogma and nonpartisan self-righteousness. But on April 4, 1997, as he approached Armanti on the witness stand for the first time, Kuby had not yet begun that chapter of his career. He was, nonetheless, every prosecutor's worst nightmare: a defense attorney who could charm and incite a jury, and bully most any witness. Not to mention his gift for making cops look like liars and fools.

It was Kuby who had fought to keep the courtroom open, a guerrilla tactic that he had hoped to use to keep Armanti miles from the witness stand. Now, after Judge Richard Lee Price's decision to limit the view of the witness stand, Kuby's only real hope was to demolish the man behind the screen. From the moment the two men first faced each other down, Kuby tried to trip Armanti up with details, asking him about strategy meetings he'd attended regarding the Lieutenant Williams case, about meetings he hadn't attended, and the decisions that had led investigators to target Tocco. There was so much evidence that Tocco had sold the cocaine, Kuby had few options other than to argue that the police had coerced his client into doing the deal. Armanti countered by clinging to his documents, sticking painstakingly, occasionally maddeningly, close to the facts. He called Kuby "sir" so often that the defense counsel might have been mistaken for the commandant of cadets at West Point.

Kuby quickly recognized that Detective #4126 and his duffel bag would not be easily led astray. So he switched gears, attempting to use Armanti's hypercompetence against him. He strove to convince the jurors that Armanti was an intimidating, all-powerful Svengali who had entrapped Tocco, luring him into a drug sale he would have never otherwise considered. As Tocco sat sneering at Armanti, Kuby pointed to a transcript that described Vinnie Blue Eyes teasing Tocco for trying to get an honest job selling toy robots on the street corner. He also focused on the first time Tocco and Armanti had discussed cocaine—when Vinnie Blue Eyes had pretended to be enraged that Joe Red had backed out of a drug deal. Kuby wanted to convince the jurors that Tocco had offered the coke only because he feared that Vinnie Blue Eyes was a homicidal maniac.

"Isn't it true that you said you were going to fuck up Joe Red?"

"No, sir," Armanti replied.

"Isn't it true that you threatened to kill Joe Red and did that in Thomas Tocco's presence?"

"No, sir."

"And isn't it true," Kuby boomed, "that you knew—*you knew!*—that Mr. Tocco was particularly susceptible to threats to kill his friends? Isn't that right?"

"No, sir."

"Well, Mr. Tocco had told you, had he not, that his best friend, Eric Mergenthal, was dead, is that correct?"

"Yeah," Armanti replied. "They killed him."

"And he had said that *they*—not *we*, but *they!*—killed him, isn't that right?"

"On one day, yes, he said they killed him."

"He said *they* killed him," Kuby sneered, gradually pacing closer to Armanti's seat in the witness box.

"That is correct."

"Did you ask him who *they* were?"

"No, sir," Armanti said, wondering how many more steps forward Kuby would take.

"Did you say to Mr. Tocco, 'Well, your friend got killed, *they* killed him. Who are *they*?' You never said anything like that?"

"In the course of that," Armanti said, "I don't think it fit in when I was speaking to him."

"You never said anything like that, is that correct?"

"No, sir."

"You never asked who *they* were?" Kuby bellowed, edging almost close enough for Armanti to smack.

"That is correct, sir."

"You knew, did you not, that Eric Mergenthal was being, was being allowed to use drugs in the course of his undercover work, isn't that right?"

"I never met Eric Mergenthal, sir," Armanti said, steadily. "I don't know what he was doing."

"Did you know," Kuby raged, "that Eric Mergenthal was being allowed to use drugs in the course of his undercover work with the police?"

"No, sir."

"Now going back to the bar, going back to the bar, when you kicked the bag, Thomas Tocco said to you, 'Calm down,' isn't that right?"

"Objection!" Zalenka shouted, fully aware that Tocco had said no such thing.

"Sustained," said the judge.

Kuby kept right on rolling: "You said to Mr. Tocco, did you not, that unless somebody made this fucking thing right, you were going to fuck up Joe Red, isn't that correct?"

"That is incorrect, sir," Armanti said stubbornly.

For four days Kuby flailed away with facts, distortions, keen observations, fanciful speculation, kidney punches, low blows, roundhouse kicks. But Armanti never allowed Kuby's goading to distract or incite him. He fended the attacks off with politeness, paperwork, and determination, even when Kuby needled him about his prized color-coded files. But Kuby kept right on coming. When Armanti gave what the attorney considered ambiguous answers, Kuby had the court stenographer read back both the question and the reply, then demanded clearer responses. He demanded to know how much Armanti drank on the set, whether he'd ever snorted cocaine while in Sebastian's, or if he'd ever seen a psychiatrist.

Armanti answered calmly: He averaged two drinks a night, had never done cocaine, and the only shrink he'd ever seen was the one who'd conducted the NYPD's routine psychological screening. When Kuby asked whether Armanti played poker with Tocco and the Ferrantis, Armanti leapt at the easy opportunity to offer a touch of comic relief.

"And approximately how frequently did you gamble?" Kuby asked.

"Maybe on four or five different occasions, sir."

"Did you win? Did you lose?"

"No, sir," Armanti said playfully. "I'm a loser."

"You lost every time?"

"Yeah," Armanti replied, with a smile that brought chuckles from several jurors.

When court adjourned each day, Armanti returned to his bulletproof vest, got his escort to police headquarters, then drove home to Staten Island himself.

That was when things always got bad. The worst moment was at home, when he pulled into his garage—a dark, enclosed space with nowhere to hide. Inside the house, he'd prepare a meal, drink a glass of wine, and study his notes to be certain he was prepared for the next day. He refused to get spooked, to think about what could happen, to answer the phone, read the papers, or turn on the TV. After a few hours of sleep, he'd dress in a different suit, the same bulletproof vest, and make the ninety-minute drive back to the Bronx for the next round of hand-to-hand combat.

After a few days of pawing and sparring, Kuby inevitably tried to use the IAB investigation to sully Armanti. Sarcastically, he hinted that Armanti was paranoid and, after making dismissive references to his accusations against IAB, gloated over the fact that no one had been disciplined or prosecuted: not the Wrynns, not the IAB detectives, not a soul.

"None of these people, to the best of your knowledge, were prosecuted in any fashion— isn't that correct?" Kuby leered.

"I'm just aware of a federal probe into police corruption being done by the United States Attorney's Office, sir."

"This is a probe that's been going on for years," Kuby shot back. "My question is, To the best of your knowledge, nobody has been prosecuted?"

"That is correct, sir."

"You haven't been prosecuted either, have you?" Kuby said slyly.

"Why would *I* be prosecuted, sir?" Armanti answered coolly.

"We're getting there," Kuby said.

Kuby withdrew the remark before Zalenka could object, and the judge chastised Kuby for the cheap shot. Armanti couldn't hear a thing—he was too busy fighting the impulse to leap from the witness box, grab Kuby's ponytail, and flail him until his skull was pulp. After a brief flash of his serial-killer look, Armanti laughed and regained his composure, reminding himself that whatever Kuby might throw at him, he would have the final say.

When Kuby completed his cross-examination, Zalenka was allowed redirect to respond to any new issues that had arisen. Early on, Armanti had worried that Zalenka's mild-mannered Clark Kent approach would be drowned out by Kuby's theatrics. Once the case heated up, however, Zalenka and Armanti made a fierce tag team. One of Kuby's craftiest maneuvers was an attempt to discredit Armanti by bringing up a Brooklyn case he'd handled in 1993 involving a suspect named Salih who'd asked him to carry out a hit.

"Do you recall being asked this question and giving this answer," Kuby said, reading the transcript from Salih's trial. "Question: 'All right, you let Salih understand that you were connected with people, and through your people, if necessary, you could whack somebody, you could kill somebody, correct?' Answer: 'Yes.'"

"That is correct, sir," Armanti said.

Kuby abruptly turned and headed back to the defense table.

"I have no further questions. Thank you, Judge," he said, leaving the jurors wondering whether Armanti might have gratuitously blown away some drug dealer.

Zalenka sprang from his seat and launched into redirect.

"Would you please tell the members of the jury what the Salih case was about," he said.

"Yes, sir," Armanti replied. "I had—I was making a purchase of two million dollars of heroin from that subject, and during the course of that investigation, he asked me to kill someone for two kilos of heroin."

"And what was your response to that?" Zalenka asked.

"That I would do it."

"Now, in actuality, did you intend to carry through on that?"

"No, we wanted to get the identity of the person he wanted me to kill," Armanti replied. "That way we could save his life."

"Were you able to do that?"

"Yes, sir."

"Eventually, were convictions obtained in that case?"

"Yes, sir."

So much for Armanti the psycho killer.

The most important doors Kuby opened during his interrogation involved police corruption. Zalenka had followed his bosses' orders and steered clear of the issue during his initial questioning, but once Kuby started in, Zalenka couldn't just let his assertions stand unchallenged. He had to allow Armanti to respond, or else the unrefuted corruption allegations might undermine his case against Tocco.

Armanti took a deep breath. The moment had finally arrived. He felt as if he were lighting a bonfire the whole world could not fail to see.

So, during redirect, Zalenka led Armanti through a step-by-step description of John Wrynn's leaks and the campaign of interference by Internal Affairs. Armanti was given the opportunity to run through a list of everyone in IAB, and at the top of police headquarters, who had betrayed or abandoned him. He got to say their names in open court and describe how, and why, he had come to mistrust them. He even got to explain how the specter of James Patrick Wrynn hovered over the entire operation.

"Let me ask you then," Zalenka said at one point. "In the hierarchy standpoint, who is more powerful: Lieutenant Shields or Inspector Wrynn?"

"Inspector Wrynn, sir."

"Now, if you knew of corruption, what is police procedure? Who is supposed to be contacted?"

"The supervisor, sir."

"And you were aware of corruption in this case."

"I felt there was corruption, sir."

"Who did you notify?"

"I approached Lieutenant Shields and I wanted to know why they were stopping the investigation when the main purpose of Internal Affairs was to get a dirty, a bad cop."

"What was the response?" Zalenka asked.

"At that point after it bubbled and there was that confrontation between me and the lieutenant, he told me he was between a rock and a hard place and it wasn't him. Don't take it out on him. And he jumped in his car and sped off on me."

After a while, it was almost as if Zalenka weren't asking questions at all. It was just Armanti telling his story, finally letting it all flow out of him as the jury, his fellow cops, the police brass, the prosecutors, and the public took it all in—every move, response, and detail. When Armanti sketched out how a succession of chiefs and commissioners had successively failed to take any action, Kuby attempted to paint Armanti as a paranoid. But every time Kuby ended recross, Zalenka was allowed redirect and Armanti was given another chance to refine his points. By the end, he wasn't angry or bitter. Just saying it all out loud made him feel like a different man. A sense of wonder entered his voice as he realized, at some late stage, that no one was stopping him.

"It's not just one incident," Armanti calmly explained. "It was a combination of incidents that took place over a three-month, four-month period. It wasn't just one thing, it wasn't one straw that broke the camel's back. Basically, it was a number of things, inconsistencies, and the problems for me that arose. It got to the point that I did not trust them."

When Armanti was finally finished, one of the cops who had escorted him from the courthouse asked why he appeared so shaken. Armanti shook his head. The sense of relief he had felt earlier had been broken. As he walked out of the courtroom, Armanti had seen Tocco high-five someone at the defense table. Armanti knew they couldn't be celebrating the pounding they'd just received inside the courtroom.

"I'm worried," Armanti said. "I think they might have gotten to a juror."

INTERNAL AFFAIRS STILL had one final insult for everyone who longed to see Lieutenant Williams's killers punished. When the prosecution rested, Kuby began his defense by calling Lieutenant Shields. Shields's testimony was their symphony of excuses, and he played each note as if convinced that his piece was Mozart. He said that IAB had never felt the least bit of pressure to protect John Wrynn. Or keep the Mollen Commission from learning about the case. Shields suggested, with a note of sympathetic concern creeping into his voice, that Armanti had become "highly stressed" as the case had progressed. He maintained that the only reason Armanti was forbidden from attending the Ferranti family barbecue—where he had expected to rendezvous with John Wrynn—was that there weren't enough backup teams available to ensure his safety.

Shields even managed to keep a straight face when he claimed that IAB had prevented Armanti from meeting John Wrynn on City Island only because it would have been a "logistical nightmare" to follow him up there. (He also added that Armanti had once said he didn't want to testify against another cop.)

Zalenka, who had long since stopped worrying about his superiors' orders to keep this saga of blatant corruption under wraps, battered Shields during the cross-examination. He made the cowed lieutenant acknowledge something that Armanti had never imagined Internal Affairs would admit—that Armanti had been an exemplary undercover, an officer who had followed orders and, contrary to Kuby's insinuations, had never been accused of the slightest misconduct.

Shields, stumbling through his attempted explanations and rationali- zations, became increasingly muddled. He was unable to defend the rationale behind Matthiessen's bumbling efforts to engage John Wrynn in conversation at the bar on City Island. When Zalenka pressed Shields for other details, like his statement about "a rock and a hard place," the lieutenant appeared to have contracted the same crippling Alzheimer's that had felled Inspector Wrynn and Sergeant Matthiessen during their testimonies before the grand jury.

During his closing arguments, Zalenka portrayed Shields as a pawn, a man who had toiled twenty-seven years in the department before finding himself saddled with the thankless task of investigating his boss's kid. He ridiculed Shields for refusing to answer a single question without por- ing over his reports.

"Lieutenant Shields basically came off as somebody who might not remember he was breathing in the summer of 1993 if he didn't have an opportunity to look at those reports," Zalenka said. "Does that strike you as somebody who feared he might be between a rock and a hard place?"

ONCE ARMANTI HAD completed testifying and returned home, he finally took the time to thoroughly review the news coverage of the trial. As he read the stories, he felt a sick, sinking feeling. The previous four years should have taught Armanti the dangers of high expectations, yet he had still hoped. But the reaction of the news media and the public was barely a fizzle.

The *New York Times* and the *Daily News* had each run two modest daily stories, but the first *Times* story had appeared on Saturday—the week's least-read paper. The others were tucked so far inside their editions that they had probably been seen only by people searching the camcorder ads. The story of Armanti's betrayal was convoluted and hard to compre- hend. There were no pictures or sound bites for TV or radio. Armanti had fired his big gun, and no sound had been heard.

The silence was deafening. Nothing had changed. *Not a thing.* Inspector Wrynn was still encamped atop IAB. John Wrynn was still on the police department payroll, pulling down the same salary as Armanti himself. On the fourth day of Armanti's testimony, Patty Kelleher began a new assign- ment as the NYPD's new first deputy commissioner—the number two job in the entire department. They were all still standing; they all had the freedom, the power, and almost certainly the desire to begin plotting their revenge.

Armanti called the *Times* reporter to ask whether he'd be writing about the verdict or doing any follow-up stories.

"I don't think so," the reporter said. "I'm not sure it's news anymore."

When the jury began deliberating on April 14, Armanti spent the day pacing around his house, occasionally peering out the window to check for menacing visitors. Zalenka called in the late afternoon, and again at about eight P.M., to say that it looked like it could be a long haul. But then, shortly after midnight, he was startled by the sound of his pager. At that hour of the night, Armanti figured, it must be trouble. He ran to the phone and dialed the number.

"There's a verdict," Zalenka said.

"Yeah?" Armanti asked.

"He's guilty," Zalenka said. "Guilty on every single count."

Armanti's body buckled and he could barely speak. He tried to squeeze out a "thank you," then hung up the phone.

When the case had begun four years earlier, Armanti and his girlfriend had been on the cusp of a new life together. Exciting career possibilities lay before him, and his abiding faith in the NYPD made the future seem like a place he could have faith in. Now he was utterly alone—a pariah to the chiefs he'd risked his life for, and an outcast in a department he no longer believed in.

Somehow, though, none of it mattered at this moment. *Lieutenant Williams took an oath, and he was willing to die for what he believed in,* Armanti thought. *I took an oath, too.* Now Lieutenant Williams's killers, the men who'd ordered and lit that fire, were off the streets, and would probably die in prison. Nothing could erase that fact. All the heartache and turmoil and danger Armanti had been through had paid off.

Armanti smiled and poured himself a glass of red wine.

I won, he thought. *I won.*

He took a sip of the wine and sat on the couch. Then he took another sip and set down the wineglass. Finally, as the clock ticked in his otherwise silent home, NYPD Undercover Detective #4126 put his face in his hands and wept.

21

"WHAT KIND OF WORLD WOULD IT BE?"

MAY – OCTOBER 1998

ARMANTI BOLTED OUT of bed at 6:30 A.M. on the morning of May 1, sprinting toward the door before he'd even finished putting on his white deck shoes. Wearing wrinkled sweats, with day-old razor stubble, he dove into the car and barreled out the driveway. It was only a half mile to the newsstand, but Armanti, gunning the engine, felt as if he were driving on a treadmill. The *New York Times* was supposedly hitting the stands with a major exposé about the Wrynns, and although Armanti wouldn't believe it until he had it bronzed, mounted, framed, and prominently displayed on the wall of his office, he still couldn't wait to get the paper into his hands.

With society safe from Tommy Tocco for four decades, Armanti had been more determined than ever to get some small semblance of New York justice in the matter of the Wrynns. During the four years since his demotion from narcotics, John Wrynn had made what many considered productive use of his stint in the property clerk's office, teaching himself enough about computer software to rate the assignment of building several simple databases for the unit. He had also been entrusted with the installation of a high-tech alarm and video-surveillance system for the NYPD's evidence warehouse in Queens. Armanti couldn't believe how perfectly fitting that was: Who would know more about subverting surveillance than John Wrynn? But Wrynn himself didn't seem to get the joke; his coworkers said he appeared to be at peace with himself, vowing, "I'm just going to stay here as long as I can."

The happily remarried Inspector was still bucking for his chief's star— despite some recurring suspicions about his associations with mobsters. In

December 1996, the home where Inspector Wrynn's parents had lived—
and where he himself had taken up temporary residence after leaving his
wife—had been sold to the son of Louis "the Whale" Inglese, the portly
gangster who had recently finished a prison term for offering a police officer a bribe commensurate with his size. (It was believed to be the single
largest bribe in NYPD history.) With all that had come out about the
Wrynns, the Inspector's neighbors and enemies had leapt to the conclusion
that the property transfer was some sort of payoff. But real estate records
showed that the Inspector hadn't actually owned the home or made the
sale—his sister had—and the purchase price was close to market value.
Rather quickly, as the Whale's offspring settled in, the incident was written
off as just another one of those coincidences involving organized crime
and its practitioners that dogged the Wrynns of Throgs Neck.

Since Tocco's conviction, Armanti's life had begun to fall back into its
own peculiar equilibrium. He had returned to action, posing as a hit man
at the Metropolitan Correctional Center for several weeks. (He hadn't lost
his touch—a member of the Latin Kings gang hired him to kill two federal witnesses.) Next, he had been slipped into South Brooklyn to investigate tips that members of the Colombo family had executed a police
officer in 1992. His supervisors begged him to watch his back—one
never knew who might be one of the Wrynns' loyalists or when they might
strike. Still, Armanti immersed himself in new cases, occasionally
obsessing about the nightmare of one day walking into work and being
introduced to a new commander, a rising star named Chief John Wrynn.

Tocco's conviction had left Armanti feeling liberated but extremely
anxious about the Ferrantis' wiseguy pals. By the time the jury foreman
had uttered the word *guilty*, Tocco had stopped his sneering. Staring
silently at his folded hands, he sat without moving as his family's uproar
had drowned out the sound of the five *guilty*s that followed. Tocco's
mother, clutching the gold crucifix that hung from a chain around her
neck, had burst violently into tears. His father, Butch, had reacted simi-
larly, slamming his hand into the bench, then jumping from his seat and
pummeling the wall. Tocco's wife, Angelique, sobbing as the jury exited,
shouted, "What if it happened to *you*?"

The wounds of these supporters apparently remained swollen and sensitive. Richard Lee Price, the judge in the Tocco case, had sued the city
after his injury in an accident when his car had hit a bad patch of road.
On the day of the proceedings, a month after Tocco's conviction, five of

the Torch's relatives had traveled to the other side of the city to watch. Members of the Tocco entourage had entered the Kings County courtroom, glaring vindictively at the judge. At some point, Tocco's father had gone so far as to rise and point a finger at the ailing magistrate. "We want *him*!" Butch Tocco had raged, before court officers had tossed the family out of the building.

But Armanti had enemies closer to home. In the years leading up to the Tocco trial, he had done his best to tone down his criticisms of the NYPD's protection of the Wrynns. He was determined not to give IAB any excuse to throw him off the force or preempt his testimony. But once Judge Price had handed Tocco the inspiring sentence of forty-four years behind bars, Armanti had felt free to prod the department openly, zealously, sometimes even obnoxiously. The only thing left to lose was his job, and he had no problem risking that; it had already, in his view, been thoroughly debased. Although the chiefs still turned to Armanti whenever they had a particularly treacherous operation, it was unmistakably obvious that some powerful forces wanted him to drop his complaint against the Wrynns.

Yet out on the streets, where police officers risked their lives each day and all through the night, Armanti's tale had struck a chord. Cops were outraged, and the outpouring of supportive calls, back slaps, handshakes, and hugs buoyed Armanti's spirits. It was as though an army of honest officers had amassed behind him and were carrying him through the moments when he might have considered walking away. Sooner or later, one of them would rise to a position high enough to do something. Armanti just needed to bide his time and get the word out. Or so he tried to convince himself.

Shortly after Tocco's sentencing, Armanti rewrote his training curriculum for new undercovers, adding a section on corruption. "There aren't as many dirty cops on the job as the media says, but you still have to be careful," he'd tell trainees. "When I was an undercover, a corrupt detective, John Wrynn, gave up my identity, and he was protected by Internal Affairs, where his father was an Inspector."

A supervisor who heard about this told Armanti to ease up. Open to advice as always, Armanti rewrote his lesson plan. During the next class, he announced, "Once, a dirty cop gave me up when I was on the set, but I'm not allowed to say who."

Then he turned to the blackboard and wrote five giant letters: W-R-Y-N-N.

Yet there were few signs that the Wrynns would ever get more than a classroom scolding. Dowd and Peil held periodic meetings with the U.S. attorney, who persisted with his hesitant approach to the case. Stamboulidis ranted about the Wrynns' transgressions, talked big about tracking down more evidence, but somehow couldn't quite bring himself to pull the trigger and press charges. Finally, in October 1997, Stamboulidis tried to break the impasse. Working with Dowd and Peil, he wrote an eleven-page memorandum to the new Internal Affairs chief, Charles Campisi. The single-spaced memo laid out the facts against the Wrynns, asserting that there was "compelling evidence of crimes and administrative violations . . . that justify the prompt termination of John Wrynn's employment."

Without mentioning the Inspector's possible promotion, the letter made clear that the U.S. Attorney's Office was prepared to humiliate the NYPD if he were elevated. A few weeks after the NYPD received the communication, the Inspector was transferred from Internal Affairs into the bureaucratic oblivion of the Communications Division. Although Stamboulidis considered this a significant victory, Dowd worried that it might be just a tactical retreat before Inspector Wrynn's promotion and return to IAB. When Dowd passed a copy of the letter to Armanti, Armanti nearly exploded.

"Why is this being written in a letter?" Armanti wanted to know. "This should be in an indictment! We're gonna tell the truth, but we're not gonna do anything about the truth? This is bullshit!"

Armanti was still fuming a month later, when the U.S. attorney had an awards ceremony for the investigators who had put Tocco and the Ferrantis behind bars. As they received congratulations and plaques from U.S. Attorney Zachary Carter, Armanti avoided giving Stamboulidis as much as a glance. After the obligatory group photo, Armanti quickly ducked out of the room. In the hallway he approached Cindy Peil.

"Did you have something to do with that piece-of-shit letter?" He was barely able to contain himself. Peil was taken aback by his vehemence.

A few weeks later, Armanti, still fuming, bumped into the *New York Times* reporter who'd covered Tocco's trial. Armanti had always worried that his reputation as an eccentric might have scared the media off his story, so he casually mentioned the letter. He considered it, if nothing else, a sort of written verification of his sanity. The reporter asked for a copy of the letter and then, a few days later, called Armanti at home.

"This is pretty incredible," he told Armanti. "We've got to try to do this one more time."

Armanti tried to douse any expectations—he didn't want to give the NYPD the chance to hack down his hopes yet again. But for the front page of the *New York Times*? He tried to muster a new attitude. Armanti borrowed Dowd's entire case file and turned it over to the reporter. During the next four months, the reporter called Armanti incessantly, asking the same questions again and again. On the afternoon of April 30, he told them the story was scheduled to run the following day.

AND SO ARMANTI had reached the May morning when, unshowered and unshaven, he raced to the newsstand. Screeching the car to a halt, he dashed to the counter without bothering to close the door. Slamming sixty cents on the counter, he grabbed a paper. The front page had a story about the scandals surrounding President Clinton and his wife, Hillary; the Senate's approval of a plan to allow the former Eastern bloc nations into NATO; a proposal to give $100 billion in aid to Indonesia; and Russian President Boris Yeltsin's new leadership team in Moscow. Not a thing about the Wrynns. Armanti felt the hope rush out of him. With global crises and world leaders' sex lives to compete against, he wondered whether the twisted saga of a Staten Island undercover would ever get heard. Later that morning, the reporter phoned in his excuse.

"Sorry," he told Armanti. "They held it for a few days. Just try to be patient."

Three days later, Armanti braced himself for more headlines about Monica Lewinsky. The reporter had called again the night before, promising that the story really would run the next day. But this time Armanti slept until eight, showered, then shaved as slowly as a man preparing for the hangman's noose. Finally, he changed into his work clothes and drove to the newsstand at a pace so leisurely that he half-expected an impatient honk from some outraged geriatric stuck behind him.

Then he picked up the paper. There it was on page one: a picture of John Wrynn caught unprepared, eyebrows arched, looking guilty and sinister. The headline was A MOLE IN BLUE: DETECTIVE'S LOYALTY IS QUESTIONED AS MOB STAYS ONE STEP AHEAD OF THE LAW. The story ran for nearly a full page inside the paper, laying out everything from the Wrynns' leaks to Eric Mergenthal's suspicious death by heroin to the Inspector being caught tearing through the offices of Internal Affairs to rip into the files detailing his son's investigation. For those too harried to read the whole thing, a graphic contained excerpts of the letter, cataloging Wrynn's misdeeds: "obstructing justice . . . making false statements to a federal officer . . . alerting criminals they were targets of ongoing covert felony investigations . . . seriously jeopardizing the safety of two undercover detectives." The article also noted that "two confidential sources were identified, one who is in fact now dead." There was even a photo from the night of the fire: five firemen covered with soot and staggering with grief after learning that Lieutenant Williams had been killed.

Armanti read the story twice, then began to laugh out loud.

The instant Armanti set foot in the special projects office in police headquarters, the whirl began. Suddenly, it was a holiday.

"Whoooooa!" shouted one of his coworkers.

"Fuck them!" screamed another. "Fuck every one of them!"

Above the laughter and cheering rose several cries of *You sick bastard!* Armanti's supervisor, shaking his head, ordered him not to leave the special projects office without another detective by his side, just in case someone tried to set him up. Armanti nodded and smiled, trying to stay cool. But he was tense, wired. It was true: They would be gunning for him now.

Armanti and Dowd were both contacted by Internal Affairs that day. Suddenly it seemed that IAB's interest had been piqued. Yet when Dowd sat down with IAB commanders, he got a news bulletin: The department wanted to transfer him into Internal Affairs to work on the case with Piel and the FBI. They promised to give him whatever help he wanted, but they had underestimated the man.

"What I want is nothing—nothing *whatsoever*—to do with *you people*," Dowd replied. Then he fled and started calling friends to ask for help in blocking the transfer.

Later, Armanti was questioned by an IAB lieutenant who ostensibly appeared to be interested in pursuing the Wrynns. But ultimately, their conversation grew so heated that Armanti called for a union lawyer to represent him.

The media pack was ravenous. Newspapers and television stations called police headquarters demanding answers: Why was the department protecting the cop who had leaked to the mob? How dare they keep mistreating the undercover who'd risked his life to avenge the fallen fireman! What the hell was going on? Armanti buzzed through the television newscasts that day and saw the front-page photo of Wrynn being shown on air a half dozen times. At the end of the week, Commissioner Safir tartly announced that the NYPD would file administrative disciplinary charges against John Wrynn, which could lead to his dismissal.

Armanti even met the special prosecutor he'd been waiting for: Richard E. Mulvaney, from the NYPD department advocate's office. Although only a sergeant, Mulvaney was far more aggressive and ambitious than the average hack police prosecutor. He'd begun his police career as a patrol officer and dog trainer in the NYPD K-9 unit, then put himself through St. John's law school and worked for three years as an assistant district attorney in the Bronx. Now he was back at headquarters, angling for a job as an assistant U.S. attorney or a position on the mayor's Commission to Combat Police Corruption. The Wrynn case offered a high-profile route to career-making notoriety.

Mulvaney's friendly blue eyes and ample jaw gave him the jovial appearance of talk-show host Jay Leno, but he had the build of a wrestler and the attitude of a street warrior. Despite his law degree, Mulvaney spoke in the same bare-knuckled, knock-around language as Armanti. It was clear he wasn't just another suit; Armanti felt as if he'd been reunited with a long-lost friend from his days brawling on Fourth Avenue in Bay Ridge.

"If anyone here was dirty, I'm going after their jobs, I'm gonna kill them," Mulvaney said during his first meeting with Armanti. "You want to kill them, you stand next to me."

Mulvaney didn't tell Armanti that the Special Prosecutor's Office had been monitoring the Wrynn case since the Tocco trial, and that the Inspector and his allies were still battling. At first, Internal Affairs had balked at turning its files over to Mulvaney. Then, once Mulvaney had the paperwork, senior Internal Affairs supervisors had tried to talk him down, conceding that John Wrynn had been trouble but trying to gloss over the charges against the Inspector. Mulvaney, who likened himself to a gladiator because he relished tangling with the toughest cases in the NYPD trial room, had quickly realized he'd have to fight solo. So he'd reached out to witnesses himself, and found a trove of evidence that the sleuths at IAB had somehow missed.

Sergeant Robert Matthiessen, who had reluctantly testified before the grand jury about Inspector Wrynn, gave Mulvaney an even more detailed—and astounding—description of the way his superior had raided the investigative file on his son. Apparently when the Inspector appeared, Matthiessen had blurted out, "Can I help you?" without thinking. Wrynn had responded to Matthiessen with a look so fierce that the sergeant described it to Mulvaney as "a death stare."

"No, Sergeant!" the Inspector had growled. "You can't do a thing for me!"

Matthiessen was so terrified by the intensity of the Inspector's bellowing that he hadn't dared attempt eye contact again. For nearly fifteen minutes, Matthiessen told Mulvaney, the Inspector had stood by the side of the desk, leafing through page after page of John Wrynn's file.

Matthiessen said he was too intimidated to testify against the Inspector at any departmental trial. But Mulvaney begged, flattered, and made countless promises to protect him from retaliation—promises that Mulvaney knew would be difficult, maybe impossible to keep. Matthiessen reluctantly agreed.

Yet if anyone thought Inspector Wrynn was going to go down with his sword still in its scabbard, they misread the man. A gladiator? Jim Wrynn had spent a career deciding who would be saved and who would be thrown to the lions. If anyone on the force had the smarts and the will to tough his way out of a desperate situation, it was he.

One night in early 1998, Matthiessen called Mulvaney in a panic: Working in lower Manhattan, he had been about to drive his car away from a curb when he'd looked up to see the daunting frame of Inspector Wrynn at his window. As he stood in the unseasonably warm night air, his body blocking the light like an eclipse, Inspector Wrynn had just smiled and said, "Hello, Sergeant."

Matthiessen had mumbled a frightened hello. But the Inspector had no time for niceties. He said that he'd heard that the department had been talking to Matthiessen, and he was troubled. Very troubled. "What kind of world would it be if we gave up our own?" Inspector Wrynn opined ominously before leaving.

Mulvaney called Internal Affairs and vowed to suspend the Inspector on the spot if he went near another witness. Nevertheless, the run-in left Matthiessen so unraveled that he refused to testify. But once the *New York Times* story broke and every TV and newspaper in town started hounding the NYPD to take action, Mulvaney felt certain that no one in IAB would have the gall to interfere. His bosses gave him the all-clear signal, assuring him that the police commissioner himself now wanted the case handled aggressively and immediately.

"I have carte blanche," Mulvaney assured Armanti the day they met. "Everyone says I can take this as far as it goes."

As Armanti began working with Mulvaney on the department case against the Wrynns, his phone wouldn't stop ringing. Friends, colleagues, and relatives called to offer support. Frank Serpico's cousin phoned to ask if he needed help. A few weeks after the story ran, Armanti and Dowd took a walk outside police headquarters with one of Dowd's friends, a sergeant who had worked closely with Patty Kelleher when he was in Internal Affairs.

"You know what this is about, right?" asked the sergeant, Michael McGovern.

Armanti's mind raced. Maybe his wildest conspiracy theories were true—maybe the wiseguys and drug dealers had a direct line into police headquarters and could order the chiefs to do anything they wanted.

"What do you mean," Armanti replied, "what is it about?"

"Kelleher," McGovern said.

Armanti stopped walking.

"What the fuck do you mean?" Armanti demanded.

McGovern stopped, looked back, then said matter-of-factly, "Wrynn helped take care of him when he wrecked his car."

As McGovern explained the story of Kelleher's crash, Armanti felt too sick to speak. But in his head, he kept repeating the same line over and over: *They tried to throw my life away, and it's all over a fucking car accident?*

THE MEDIA WOULD not be stifled this time. The *New York Times* followed up its story with an editorial, declaring that the case was a test of Mayor Giuliani's resolve to curb police corruption. Next, the paper asked the U.S. attorney to investigate the failures that had allowed the Wrynns to escape punishment for so long. *Newsday,* the *Post,* and the *Daily News* ran several follow-up stories. Whatever the intended topic of the police department's press briefings, reporters pushed Safir and his aides for an explanation, time and again.

Police officials raced to blame the feds. Walter Mack, fired as chief of Internal Affairs by Bratton three years earlier, gave interviews saying that the U.S. Attorney's Office had specifically asked him not to take any sworn statements from the Wrynns until the criminal investigation was finished. His statement was true, but incomplete: The NYPD already had more than enough evidence to fire John Wrynn, even without a sworn statement. At the very least, the department could have suspended him, sparing taxpayers the burden of his salary. Mack also failed to explain how he and other NYPD officials had justified allowing the Inspector to remain in IAB and even tried to promote him after he'd read the file on his son and threatened investigators on the case.

Police Commissioner Safir felt the heat, too. But a few days after the story broke, he scoffed at suggestions that the NYPD had dawdled to protect two of its own.

"That's how long it takes," he snapped, referring to the lengthy process.

Near the end of one press briefing, a reporter pressed Kelleher about rumors that Inspector Wrynn had come to his aid on the night of his car accident.

"As I recall, I was unconscious," Kelleher said with a nervous grin, "but there is no indication or no knowledge that he was then present. He was not there."

"You were unconscious?" a reporter asked incredulously.

"I hit a tree," Kelleher shot back.

Before anyone could ask what behind-the-scenes role Wrynn might have played or whether it had affected Kelleher's actions, Safir raised his hand and waved them off.

"Next," the commissioner barked.

The exchange received little notice in the press, and was published only as a small item in a weekly column in *New York Newsday,* which chronicled the inner workings of the NYPD. But it sent a buzz through the department, especially in Internal Affairs. A few days after the item ran, IAB Inspector Bruce Major spoke with his old friend Jimmy Wrynn to ask whether it was true.

"It's all foolishness," Wrynn said dismissively. "We went up there, Kelleher wasn't drunk. It has nothing to do with anything."

Major had known Jimmy Wrynn long enough to realize it was pointless to press him for details.

During the next three months, the NYPD's approach to the case careened between backstage anxiety and public defensiveness. On May 19, administrative charges were quietly filed against John Wrynn— more than four and a half years after he'd been accused of leaking confidential information. The department made no public mention of this until two weeks later, when a reporter inquired about it during a briefing on crime statistics. Safir became indignant at the suggestion that the NYPD had been slow to take action against John Wrynn. "The federal government had this case for five years and it resulted in no criminal charges," he said. "We've had it for five months and served him with charges."

But Safir made it clear that the NYPD was still standing behind the Inspector.

"I have no information at this point that Inspector Wrynn has been involved in any misconduct," he said, insisting that the veteran commander's sterling career should not "have a cloud over it." Safir said the Inspector still might be promoted.

Police officials and Wrynn's allies quietly launched a manhunt to find and punish the person responsible for leaking Stamboulidis's letter to the *Times*. Dowd got calls from the deputy commissioner of public information's office, asking whether he would give a follow-up interview. Clearly, it was a test of whether he'd been the source of the story. "No comment," Dowd told them. "I've got nothing to say."

Lieutenant Nancy McLaughlin, Inspector Wrynn's new wife, thought she had figured out the source of the leak to the *Times* one day in early June. One of her office mates in the Bronx Detective Bureau, Lieutenant Freddy Solomon, received a call from an FBI agent who had the same first name as the reporter who'd written the story. McLaughlin, who took a message for Solomon, began screaming that the lieutenant had ratted out her husband and his son. She was completely mistaken, but the tirade was so fiery that her bosses moved Solomon's desk to another office.

DURING THE FIRST week of June, Armanti got the most astonishing news yet: He was being promoted. The NYPD had passed him over during five previous rounds of promotions, but now, four years after it was due, he was finally going to get a bump to detective second grade. A friend in the chief's office claimed that somehow his name had slipped by, and Commissioner Kelleher was now livid. But Dowd smelled a setup: The NYPD bosses, attempting to throw Armanti a bone, were obviously hoping it would lodge in his throat and mute his hysteria when the Wrynns walked away from it all untouched.

Whatever led to the promotion, on June 18, Armanti found himself riding the elevator to the thirteenth floor of police headquarters for a private

ceremony in Commissioner Safir's office. As he made his way to the ceremony, awash in ambivalence, he couldn't stop thinking of all the times
he'd wanted to get Safir alone in a room, all the questions he had been
dying to hurl at him. But Armanti wasn't alone—he was accompanied by
his parents, several friends, and the narcotics commanders who'd fought
so hard to make that day happen. He was also entering the office of the
New York City police commissioner, a position that had once been held
by Theodore Roosevelt. Armanti didn't consider Safir worthy of mucking
out Roosevelt's horse stable, but he'd vowed to keep his complaints to
himself—at least for that day—out of respect for the institution.

Safir's welcome was as warm and cuddly as dry ice.

"Detective Armanti, here you are," Safir said, handing him a certificate and extending his hand stiffly.

They shook hands, and the commissioner posed for a few photos. Then
Safir abruptly left the office. Armanti and the others lingered in the room,
sharing small talk, savoring the moment, and waiting for Safir to return.
After five minutes or so, the police commissioner's secretary stuck her
head in.

"You can all leave now," she said.

ARMANTI MET WITH Richard Mulvaney more than a dozen times that
first month, watching him as if he were a suspect, waiting for him to
reveal himself as just another con artist. Armanti wasn't about to be
played—not at this stage of the game and not by anyone with a badge or
an NYPD paycheck. When Mulvaney asked what Armanti was hoping
for, the special prosecutor didn't flinch when the detective said he
wanted them all: John Wrynn, fired and prosecuted; the Inspector fired
and prosecuted; Matthiessen, Gagliardi, and Shields, prosecuted, fired,
or at least demoted for undercutting the Lieutenant Williams investigation; the list went on.

Of course, Mulvaney said. He had expected nothing less.

Armanti turned over the notes and reports he had amassed about the
case—one document at a time—giving Mulvaney new pages only after
making certain that he'd taken action on things described in the previous pages. But Mulvaney seemed as eager to nail the Wrynns as Armanti
himself. The two men spent so much time analyzing the case that Armanti
began socializing with Mulvaney, even setting him up on a date with a
model and inviting him into his home.

As the weeks passed, however, it became evident that Mulvaney's superiors in the Special Prosecutor's Office didn't share his fervor and weren't about to be persuaded. Mulvaney trudged back from meetings with his bosses and told Armanti about the hypotheticals they were tossing around: What if the son is fired and the father resigns? How about if the father is transferred and the son stands a departmental trial?

"I want them both fired," Armanti insisted. "And once they're gone, I want them charged! The son obstructed three investigations. The father lied before a federal grand jury. If we take them to trial, they're gonna lose. Then we've got other issues—those fucks in Internal Affairs."

Over and over, Armanti spelled out his demands, down to the last vowel. Over and over, Mulvaney said he'd have to take it upstairs to get it approved. But upstairs was the head of the special prosecutor's unit, Richard Kubick, who was negotiating with the Wrynns' lawyers and who reported directly to Patty Kelleher.

Richard Dienst, the Inspector's attorney, argued that after a stellar thirty-three-year career, James Wrynn hadn't the slightest intention of surrendering his job or his pension without waging the mother of all battles. No one explained just how Wrynn could be so unrelentingly arrogant and hardheaded; no one had to. After twenty-five years in Internal Affairs, the Inspector knew an awful lot about the department, its history, its bosses, and their vulnerabilities. If Kelleher wanted to fire Inspector James Wrynn, he'd have to give him a departmental hearing in the public forum of the police department trial room, and hope that what came out wouldn't take him down, too.

By late June, the media had moved on, and Armanti could feel it all slowing down, slipping away. Mulvaney told Armanti he wanted to take the Inspector to trial first, send a message that no one, regardless of rank, was above the law. But each time Mulvaney came back downstairs, he'd repeat one of his commanders' latest attempts to absolve the Inspector. He's only guilty of being a father. . . . He was just protecting his son. . . . He did what any father would do.

"What about Mr. Mergenthal's son?" Armanti demanded. "What about my father's son? What about the other undercover he gave up?"

In early July, the department settled on its battle plan: Try the son first, on charges of obstructing an investigation and leaking information to suspects, then work on Inspector Wrynn and his IAB associates later. But for all Mulvaney's good intentions, Armanti could hear the silence coming from the upper echelons of the NYPD. Still, he and Mulvaney met three times a week as the trial date approached, compiling lists of questions for each witness and preparing Armanti to testify once more.

Mulvaney caught a major break in the weeks before the trial when one of his old colleagues from the Bronx DA's office called to say that a guy named Myron Dobbs had been arrested. Dobbs, Armanti's friend from Sebastian's bar, was now looking to cooperate and said he had information about a dirty police officer from his neighborhood: John Wrynn. Dobbs told Mulvaney that Wrynn was a frequent guest in the bar during after-hours cocaine parties. In early 1993, Dobbs said, Wrynn warned him to stop selling coke in the bathroom because the police were watching the place.

"He told me, 'No more hand-to-hands at the bar,'" Dobbs said, at last divulging how he'd learned the words Armanti had written on his report. "He said they had me doing hand-to-hands."

As the day of the department trial neared, Armanti was ablaze with anxious energy. Once the workday ended, he would drive off to Brooklyn in zigzagging, roundabout routes, still checking, as he had been for the last five years, to see whether he was being tailed. For two weeks, he stayed with a friend, terrified that Internal Affairs might set him up, arrest him for DWI, do anything to prevent him from testifying against the Wrynns.

He could feel the machine in motion, hear the gears clicking, but he just had to make it into the courtroom. That way, even if the NYPD had the audacity to let the Wrynns go, he'd at least have a written record of the evidence—something to take to the attorney general, the White House, someone.

On the morning of July 18, Armanti woke early in the quiet house where he had taken refuge and prepared to head to the department trial. Opening his suitcase, he took out a blue three-buttoned suit and a dark, solid-colored tie—something conservative, predictable, impressive. All the things he feared he had never been. Then he strapped a tape recorder inside his suit jacket; its sensitive built-in microphone would capture his testimony just in case the trial minutes were misplaced. Armanti looked in the mirror and slicked back his hair. It was odd to think how much easier it was to suit up before entering a set full of drug dealers or mobsters. At least out there, he could keep his enemies in front of him.

Driving to police headquarters, Armanti couldn't resist the impulse to speed. He knew there was an IAB car around somewhere, looking for any excuse to pull him over, but he hit the gas anyway; waiting had become impossible. Let them come.

Mulvaney was in a meeting upstairs when Armanti arrived, so the prosecutor's coworkers offered Armanti a seat and a cup of coffee. A few minutes later, Armanti's cell phone rang. It was Mulvaney. There had been a change of plans, Mulvaney said. Armanti wouldn't have to testify today after all.

"It looks like the kid is going to resign," Mulvaney said. "It's definitely not going to be today."

"Resign!" Armanti repeated, incredulous. "What do you mean *resign*? You can't just resign when you're facing departmental charges—the police commissioner can refuse the resignation and make sure he's fired!"

Mulvaney said he'd explain later; he had to get back to his meeting. Later that week, Armanti learned the terms of the deal. John Wrynn had been allowed to resign with the permission of the police commissioner.

It was the NYPD's equivalent of an honorable discharge.

Mulvaney was livid that his bosses had deprived him of the chance to tear apart John Wrynn in the trial room, but he still figured he had one last shot: Inspector Wrynn. He called the U.S. Attorney's Office and asked whether the feds would finally sign off and let the NYPD start administrative action. A month passed with no response, then another.

Finally, in late September, Stamboulidis said that the U.S. attorney had decided not to prosecute. He gave the department the go-ahead to proceed with administrative action. Mulvaney began assembling his witness list. He would call Sixto Santiago, one of the IAB investigators who'd seen the Inspector rampage through Internal Affairs. And if Matthiessen balked, he'd swear out a subpoena, force him to appear.

But one morning in early October, Mulvaney arrived at his office in the basement of headquarters only to find it had all vanished. The three cardboard boxes stuffed with evidence against Inspector Wrynn had been taken from under his desk. Mulvaney called up to Internal Affairs, demanding to know what had become of the boxes. A lieutenant told him that they had been moved to the Internal Affairs office. Internal Affairs, the people who couldn't prevent the Inspector from looking through his own son's file, had snuck into Mulvaney's office under the cover of night and hauled the evidence away. And they had the nerve to say they were doing it for safe-keeping.

Mulvaney barreled into the office of the head special prosecutor, Richard Kubick, demanding to get the boxes back. Kubick watched Mulvaney storm for a minute or two, then put up his hand.

"What do you want me to tell you?" Kubick said. "Obviously, we're not going to go on with it. It's over."

THE SUN SHONE so brightly over the East River that reflected flickers of light managed to make their way to the dark corner of the barroom where John Wrynn sat whispering into a cell phone. Wrynn, now thirty-six years old, was seated in Sequoia's, a fashionable-enough restaurant on the third floor of the South Street Seaport. Because of the weather, the piers and boutiques were pulsing with tourists, shoppers, and Wall Street traders wearing their dark, expensive suits. Yet also scattered among the crowd on that spectacular afternoon were dozens of NYPD officials, men in older, not so costly jackets, who had walked the six blocks from police headquarters for a luncheon to honor one of their own.

After thirty-three years on the force, Inspector James P. Wrynn was retiring, and nearly one hundred of his colleagues, mainly men like himself who had spent their lives in filthy, smoky police stations, had gathered to lift a glass and offer the kind of farewell police commanders customarily provide one another—brief, stiff, unsentimental, but well lubricated.

John Wrynn's own departure from the department in 1998 had been a far different occasion for the Wrynns, although even then their family loyalty had remained unshakable. By the time he was forced off the job, the Inspector's son had spent five years pulling down an NYPD salary in the property clerk's office, mouthing cocky predictions that seemed less and less in sync with reality. But once the department was finally pressured into filing administrative charges against him, he'd realized that the situation was something that even his father's Herculean resolve could not repair. His lawyers, provided by the Detectives Endowment Association, had tried to negotiate a settlement that would allow John to keep his pension. But there was so much concern that federal prosecutors might press criminal charges that the younger Wrynn received an ultimatum: Quit or face a department trial.

John's lawyers told him they were willing to fight it out, but they pulled no punches about the fact that a departmental hearing would definitely be ugly. And it would almost certainly be for naught. There were cops willing to testify about John's leaks in the Lieutenant Williams case and the Operation Big Shot investigation. Then there were Tocco's statements, plus Wrynn's own damaging admissions to the FBI. Cindy Peil had also agreed to testify, as had Armanti. Myron Dobbs was available to take the stand. The ordeal was practically destined to end with Wrynn being fired. If he was prosecuted criminally, Wrynn could end up doing time.

When John Wrynn heard this stated straight out, he knew that such a scene would undoubtedly stir up a new public outcry to oust his father. So he shook his head. "I've put him through enough," John said.

Once he'd agreed to resign, the former detective walked back to the property clerk's office to clean out his desk and say good-bye to his coworkers. Five years of his charming "Who, me?" routine had led many in the office to affectionately refer to Wrynn as a "fallen angel." They were stunned that he had actually been forced off the job. "It's a lot more complicated than you think," he said as he strolled out of the office, looking a bit less certain than the young officer who once roared through the quiet nights of Hosmer Avenue on his motorcycle.

Within the Wrynn family, there was no glossing over the shame he had brought upon his father and himself, but John had at least prepared himself for life after the NYPD. His interest in software had developed into a marketable skill, and within a year of leaving the NYPD he had formed Eclipse Systems, his own computer-consulting firm in Westchester County. In 1998, the high-tech bubble had not yet burst, and there was room for one more self-educated software technician to try to eke out a few bucks by helping small companies set up their computer systems and Web sites.

ALTHOUGH THE INSPECTOR'S clout could not save his son's job on the police force, the timing of Jimmy Wrynn's send-off was a sign that he'd at least made good on his promise to leave the department on his own timetable. He had lasted three years since the stampede caused by the

New York Times article. But by the day Inspector Wrynn's friends gathered to mark his retirement, his power on the NYPD had diminished substantially. In 1997, the Inspector had been banished from his enviable position in Internal Affairs and dispatched into the oblivion of the Communications Division, where his influence no longer extended beyond his fiefdom. Later he had been assigned to the Office of Technology and Systems Development, charged with the thankless task of trying to oversee the NYPD's motley jumble of outdated computer and telecommunications systems. Although the Inspector had no computer experience (and had testified that he was too technologically inept to understand IAB's primitive computer printouts) it was obvious, even to him, that the NYPD's technology gap could be closed only with the kind of massive infusion of money and manpower that the city had no intention of committing.

People who worked under Inspector Wrynn noted that he showed little interest in the task. He had spent much of his time reading—mostly biographies and military history—and grousing that he'd been mistreated by one chief or another. He had even allowed weekly reports to be filed on a sporadic basis, revealing the kind of relaxed approach that Jimmy By-the-Book Wrynn would never have tolerated in the days when he'd demanded the utmost of himself and all those who surrounded him.

But the Inspector, who had reluctantly reconciled himself to never wearing a chief's star, had tenaciously bided his time. In early 1999, he even attempted a minor comeback when the department was embarrassed by news reports that a group of supervisors in the Management Information Systems Division had glommed more than $1 million in overtime while preparing the NYPD for the Y2K computer glitch. Patty Kelleher, still angling to become police commissioner, had transferred out the old commander and brought Jimmy Wrynn in to clean up one more mess. At MISD, Wrynn supervised 340 civilians and technicians, but years of neglect had left the department's hardware and software hopelessly obsolete. During October of the following year, the new police commissioner, Bernard Kerik, vowing to make technology a top priority, shoved Inspector Wrynn aside at MISD and transferred him back into the lowly Communications Division. Even then, with his exile beginning to resemble a humiliating forced march, the Inspector had appeared unbowed and determined not to leave the department before he was good and ready.

One warm afternoon in the spring of 2000, the Inspector was walking across a long courtyard toward police headquarters when the building's revolving door spun to reveal Richard Mulvaney, the department prosecutor. Mulvaney did not avert his glance as the two men strode toward each other like gunslingers. Inspector Wrynn stared straight through Mulvaney until they were ten feet apart. Then, as the two passed, Wrynn's dour face curled ever so slightly into a jaunty smile. The Inspector tossed back his head in a self-satisfied gesture that Mulvaney interpreted as "Nice try, kid." Mulvaney turned to the friend he was walking with and burst into laughter.

In the days after John was forced to resign, the Inspector had confided to friends that he wanted to wait at least three years before retiring himself, so no one could claim he had been hounded out of the department because of the investigation. And like clockwork, when the magic, self-imposed deadline had finally arrived, in June 2001, Inspector Wrynn put in his papers. He had served thirty-three years on the NYPD and had seen it all, fought the best and the worst, and survived.

On the day of the Inspector's retirement party, John arrived early, helped set up a table at the door, then took his seat at the bar, where he could watch the entryway. He was determined that no uninvited guests, no personae non grata, would disturb his father's final hours as a policeman. Shortly after two P.M. John spotted the *New York Times* reporter who had written about him. Glaring at the uninvited guest, Wrynn walked back to the entry table, whispered something to the retired cop at the door, then returned to his seat at the bar. When the reporter tried to enter the party a few minutes later, he was refused one of the sixty-dollar tickets.

"It's a private party," he was told.

After all Inspector Wrynn had done to protect his son over the years, John had found his own small way to return the favor.

Inside the restaurant, the mood was as festive as might be expected, given the stern deportment of Jimmy Wrynn. Even the rays of sunshine couldn't lighten the slightly subdued ambience of this occasion. The Inspector was seated beside his wife, Nancy, with whom he had moved to the upstate town of Pleasantville. (They also bought a home on the Jersey shore.) Around the couple were gathered former colleagues from the Bronx and Internal Affairs, the police academy, the Communications Division, MISD, and an assortment of the other investigative units where he'd worked. After lunch and a few speeches, the Inspector was presented with several photographs, a plaque, and a gift certificate from Barnes & Noble bookstores. He had never been one for public displays of emotion, but at least two guests saw tears welling in his eyes as he looked back on his career and thanked everyone who had stood by him so dependably.

"Working with you people has been an honor," he said.

Considering the rough ending to Inspector Wrynn's career, a respectable number of high-level police commanders made it to the event. One notable absence was Patty Kelleher, who had retired himself the previous year, after being lavished with the kind of bureaucratic pomp usually reserved for commissioners. Mayor Giuliani had held a press conference to announce the departure and had attended the fare-well dinner at the New York Hilton. "When the history is written of the extraordinary success of the New York City Police Department at reducing crime, special credit will belong to Patrick Kelleher," he said.

The *Daily News* speculated that Kelleher's departure might be little more than a short sabbatical before his triumphant return as Safir's successor as police commissioner. But when Safir announced his own retirement several months later, Giuliani passed over Kelleher and chose one of his former bodyguards, Corrections Commissioner Bernard Kerik. The move touched off a tempest of speculation within the NYPD. Kelleher's friends, enemies, allies, and admirers all tried in vain to divine what might have inspired Giuliani's snub. There was an apparent explanation: At the time of Kelleher's retirement, it seemed, several highly publicized scandals had prompted the U.S. Attorney's Office to launch a lengthy investigation into the NYPD disciplinary system controlled by Kelleher. The inquiry had determined that the NYPD's handling of corrupt and brutal cops was so lax and arbitrary that, at the time of Kelleher's departure, some Justice Department officials were still pushing for a federal monitor to oversee the force. But Kelleher, who had often said that he saw his job as protecting the image of the department, insisted that the federal investigation had nothing to do with his decision to leave the NYPD. And when the Giuliani administration vowed a court challenge to any outside monitor, the Justice Department caved.

There was certainly little to suggest that Kelleher's handling of the Wrynn case had met with disapproval from city hall. In fact, Giuliani's handpicked Commission to Combat Police Corruption (created to blunt the Mollen Commission's call for an independent monitor) managed to deliver the administration's final verdict on the Wrynns without ever actually mentioning the family name. In a September 1998 report that

urged the NYPD to curb off-duty drinking by officers, the commission
made a brief reference to the Wrynns, referring to them only as Detective
A. and Inspector B. Doe "in the interests of privacy." Federal prosecutors
were blamed for the lengthy delays in the case. But the report did not
question the NYPD's decision to leave Inspector Wrynn in Internal
Affairs after he threatened the investigators examining his son and gave
dubious sworn testimony before the grand jury. Also left unmentioned
were Kelleher's vow to get Armanti's head on a silver platter and numerous other infractions.

Kelleher's disappointment at being passed over for the commissioner's
post might have been soothed by the fact that he had landed the city's
premier private security job. His new position as director of worldwide
security at Merrill Lynch paid $300,000 a year, more than double the
commissioner's salary. Merrill Lynch's location at the World Financial
Center, just across the street from the World Trade Center, made Kelleher
a constant presence during the cleanup after the September 11, 2001,
terrorist attacks leveled the towers. The State of New York later named
him to a special commission formed to identify other terrorist targets.

At his retirement party, Kelleher had been gracious and effusive. He
thanked the many commanders who had taught him the secrets of policing, and he paid tribute to the officers who risked their lives every day. In
a stirring farewell address, Kelleher read off the names of the officers
killed in the line of duty during his tenure as first deputy commissioner.
He spoke of the anguish he felt knowing that other officers would
inevitably give their lives.

"Another death. Another hospital. Another visit to a widow," he said
solemnly.

DOWD AND ARMANTI each spent years trying to peel away the layers of
intrigue surrounding the Wrynns' miraculous deliverance. To Dowd, who
was passed over for several promotions and bounced around several low-
profile Queens detective squads, Wrynngate came to be known as "The
Case That Cost Me My Career." For years, he and Cindy Peil filled their
stolen moments by pounding away at the Bruce Bailey murder and Eric
Mergenthal's death. Along the way, they stumbled across new allegations
against Detective Wrynn but did not find enough evidence to verify them.
After John Wrynn got his honorable discharge, new tips came in—information suggesting that Wrynn had leaked NYPD secrets to other neigh-

borhood thugs and had been involved in an assortment of nefarious deals with the Ferrantis before joining the force. But no one in the department wanted to hear about it. So much time had passed that faulty memories had erased what the top brass had not managed to eviscerate.

Dowd tried to rehabilitate his image with the bosses by carrying a heavy caseload, taking on cold cases—anything he could get his hands on. In 1999, he solved the high-profile murder of a young woman killed in a drive-by shooting on the Long Island Expressway on Christmas Eve. He was finally promoted to second-grade detective, five years or so after his peers and immediate supervisors had expected it. But by the time he made the grade, he was just a few years shy of retirement. Any hope of advancing in the department had passed him by. "You made enemies," his lieutenant said. "Enemies with long memories and a lot of friends."

In the summer of 2000, Dowd got a hysterical call from his wife, who had just answered the door of their home to find a pair of private detectives. They had, it turned out, been hired by Jack Ferranti and sent to deliver a subpoena to Dowd's house.

"How did those animals find us!" asked Dowd's wife, who was pregnant with child number four. (Mrs. Dowd gave birth to the couple's fifth child in 2002.)

Dowd raced home to calm her, but when he looked at the subpoena, he saw that the court hearing it referred to had taken place months earlier. Dowd spent three days prowling around Brooklyn and Queens before he found one of the private investigators and dragged him into the precinct. "What the fuck are you doing?" Dowd demanded, throwing him against a set of lockers in the squad room.

"They just wanted to send a message," he was told.

Dowd alerted the NYPD, and his home was put under surveillance. He tried to reassure his wife that it was just an idle threat. "Eddie," she told him. "It's time to let go."

Dowd sighed. After eight years, maybe it was time to let the Wrynns and the Ferrantis become someone else's headache. As he prepared to mark his twentieth year on the force in April 2003 (an anniversary that would entitle him to retire with full pension benefits) Dowd was uncertain how much longer he would remain on the job.

But even if Dowd and Peil had managed to cobble together enough evidence to push for an indictment against the Wrynns, they would have had to find a new prosecutor. By the spring of 1999, Assistant U.S. Attorney

George Stamboulidis had been temporarily transferred to New Mexico for the case of Wen Ho Lee, a scientist at the Los Alamos nuclear lab accused of leaking atomic secrets to the Chinese. Lee had been vilified as the most damaging nuclear traitor since the Rosenbergs. But while the FBI kept him in solitary confinement, without providing much evidence against him, he picked up some support. His colleagues in the scientific community began to argue that he had been railroaded because he was an Asian-American. Eventually, Stamboulidis had to allow the scientist to plead guilty to a single count of improperly copying files. The entire episode was a colossal embarrassment for the FBI. In 2001, Stamboulidis joined the New York office of the law firm Baker & Hostetler, where he specializes in white-collar defense work.

"THEY'VE GOT ME doing hand-to-hands . . ."

It had taken five years of Armanti's life to make John Wrynn pay for leaking those words—five agonizing years of fear, unrelenting work, anger, and questioning everything he'd ever believed in. Now he was almost forty years old. He would never have those years back, never be the same person he had been before it had all happened. Sometimes, when his struggle had seemed most hopeless, he had bucked himself up with some soothing fantasies. They all had one scene in common: Armanti tracking down Wrynn at some police promotion party, beating him bloody, then dragging him center stage, shouting, *This is the low-life who gave up an undercover!*

But as the case languished, Armanti had forced himself to face the inexplicable possibility that both father and son, not to mention their sympathizers in Internal Affairs, might escape prosecution altogether. *How could he possibly continue risking his life for an institution that had no regard for his life? How could he keep taking orders from chiefs and commanders who had spit at their oath? How could he resist throwing his shield on his desk and walking away forever?*

Once the worst-case scenario actually played itself out, however, anger and dismay were only part of the torrent of emotions overwhelming Armanti. He marveled at all the honest cops who had tried to help him at every important juncture. He found consolation in the fact that four different officers had reported John Wrynn's corruption, hoping that the frauds in Internal Affairs might actually have the conscience to do something about it. He was inspired by the narcotics detectives and supervisors who had tried to help him maneuver his complaint against the Wrynns through the thickets inside police headquarters. He would never forget that when the NYPD had denied him a bodyguard, two cops had gone to court with him, on their own time, willing to take a bullet to protect him.

Armanti was sitting at his desk a few weeks after John Wrynn's great escape—staring at his Teddy Roosevelt plaque with the quote about the valiant men who risked their lives in the arena and the cold timid souls who remained on the sidelines—when a colleague asked him why he hadn't left. "How do you still go out there?" he asked, as others often did.

Armanti thought of Detective Louis Miller, who had trained him as a rookie and who had remained on the streets after he'd turned sixty. He had been killed while defending other officers in a shoot-out. "It's what I do," Armanti said. "That's who I am. What *they* did, protecting those guys, that's who *they* are. If I walk away I become like them. A coward."

He would never stop trying to get out the truth about the Wrynns and the bosses. But Armanti would not let them stop him from doing what he had taken an oath to do. He promised himself that he would reclaim his life. At work he concentrated on high-profile cases, investigations where narcotics chiefs could protect him from interference by anyone else inside the department. At home, he was more careful about whom he trusted, but he was determined not to let his worries about reprisals from the Ferrantis and IAB make his existence hollow. While vacationing at Club Med in Martinique near the end of the whole ordeal, he met a woman and soon found himself in the first serious relationship he'd been able to handle since before he had set foot in Throgs Neck. She didn't seem to mind the danger of his job, and Armanti was relieved to learn that she lived in Connecticut, an hour's drive and a world away from the NYPD's madness. Armanti gave her strict orders not to offer the slightest bit of biographical information about herself to anyone inside One Police Plaza. When one of his fellow detectives asked where she came from, he cut off the conversation.

"None of your business," he shot back.

Before his retirement, Patty Kelleher's disdain for Armanti had become a running joke inside the narcotics unit, which remained the undercover's home turf. Armanti made sure to laugh while everyone was watching. But he had privately added a new vocation to his formal job duties: trying to find evidence that would convince Justice Department officials in Washington to overrule the Brooklyn U.S. attorney's decision not to prosecute the Wrynns.

The key to that search was solving the mystery of Pat Kelleher's 1990 car accident—which had been investigated by Jimmy Wrynn and, Armanti believed, had left Kelleher beholden to the Inspector. Attempting to find paperwork about the crash was like grasping at a mirage. The Department of Motor Vehicles and New York State Police both purge their records after five years. By 1998, when Armanti had learned of the accident, their files had been wiped clean. The NYPD's Motor Transport Division claimed it could not locate its copy of the crash report. The department also refused to release the Narcotics Division's review of the accident.

Armanti just kept searching. NYPD guidelines require that the department's various commands save their logbooks for fifty years, but the undercover found some thought-provoking lapses. The Manhattan South Narcotics Unit, where Kelleher had been working at the time of the wreck, had kept some logs from 1990. But the volume from the fall of that year, when Kelleher and the tree had had their fateful meeting, had been removed from the box, leaving a gap like a missing tooth. The NYPD's Operations Unit, which had taken the call from the state police the night of the crash, was missing records for the entire year of 1990. In Bronx borough headquarters, which was required to track the movements of supervisors responding to accident scenes, the telephone and sign-in logs were gone, too.

Every now and then new shards of information about the wreck would find their way to Armanti. He found a narcotics investigator who'd been called to the crash scene to help clean up the mess. He met several people who claimed they had seen Kelleher at a party before the crash. Still others came to Armanti to describe Inspector Wrynn's role in the exceedingly discreet investigation. But when asked whether they'd go public, even cooperative officers were afraid to antagonize Kelleher's powerful friends on the police force. Even Kelleher's former aide Mike McGovern, who first told Armanti about the accident, refused to step forward. "I've got to worry about my paycheck," he said.

Armanti didn't have an ounce of naïveté left. But he still kept finding himself surprised. During his twenty years on the force, he had exposed the secrets of drug gangs, murderers, bank robbers, terrorists, and mobsters. Finally he had found a clan so cunning and fiercely protective that even he couldn't penetrate it.

ARMANTI TOOK A long drag off a Newport Light cigarette as he parked his car near the corner of Shore Parkway and Homecrest Avenue in Brighton Beach. The neighborhood was so heavily populated with Russian immigrants that street vendors sold tins of black market caviar on the corners, but Armanti was again playing the role of Charlie Scadero, an Italian wannabe from Brooklyn. He wore a black velour warm-up suit and a pair of brand-new, white Fila sneakers. The car was a Lexus GS 300, black-on-black with tinted windows, and there were several thousand dollars of buy money in the console. Out of the shadows walked a man in a three-quarter-length black leather jacket.

"You Charlie?" he asked in a thick Russian accent.

"Yeah," Armanti said. "Get in."

Armanti had been working a case in Gravesend, Brooklyn, investigating a crew from the Colombo crime family suspected in a series of gangland-style killings, including the double murder of a pair of identical twins. But when an informant had introduced him to a Russian who was eager to move coke Armanti wasn't about to pass up an easy mark. Four years earlier, less than half a mile away, Police Officer Ralph Dols had been shot and killed execution style, and the police suspected that either Italians or Russians were responsible. Armanti's unit was always looking for the chance to squeeze any neighborhood criminal for information that might help them solve his murder.

While waiting for the cocaine to arrive, Armanti glared at the suspect and warned him, "This better be legit!" Then Armanti's pager began rattling, flashing a number from police headquarters, followed by the code 9-1-1.

"I've gotta make a call," he said, getting out of the car.

He was sure he'd been burnt again. If headquarters was calling, that probably meant that the DMV computer had picked up someone trying to run the license-plate number of his undercover car. The call, he figured, was a warning. But when Armanti phoned in, a woman in the Chief of Department's office ordered him to appear in the police commissioner's office at 11 A.M. the next morning. He was to dress in business attire.

"What did I do this time?" Armanti asked, feeling the dread start to boil up inside him again.

"You're getting promoted to first-grade detective," she said. "Congratulations."

Armanti thanked her, hung up the phone, then finished making his buy.

The next day, March 23, 2001, he stood in the police commissioner's office, near Teddy Roosevelt's old desk. His previous promotion, three years earlier, had felt like it was being given through gritted teeth. But this ceremony was the real thing—complete with a warm welcome and generous praise from Police Commissioner Bernard Kerik. Armanti's father beamed as he watched his son, a kid who many people thought would leave the streets of Sunset Park only in handcuffs, receive one of the highest honors the NYPD can bestow upon a detective. His colleagues from narcotics were amazed.

"Hey, Commissioner," one detective asked Kerik. "When's the last time you promoted someone who was out buying half a kilo of cocaine the night before?"

Armanti forced a laugh. For more than seven years, he had been forced to go to war with the NYPD simply because he wanted to do his job. Now, finally, the department was coming to him with an honor that seemed genuine. But he could not escape the feeling that his troubles weren't over; when he thought about the future, all he saw were the shadows. During fifteen years as an undercover, hundreds of people had fallen into his traps. Every day, some hit the streets, fresh from Rikers Island, Attica, or some other godforsaken place. The one who haunted him most, Mario Ferranti, was scheduled to be paroled in a few months, and Armanti knew that they would meet again.

Let them come, Armanti thought as he rose to shake hands with the commissioner. *Let them come.*

PROLOGUE: DEADLY ECHO

The detail in the opening scene comes from Armanti's sworn testimony at the Tocco trial, along with his daily police report from 9 June 1993, and extensive interviews. Other sources include Dowd's investigative work sheets, the handwritten memos of FBI Agent Cindy Peil, plus interviews with Fire Marshals Bobby Thomson and James Desocio.

1: NO ACCIDENT

Descriptions of the fire come from a review of thousands of pages of testimony from the Ferrantis' arson trial, plus hundreds of pages of fire department reports, the insurance adjustors' investigation, and more than one hundred photos of the crime scene.

The portrait of Lieutenant Williams, and his final shift at Rescue 4, comes from sworn testimony Firefighter Michael Milner gave during the Ferrantis' trial in August 1995, plus interviews with Milner and Rescue 4 firefighters Ray Strong, Richard Euler, and Doug Sloan.

The account of the origins of the arson investigation come from interviews with Fire Marshals Bobby Thomson and James Desocio, plus a review of hundreds of pages of FDNY incident reports, Detective Ed Dowd's investigative file, and testimony from the Ferrantis' arson trial.

The material regarding Eric Mergenthal's work as a confidential informant is based on tape-recorded conversations between Mergenthal and various targets of the investigation and FBI transcripts of his discussions. Other details about Mergenthal's activities as an informant are drawn from interviews with Fire Marshal Bobby Thomson and NYPD investigative reports prepared by Detective Dowd.

Details of the Ferrantis' alleged criminal past come from NYPD incident reports about the murder of Bruce Bailey, the shooting of mortgage broker Robert Cohen, and the shooting and subsequent death of Patrick Donnelly. Other sources include interviews with two former tenants of the Ferrantis, who spoke on condition of anonymity, plus testimony given by FBI Agent Cindy Peil during the Ferrantis' detention hearing in federal court.

Material regarding Michelle and Shelly Anthony's escape from the fire, and their observation of Tommy Tocco lurking outside the building, comes from their sworn court testimony and extensive interviews with Michelle.

The description of Jack Ferranti's statement to the police is drawn from the NYPD investigative report of the interview.

Written sources include: *Village Voice*, 25 April 1995; *New York Newsday,* 16 July 1989, 26 February 1992, 28 February 1995; *New York Times,* 26 August 1993, 2 March 1995; *New York Daily News,* 1 March 1995.

2: ONE LAST CASE

The description of Armanti's background is based on interviews with more than one hundred friends, relatives, coworkers, fellow narcotics detectives, and supervisors, along with statements made by several of the criminal suspects he arrested and their families.

Written sources include annual NYPD performance reviews, the incident reports from Armanti's shooting incidents, previous arrests, and trials.

Other written sources include: *New York Daily News,* 27 October 1989, 23 May 1991, 31 May 1991, 24 September 1993; *New York Newsday,* 24 September 1993; *Brooklyn Home Reporter and Sunset News,* 2 August 1991, 8 October 1993; *Brooklyn Spectator,* 12 January 1989, 19 June 1991, 1 November 1991, 6 October 1993; *Bay Ridge Paper,* 28 July 1991.

3: BOTH ENDS

The details about Tommy Tocco's activities in Throgs Neck came from police reports, interviews with Armanti and Fire Marshal Bobby Thomson, the sworn testimony of Vincent Marziano, and interviews with several of his friends, relatives, and neighbors, who spoke on condition of anonymity.

The allegations that the Ferrantis fixed criminal cases with various officials in the Bronx district attorney's office and U.S. attorney's office came from written reports filed by former federal agent Anthony Lombardi.

Detective Benjamin Gozun did not return repeated calls requesting comment. The description of his confrontation with Armanti comes from interviews with Armanti, Fire Marshals Desocio and Thomson, plus FBI Agent Cindy Peil's handwritten synopsis of the case and an IAB daily case report that made reference to the disagreement.

4: "A GOOD GUY"

John Wrynn declined numerous requests for an interview, which were made via telephone, mail, and e-mail. Descriptions of his background are derived from more than seventy-five interviews with friends, relatives, colleagues, classmates, clergymen,

and coworkers, along with records from Monsignor Scanlan High School and his
NYPD personnel file.

Conversations between John Wrynn and his father were taken from the Inspector's sworn testimony before the federal grand jury in the Eastern District of New
York on 18 August 1994.

The description of Detective Wrynn's actions at the party in Chris Stolz's house is
based on a written transcript of statements that his boyhood friend Steven Turuk
made to the NYPD while acting as a confidential informant.

Material about John Wrynn asking other investigators for information about drug
investigations involving his friends is derived from written reports of FBI interviews
with Assistant Bronx District Attorney Linda Nelson, NYPD Detective Elizabeth
Rye, and NYPD Detective Vincent Flynn.

Wrynn's admission to giving a "heads up" to the subject of a criminal investigation came from an FBI report summarizing his interrogation by Agent Cindy Peil on
11 January 1994.

5: "THESE GUYS ARE MINE"

The dialogue between Armanti and Myron Dobbs is taken from FBI transcripts of
their secretly taped conversations and transcripts of Armanti's testimony at Tommy
Tocco's trial in Bronx State Supreme Court. Other details of the conversations are
derived from Armanti's daily reports, plus extensive interviews with Armanti and
Fire Marshals Bobby Thomson and James Desocio.

Jack Ferranti's arrest for patronizing a prostitute comes from an NYPD incident
report and Bronx court records.

"Joey Scams'" description of the dismemberment murder was secretly taped by
Armanti and is summarized on Armanti's daily work sheets.

Written sources include: *New York Daily News*, 17 March 1987, 16 February
1990; *New York Times*, 12 March 1987.

6: THE HUNTER, HUNTED

Inspector James Wrynn has declined repeated requests for an interview since 1997.
Biographical details of his life were gathered from records at the U.S. Immigration
and Naturalization Service, Fordham University, the NYPD Personnel Bureau.
More than fifty of his colleagues, friends, relatives, and neighbors were also interviewed, most of whom spoke on condition of anonymity,

The Inspector's description of his family problems and the dialogue of his conversations with John are taken from a transcript of his sworn testimony before a federal
grand jury in June 1994. The description of the conversation between Inspector
Wrynn and the anonymous phone caller was also taken from the Inspector's sworn
testimony before the grand jury.

Material on the problems in Internal Affairs in the early 1990s and the origins of
the Mollen Commission come from my own observations and reporting published in
New York Newsday and the *New York Times*. Other written sources include: *New York*

Newsday, 1 September 1990, 13–18 November 1991, 22 January 1992, 16 May 1992, 18 July 1992, 17 December 1992; *New York Times,* 25 September 1986, 17 November 1992, 3 October 1993, 7 July 1994; Associated Press, 26 September 1993, 16 April 1994.

7: 911

The account of Internal Affairs detectives refusing to allow Armanti to meet with John Wrynn is derived from interviews with Armanti, Detective Sixto Santiago, Assistant U.S. Attorney George Stamboulidis, and Fire Marshals James Desocio and Bobby Thomson.

Internal Affairs Sergeant Robert Matthiessen declined requests to be interviewed. But he gave sworn testimony about the unsuccessful Internal Affairs undercover operation on City Island during his appearance before the grand jury, and a transcript of his statements was used to prepare the account in this book.

IAB Lieutenant John T. Shields also did not return repeated calls requesting comment, but he gave sworn testimony about the incident when he was called as a defense witness during the cocaine trial of Tommy Tocco in 1997.

8: FIRST BUY

The depiction of Armanti's cocaine purchase from Tommy Tocco on 1 July 1993 comes from Armanti's sworn testimony at Tocco's trial in Bronx State Supreme Court, plus NYPD incident reports. Some of the dialogue was derived from an FBI transcript of the secretly recorded conversations between Tocco and Armanti. But the NYPD's tape recorders did not capture all of their conversation, so part of their exchange was reconstructed using the daily reports filed by Armanti, Internal Affairs, and the FBI on 1 July 1993. The description of the sale also relied on details of the incident recorded in the handwritten notes from Detective Ed Dowd and Agent Cindy Peil, along with interviews with Armanti and Fire Marshals James Desocio and Bobby Thomson.

9: "THERE'S GONNA BE TROUBLE!"

Although Inspector Wrynn gave sworn testimony to the grand jury denying that he ever made any efforts to intercede in the investigation, the account of his foray into the IAB Special Projects Unit where his son's investigative file was kept is based on the ample evidence to the contrary.

In an IAB report about a September 1993 meeting between Internal Affairs supervisors and Assistant U.S. Attorney George Stamboulidis, IAB officials concede that Inspector Wrynn did indeed make an unauthorized visit to the detectives investigating his son (although they steadfastly denied that he saw the investigative file or threatened the detectives handling the case).

Other details are taken from the sworn grand jury testimony and subsequent statements of two IAB detectives present during Inspector Wrynn's visit to the Special Projects Unit office. Detective Sixto Santiago testified that Inspector Wrynn charged into the office where the file was kept, stayed there for several minutes, then left, shouting, "There's gonna be trouble!" Santiago reiterated that account in interviews with me in 2003.

Sergeant Robert Matthiessen testified that he was sitting in the office where the file was kept when Inspector Wrynn made his unexpected visit. Matthiessen was also quoted as making more detailed statements about the incident, according to Detective Ed Dowd, Armanti, and Fire Marshals James Desocio and Bobby Thomson. Records in the NYPD Department Advocate's Office indicate that in 1997 Matthiessen also gave a similar account of the incident to Richard Mulvaney, an assistant special prosecutor investigating the Wrynn case.

The dialogue between Inspector Wrynn and his son is taken from the Inspector's grand jury testimony.

10: ARE YOU HOT?

The account of Eric Mergenthal's activities as a confidential informant is taken from secretly tape-recorded conversations involving Mergenthal and Tommy Tocco, Steve Turuk, and other associates in Throgs Neck. Other details come from recordings of Mergenthal's conversations with Detective Dowd and Fire Marshal Bobby Thomson, along with interviews with Mergenthal's mother, Millie, and brother, Artie, plus notes Mergenthal had written before his death.

Tocco has given contradictory statement's about Eric Mergenthal's death, but the dialogue cited in this chapter is taken from an FBI transcript of a secretly recorded conversation he had with Armanti on 17 July 1993.

The quote attributed to John Wrynn, in which he bemoans the tragic fate of his friends, is taken from an FBI report of Agent Cindy Peil's interview with John Wrynn's former girlfriend Linda Nelson.

Detective Ed Dowd's assertion that Lieutenant John Shields was overheard discussing the case with the chief of IAB comes from Peil's written synopsis of the case, Dowd's handwritten notes, plus interviews with Armanti and Fire Marshals James Desocio and Bobby Thomson.

11: "A ROCK AND A HARD PLACE"

The description of Tommy Tocco's shooting of Fahed Bashdar is drawn from various police reports about the incident, made in August 1993. The statements about the shooting attributed to Tocco and Mario Ferranti are drawn from secretly recorded conversations with Armanti and the FBI transcripts of those exchanges.

Mario Ferranti's statements about cocaine dealing and receiving confidential information about drug busts from within the police department are drawn from secret tape recordings Armanti made of their conversations and Armanti's daily reports.

The description of Lieutenant John Shields saying he was "between a rock and a hard place" comes from Armanti's written reports, and interviews with Fire Marshals James Desocio and Bobby Thomson. When Lieutenant Shields was called as a defense witness during Tocco's trial in Bronx State Supreme Court in 1997, Assistant Bronx District Attorney William Zalenka asked whether he made such a statement and Shields gave sworn testimony that he could not recall.

The description of the 30 September 1993 meeting in which IAB detectives are chastised for interfering in the case is taken from an IAB daily work sheet prepared and signed by Lieutenant Shields. Other details of the meeting are drawn from interviews with Armanti, Assistant U.S. Attorney George Stamboulidis, and IAB Chief Walter Mack.

The description of John Wrynn poring over entries in the NYPD's top-secret DECS book of sensitive narcotics investigations is drawn from a report filed by Lieutenant John Fischer, the integrity control officer for the Organized Crime Investigation Division. The incident is also referenced in an IAB internal report, prepared and signed by Lieutenant Shields in September 1993, plus a memo written by Assistant U.S. Attorney George Stamboulidis in 1997.

12: "COMING FROM THE TOP"

The conversation in which Carlo Cuzzi and Joe "Red" Bastone solicit "Vinnie Blue Eyes" to rob and kill a man whom they owed $21,000 was secretly recorded. The portrayal here is based on an FBI transcript of that conversation, along with Agent Cindy Peil's handwritten synopsis of the case and interviews with Armanti.

The portrayal of Deputy Chief Al James declaring that police officers who cooperated with the Mollen Commission were "psychopaths" was taken from my own reporting of the incident in *New York Newsday*.

The conversation between Detective Ed Dowd and Lieutenant Pooley is based on Dowd's notes, plus interviews with Armanti, and Fire Marshals Thomson and Desocio.

13: "ONE SHOT, ONE KILL"

The confrontation between Armanti and Tommy Tocco comes from Armanti's sworn testimony at Tocco's trial; interviews with Armanti, and Fire Marshals James Desocio and Bobby Thomson; plus assertions that Tocco's wife, Angelique, made in court papers about the incident. The dialogue between Tocco and Armanti was taken from FBI transcripts of their recorded conversation and interviews with Armanti.

The meeting between the Internal Affairs officials and the U.S. attorney is based on an IAB report of the encounter, prepared by Lieutenant John Shields, plus interviews with George Stamboulidis and Walter Mack.

The description of the Mollen Commission hearings and the testimony given by Joseph Trimboli before the Mollen Commission were derived, in part, from my personal observations while covering the proceedings. In addition, I interviewed two Mollen Commission investigators and two of its members.

Written sources include: *Good Cop, Bad Cop*, by Mike McAlary; *New York Times*, 28 September 1993, 29 September 1993, 30 September 1993, 1 October 1993, 2 October 1993, 3 October 1993, 4 October 1993, 5 October 1993; *New York Daily News*, 28 September 1993, 29 September 1993, 30 September 1993, 1 October 1993, 2 October 1993, 3 October 1993, 4 October 1993, 5 October 1993; *New York Newsday*, 28 September 1993, 29 September 1993, 30 September 1993, 1 October 1993, 2 October 1993, 3 October 1993, 4 October 1993, 5 October 1993; Associated Press, 2 October 1993, 4 October 1993, 5 October 1993; *New York Law Journal,* 4 October 1993; *New York Post,* 3 October 1993, 5 October 1993.

14: "A HEADS UP"

The portrayal of John Wrynn's interrogation by the FBI was based on a written FBI report of the encounter, plus interviews with Armanti and Stamboulidis, who were briefed about the encounter by Agent Peil.

The dialogue between Inspector Wrynn and John Wrynn is drawn from a transcript of the Inspector's sworn testimony before the grand jury.

The description of John Wrynn's inquiries about various Bronx drug investigations is derived from FBI reports of interviews with NYPD Detective Elizabeth Rye and Bronx Assistant District Attorney Linda Nelson, plus interviews with two officials in the Manhattan district attorney's office, who spoke on condition of anonymity.

Written sources include: *New York Daily News,* 23 January 1994; *New York Times,* 22 January 1994.

15: "WHAT ANY FATHER WOULD DO"

The description of Inspector Wrynn's appearance before the grand jury, and the grand jurors' comments about his testimony, come from transcripts of the proceeding.

The description of Sergeant Robert Matthiessen's statements before the grand jury, and the grand jurors' comments about his testimony, are taken from a transcript of the court hearing.

The description of Armanti's dealings with Internal Affairs officials assigned to investigate his official complaint against the Wrynns is based on secret tape recordings Armanti made of his conversations with IAB officials. The meeting between Armanti and Walter Mack is based on a secret tape recording Armanti made of that conversation.

16: "GUYS WHO'LL TAKE CARE OF THIS"

Material about the harassing telephone calls to Armanti's home is drawn from interviews with Armanti, FBI reports prepared by Agent Cindy Peil, plus sworn testimony both made about the incident. Other details come from the court papers filed in Bronx State Supreme Court as part of Tommy Tocco's appeal.

The description of the firebombing outside the home of two witnesses preparing to testify against the Ferrantis was based on a police report about the incident and interviews with Fire Marshal Bobby Thomson, FBI Agent Cindy Peil, and Assistant U.S. Attorneys Sean O'Shea and Lauren Resnick.

The portrayal of Jack Ferranti's courtship of Miriam Breyer is based on a letter she wrote to Judge Jack B. Weinstein, which is part of the court file. The description of Jack's interaction with the Breyer family is drawn from letters her sister and parents wrote the judge before Ferranti's sentencing in 1996.

Details about the arrest of Jack Ferranti are drawn from the arrest report, interviews with two law enforcement officials who participated in the arrest, sworn testimony at Ferranti's criminal trial and detention hearing, plus Miriam Breyer's letter.

Written sources include: *New York Daily News,* 1 March 1995; *New York News-day,* 27 February 1995, 28 February 1995.

17: "A TEST OF THE DEPARTMENT'S WILL"

The description of the rampage by police officers attending the Washington Memorial is based, in part, on my own reporting of the incident for *New York Newsday.* Material was also taken from an interview with IAB Inspector Bruce Major plus the NYPD's written decision describing the evidence presented in the departmental trials of Officers Hagmaier and Morrow, who were fired for their roles in the mayhem.

Written sources used include: *New York Newsday,* 20 May 1995, 23 May 1995, 24 May 1995, 27 May 1995, 9 June 1995, 12 July 1995, 24 February 1996; *New York Times,* 21 May 1995, 22 May 1995, 29 May 1995, 4 June 1995, 28 February 1996; *New York Daily News,* 20 May 1995, 21 May 1995, 25 May 1995, 14 June 1995, 19 June 1995, 11 July 1995, 12 July 1995, 25 October 1995.

Patrick Kelleher declined to be interviewed, but details about the crash were prepared using records from the New York State Department of Motor Vehicles, plus interviews with more than a dozen people involved in the NYPD's response to, and investigation of, the crash. Most of those individuals spoke on condition of anonymity, but Organized Crime Control Bureau Chief Anthony Voelker and Narcotics Bureau Commander Frank Biehler gave on-the-record interviews.

18: "I DO WANT JUSTICE DONE"

The portrayal of the Ferrantis' trial was prepared using more than four thousand pages of transcript and court papers from the case. It also relies on information gathered in interviews with defense lawyer Marion Seltzer, Assistant Prosecutors Sean O'Shea and Lauren Resnick, Fire Marshals Bobby Thomson and James Desocio, and witnesses Michael Milner and Michelle Anthony.

Other written sources include: *New York Times,* 16 August 1995; *New York Newsday,* 3 August 1995, 5 August 1995, 12 August 1995, 16 August 1995, 19 August 1995, 23 August 1995, 25 April 1996; *New York Daily News,* 16 August 1995, 24 April 1996; *Village Voice,* 24 March 1998; *New York Law Journal,* 9 February 1998.

19: "HEAD ON A SILVER PLATTER"

No written transcript was made of Tommy Tocco's proffer session, and Tocco declined repeated requests to be interviewed. But Tocco has filed court motions in which both he and his wife, Angelique, make reference to the discussions. Other details about the discussions are drawn from interviews with two people present in the room, who spoke on condition of anonymity.

The description of Police Commissioner Howard Safir's telling Armanti, "It's a shame about what they've done to you," is drawn from interviews with Armanti and Fire Marshals Bobby Thomson and James Desocio.

The account of Captain William Plackenmeyer's meeting with police department officials is based on interviews with Plackenmeyer and Armanti.

The account of Patrick Kelleher's drive home up the FDR Drive is derived from an interview with his driver at the time, IAB Captain William Gorta.

The assertion that Patrick Kelleher declared that he wanted Armanti's "head on a silver platter" is based on interviews with IAB Detective Jerry Walker, Assistant U.S. Attorney George Stamboulidis, and Armanti.

20: "I TOOK AN OATH"

Material used to describe the Tommy Tocco trial is drawn from personal observations and notes I made while covering the proceedings, plus the stories I wrote about it for the *New York Times*. The dialogue quoted in the trial is taken from the trial transcript.

Written sources include: *New York Times*, 29 March 1997, 8 April 1997; *New York Daily News*, 29 March 1997.

21: "WHAT KIND OF WORLD WOULD IT BE?"

Assistant Special Prosecutor Richard Mulvaney declined to be interviewed. Descriptions of his actions in the case—and the evidence he gathered regarding Inspector Wrynn, John Wrynn, and Sergeant Robert Matthiessen—are based on interviews with Armanti, plus more than one hundred confidential documents from the NYPD Department Advocate's Office. I also gathered information from three other lawyers involved in the case, who spoke on condition of anonymity.

The description of Patrick Kelleher's response to questions about his auto accident is based on personal observations and published accounts of the press briefing.

The description of Lieutenant Nancy McLaughlin's attempt to ascertain the source of the news leaks about the Wrynns is drawn from interviews and an account of the incident published in *New York Newsday*.

Written sources include: *New York Newsday*, 25 May 1998, 15 June 1998, 17 August 1998; *New York Times*, 4 May 1998, 12 May 1998, 31 July 1998; *New York Daily News*, 4 June 1998.

EPILOGUE: IN THE ARENA

The portrayal of John Wrynn's actions watching over the entryway at his father's retirement party is drawn from personal observations. The description of the party itself is drawn from interviews with four people who attended the luncheon and spoke on condition of anonymity.

The description of the negotiations leading up to John Wrynn's resignation are drawn from hundreds of pages of records from the NYPD Department Advocate's Office, and interviews with lawyers involved in the discussions, who spoke on condition of anonymity.

The Mayoral Commission's analysis of the Wrynn case is contained in the Commission to Combat Police Corruption's Third Annual Report, released in August 1998.

The description of Kelleher's statements at the two retirement parties is drawn from interviews with guests at the events and press accounts of the festivities.

Other written sources include: *New York Daily News*, 14 July 2000, 9 August 2000, 1 October 2000; *New York Newsday*, 14 July 2000, 17 July 2000, 24 July 2000, 20 August 2000, 25 June 2001, 14 January 2002, 17 July 2002; *New York Post*, 14 July 2000, 8 August 2000.

ACKNOWLEDGMENTS

THIS BOOK COULD not have been written without the sacrifices of many men and women in the New York Police Department and the New York Fire Department and the support of my family, friends, and colleagues at the *New York Times.*

I am honored that Undercover #4126 entrusted me with his story, and grateful that he patiently sat through the many hours and innumerable questions it took for me to tell it. Although the NYPD never gave Detective Ed Dowd permission to speak to me, I was fortunate that his colleagues granted me access to his many files and insights. I will forever be indebted to John Perry, one of the NYPD's lost heroes of September 11th, for teaching me about the machinations of the police department and its disciplinary system. Fire Marshals Bobby Thomson and James Desocio were exceptionally generous with their time, their recollections, and their case files. And I feel special gratitude to the friends and relatives of Fire Lieutenant Thomas A. Williams, and the men at Rescue 4, for being so gracious and forthcoming in sharing their memories with me.

It is unfortunate, though understandable, that many of the police officers and firemen who provided crucial support for this book were so fearful of reprisals that they had to ask that their names not appear in its pages. They know who they are—I can only hope that they realize just how deeply I appreciate their contributions.

At the *New York Times,* I am grateful to Matt Purdy, who helped me shape the original newspaper story, to Joyce Purnick, Bill Keller, and Joe Lelyveld, who saw to it that those words made their way into print, and to Bill Schmidt, who permitted me to explore the possibility of developing it into a longer work. My colleagues in the *Times* police bureau, Michael Cooper and Kit Roane, offered encouragement and assistance. During the years I spent working on the manuscript, my editors Jim Roberts, Peter Applebome, and Jon Landman have taught me volumes about writing and reporting, and Adam Liptak, George Freeman, and David McCraw have given astute legal advice. Through it all, Willie Rashbaum has been both a loyal friend and an incomparable resource.

At Henry Holt, John Sterling was incredibly enthusiastic about the potential of this book and I owe him thanks for providing the time, help, and resources to see it through. Jack Macrae and Jennifer Barth both gave me invaluable guidance. My editor, George Hodgman, was a constant source of insight and support. His thoughtful editing and dedication, cheerleading, patience, and sense of humor were irreplaceable.

I am fortunate that Amanda Urban is my literary agent; she was unwavering in her support and unerring in her keen observations about the proposal and manuscript.

I am also grateful to Jason Epstein for reaching out to offer his kind words and counsel.

Thank you to my friend Peg Tyre, who was there, as always, with encouragement and shrewd advice. Bryan Gruley gave me the benefit of his passion for writing. Bud Anzalone was a sensitive, perceptive editor and his unflagging belief in me was uplifting.

I also want to extend my sincere thanks to Millie Mergenthal for having the courage and consideration to open her home to me and share the painful memories of her son's death.

I would also like to thank Donald Armanti, Bobby Thomson, and Charlotte Mergenthal for the use of the images contained in the photograph section.

Because this book was written on weekends and vacations over the course of more than three years, my wife, Denise Barricklow, endured my long hours and frequent distractions and I am grateful for her sacrifices. Her mother, Daphne Mroz, provided invaluable help pinch-hitting for me at home. My daughters, Katia and Devin, gave me comfort and inspiration even though they were too young to completely understand why I needed it. I look forward to the day they are old enough to read this, so they will know how much it meant to me. Finally, I want to thank my mother, Esther Wojtan, my brother, Greg, and my four sisters, Linda, Eileen, Sue, and Karen, for all the love and support they have given me.

David Kocieniewski has been covering the New York City Police Department since 1990, first at *New York Newsday* and then at *The New York Times,* where he was police bureau chief. He is currently the Trenton, New Jersey, bureau chief for *The New York Times*. He lives in Bucks County, Pennsylvania.